Catholic Schools
at the Crossroads

SURVIVAL AND
TRANSFORMATION

Catholic Schools at the Crossroads

SURVIVAL AND
TRANSFORMATION

Edited by James Youniss & John J. Convey

TEACHERS
COLLEGE
PRESS

Teachers College, Columbia University
New York and London

Published by Teachers College Press, 1234 Amsterdam Avenue, New York, NY 10027

Library of Congress Cataloging-in-Publication Data

Catholic schools at the crossroads : survival and transformation / edited by James Youniss & John J. Convey.
    p.   cm.
  Includes bibliographical references and index.
  ISBN 0-8077-3909-X (hardcover : alk. paper)
    1. Catholic schools—United States. 2. Catholic Church—Education—
United States. I. Youniss, James. II. Convey, John J., 1940–
  LC501.C3495 2000
  371.071′273—dc21   99-049571

ISBN 0-8077-3909-X (cloth)

Printed on acid-free paper
Manufactured in the United States of America

07 06 05 04 03 02 01 00   8 7 6 5 4 3 2 1

Contents

Acknowledgments

THIS BOOK IS ONE RESULT of the project "Legacy at the Crossroads: The Future of Catholic Schools." The project, which is still ongoing, was sponsored through the generosity of the Lilly Endowment, whose officers, Sister Jeanne Knoerle, Fred Hofheinz, and Craig Dystra, provided their counsel and support. Projects such as these are successful to the degree that teams of scholars collaborate in a system of intellectual and political checks and balances. Although the two of us did the editorial work that made the present book possible, David Baker, now at Penn State University, helped to write our original proposal and to organize the conference at which the material in these chapters was discussed. Other colleagues, especially Carl Pieber and Louis Crishock, helped at various phases by contributing their knowledge of the political structure and religious commitment that sustains these schools. All deserve credit for the successes of this project, and we acknowledge their contributions with gratitude.

We thank also Dot Kane for managing the paperwork, editing, and communications this project entailed. Woinishet Negash was a constant supply of help whenever we asked. We also thank principals and teachers at Catholic schools and officials of educational organizations who gave us valued feedback throughout. Finally, we dedicate this book to the thousands of educators who are responsible for establishing and maintaining Catholic schools, which were and remain an essential part of education in the United States. It is their legacy that we believe is worth sustaining and the reason why the future of these schools merits attention.

Introduction

JAMES YOUNISS

FOR THE PAST TWO DECADES Catholic schools have been the focus of considerable interest and controversy among educational researchers and policy makers. The work of James Coleman and his colleagues is in part responsible. Coleman and Hoffer (1987) and Greeley (1982), for example, used data from the High School and Beyond survey to argue that Black inner-city students who attended Catholic high schools were more academically successful than their peers who attended public schools. This claim has been seriously challenged (e.g., Alexander & Pallas, 1983), but has stood up to methodological scrutiny at least to the satisfaction of some scholars (Bryk, Lee, & Holland, 1993; Hoffer, Chapter 5, this volume; Riordan, Chapter 2, this volume).

Had this controversy remained solely a matter for researchers to determine, it probably would have died down by now. But the work of Coleman and others was drawn into a larger assault on public schools and the philosophy behind them, and on teacher unions and the logic for them. What might have been settled in the court of scientific review became a public issue that is still being played out in the media and on political platforms. As a result, Catholic schools have been pictured variously as the alternative to the monopolistic hold of teacher unions, a prime rationale for school choice, and the cause celebre for breaking down the historical wall between church and state. As if these roles were not sufficient, Catholic schools in some cities have been portrayed as the best hope for the Black underclass, with some public school administrators threatening to remove their own school staffs for comparative non-performance.

Whether Catholic schools actually succeed with students who otherwise are recognized as being at risk for educational failure, is certainly important. But our view is that this issue has distracted researchers and policy makers from addressing the more fundamental matter of the survival and future form of Catholic schools themselves. To wit, in 1965, 13,300 Catholic schools, with 114,000 religious teachers, enrolled approximately 5.6 million students. In 1995, 8,200 schools, with 15,600 religious teachers, enrolled 2.6 million students. Parishes, which historically supplied the bulk of school costs, had, by 1995, reduced their contribution appreciably, forcing a spiraling rise in tuition to make up the difference (Harris, Chapter 3, this volume). As a consequence, the very inner-city Catholic schools that have been the focus of controversy are at risk for closing due to decreasing parish income, increased cost for lay teaching staffs, and rising tuition (Nelson, Chapter 8; O'Keefe & Murphy, Chapter 6; Polite, Chapter 7, this volume). Those inner-city schools that remain open may have to charge a tuition that would rule out enrollment for many low-income students.

Given just this set of data, although more will be provided in the various chapters of this book, it should be immediately evident that narrow focus on the Catholic versus public school achievement question directs attention away from more fundamental issues about the survival and future structure of Catholic schools. Little good it does to argue about the right to choose one's school, or which kind of school serves minorities better, when Catholic schools in the inner cities may go out of existence. More fruitful challenges for researchers would be to learn why enrollment has declined, why religious teachers have left the schools, and why parish income has decreased. Equally challenging are questions regarding the implications of these data; for example, can the decline in enrollment be attributed to a mismatch between the historical location of Catholic schools within cities and the migration of the Catholic population to the suburbs (McLellan, Chapter 1, this volume)? If this is the case, how long will Catholics in the suburbs continue to support inner-city schools, in particular, schools that serve non-Catholic, minority students? Moreover, if the success of Catholic schools is attributable to the religious teachers who view their work as a vocational mission rather than a job, how has their withdrawal and their replacement by lay teachers altered the nature of the schools? With 90% lay teachers, can the schools retain their Catholic character, or will they come to resemble secularized private schools, as occurred with many Protestant denominational schools a century ago?

It seemed to us that addressing the problems and challenges of Catholic schools should take precedence over questions of school choice, tax credits, vouchers, and the like. One might even argue that in focusing on the latter rather than confronting immediate and real issues facing Catholic schools, researchers are complicit in allowing Catholic schools to be used for ulterior purposes. With survival and transformation at stake, there is a need to gather basic information that is requisite for sound policy regarding the schools' future. Catholic schools undoubtedly have changed in numerous ways over the past 40 years (McLaughlin, O'Keefe, & O'Keefe, 1996). It is important to understand why they have changed and how they have changed. Further, the processes that propelled these changes are probably still at work, so the transformation continues. Hence, the need for focus on basic issues and for sound information was never more apparent and essential for the sake of intelligent policy.

BACKGROUND TO THE BOOK

With the above considerations in mind, we designed a project that would synthesize available empirical evidence on the schools. A team comprising the two editors, plus David Baker and Carl Pieber, met for several months to lay out the dimensions of the problem. With a grant from the Lilly Endowment, the team interviewed policy makers in Catholic education, administrators, bishops, pastors, principals, teachers, and researchers. The goal was to verify and refine our list of central topics.

On the basis of this work, we then invited about 30 scholars from various universities and agencies to review the literature in the selected areas of interest. A year later, a conference was held in Washington, D.C., at the Catholic University of America, at which about 100 participants discussed the results and debated their implications.

The present book is one result of this project. The goal is to present an up-to-date portrait of the schools that is focused on the subset of the empirical syntheses that deal with the operational aspects of Catholic schools. Part I of the book deals with the meat-and-potato topics of enrollment, income and costs, personnel, and achievement. Part II deals explicitly with urban schools and their mainly minority, often non-Catholic students. As was noted, these schools and this population were crucial in recently bringing Catholic schools into the spotlight. But also as noted, the problems of money and changing teaching staffs have placed these very schools at risk for closing. To conclude the book, Maureen Hallinan masterfully reviews the chapters in Parts I and II and reflects on their meaning for the philosophy behind Catholic education and implications for policy. She synthesizes the findings, which are surprisingly congruent, but more important, she articulates questions that Catholic school officials can gainfully address. With limited resources available, Catholic schools can no longer be asked to be all things to the entire population that might use them. Hallinan lists several options, with advantages and disadvantages for each. This articulation is as sharp a conclusion as one can hope to reach in an enterprise as complex as the one we set out to study.

The coverage in this book, of course, does not exhaust what could be learned about the schools. Some of the important elements that are missing, however, can be gotten from other sources; for example, Guerra's (1999) report offers information on the secondary school curriculum, an important topic. Further, in a companion book from this project that is now in preparation, we present a close look at the religious dimension, or *The Catholic Character of Catholic Schools* (McLellan, Youniss, & Convey, in press).

A CONTEXT FOR UNDERSTANDING CATHOLIC SCHOOLS

Before presenting the chapters with their novel syntheses of the data, we believe it is useful to offer a background sketch of Catholic schooling in the United States. We begin with a description of the jurisdictional status of these schools, then review recent historical trends, and next turn to key policy matters. In reading the literature on achievement differences, we noted a number of points of possible confusion whose clarification might help sharpen questions and enhance understanding. Catholic schools and public schools share the function of education, but they do not necessarily go about this task in the same way. Our aim is to help frame the reader's perspective so that what is commonly known about public schools is not simply generalized to the Catholic school domain but is properly conditioned.

Administrative Structure

Bryk, Lee, and Holland (1993) proposed a list of characteristics that they believe differentiate Catholic from public schools and provide the basis for the former's relative success in promoting academic achievement. Local autonomy, symbolized in the authority of the principal (Schaub, Chapter 4, this volume), is a major characteristic. How does this authority fit within the broader structure of Catholic education?

To an outsider, the Catholic Church seems like a textbook case of a hierarchically organized institution. In principle it is, from a theological perspective. But administratively, it is not. There is no single official Church body that is administratively responsible for the schools. There is instead a criss-cross pattern of authority. First, bishops are canonically in charge of education within their dioceses. There are approximately 174 dioceses in the United States and, therefore, 174 seats of authority. Second, dioceses have education offices with a superintendent and staff, who report to bishops. Third, pastors of parishes also have canonical authority over parochial, or parish-based schools. They hire principals and have fiscal responsibility for their schools.

Fourth, not all schools are controlled by a parish. Of all the elementary and secondary schools, many are parochial schools that offer pre-K through grade 8 classes. But there are also *interparish* schools, which are governed by several pastors and school boards; *diocesan* schools, which are controlled from a bishop's office; *private* schools, which are managed by religious orders that have cross-diocesan jurisdiction; and *charter* schools, which are Catholic in purpose, but are autonomous from the diocese or religious orders.

Religious orders, also called congregations of religious women or men, add another layer of jurisdiction. They have official canonical status that cuts across diocesan and parish lines. Orders of teaching sisters, for example, are organized in geographical provinces and may send personnel to teach in various parishes. Their presence in any school or parish is voluntary, and they may withdraw for good reason. One can get a view of their autonomy from the historical record during the expansion phase of Catholic schools. Bishops competed with one another and used sophisticated personal networks to secure sorely needed teachers (Wittberg, 1994).

Orders are probably best known for their private secondary schools and universities. For instance, during the nineteenth century, Jesuits established prep schools and colleges in several major cities in the United States. The result was a network of schools with an identifiable philosophy and overarching loyalty to the Society of Jesus (Leahy, 1991). Each order has a differentiating educational philosophy and history, thus giving the term *Catholic school* multiple meanings rather than a homogeneous cast. While a bishop has authority within his diocese, order-run, private schools are linked authoritatively to their province. For example, in recent years, as members of religious congregations have declined significantly in numbers, provincial authorities have either closed their schools or given up primary responsibility by becoming sponsors who sit on a school board, perhaps make an annual financial contribution, and try to perpetuate their initiating philosophy (Mueller, in press).

It is clear that local control and authority are real for Catholic schools in ways that are not possible for public schools. The latter are organized according to political units that collect the public funds through which schools are managed. Thus, there is only a dim parallel between a public school superintendent and school board and a diocesan superintendent who reports to the local bishop. The former have authority to hire, fire, determine curriculum, and the like. The latter has the right to persuade parish and private schools and the responsibility to support them in whichever ways are feasible. So, indeed, Bryk and colleagues' observation of the autonomy of Catholic schools accurately reflects this complex set of arrangements. For this reason, insiders use the term *Catholic system of education* rather than *Catholic school system* for these multiple canonical units. The Catholic system symbolizes a unifying philosophy and history, but does not imply uniform, coherent, hierarchical governance.

Starting Points of the System

By the end of the Civil War, Catholicism was already the largest single religious denomination in the United States (Smith, 1957). At the nation's founding, the Catholic population was sparse. It grew during the early part of the nineteenth century mainly from Irish and German immigration. There were relatively few Catholic schools at the time, and in some states, such as New York and Minnesota, Catholic schools received state aid in various forms. Historians have covered this period well and generally agree that financial relations between Catholic schools and the state were formed through a series of experiments and challenges that, by the end of the century, took the form of separate and independent systems (Walch, 1996).

However, there is scant quantitative information on Catholic schools during the nineteenth century. It is evident that Catholic schooling expanded after 1870 when a new wave of immigrants arrived from Catholic countries such as Italy, Poland, and other areas of southern and Slavic Europe. Population growth alone does not explain why Catholics desired to establish schools apart from the parallel burgeoning system of public schools that were supported with public money. Two common explanations are that Catholics were offended by the overtly Protestant ethos of public schools and that various Catholic ethnic groups sought to preserve their respective cultural traditions.

It is not clear how offended Catholics were or how offensive the public schools were. Individual cases, such as New York around the mid-nineteenth century, offer interesting evidence (Ravitch, 1974). But as the century wore on, the nation became less overtly Protestant and religious, while the public schools made conscious accommodations that would make the immigrant Catholics feel welcome. As to ethnic competition, Baker (1993) has shown how respective groups, in establishing national parishes, participated in a dynamic that generated separate parishes with accompanying schools. For example, when German immigrants established a parish and school in a city, Irish or Polish immigrants were likely to open their own parishes and schools. In each, religious services and educational instruction were conducted in the native language, with the goal of preserving the native culture. Hence, several schools were spawned with preservation of ethnicity, of which religion was a fundamental part, as the driving motive.

Walch (1996) has provided a crisp history of this era with identification of the forces that impelled school growth. A key event occurred in 1884, when the U.S. bishops, at their annual meeting in Baltimore, made it mandatory for every parish to open a school and binding for parents to send their children to these schools. This edict and continued immigration guaranteed expansion. By 1900, an estimated 1,000,000 children were attending Catholic schools. This growth required logistics that are still mostly unexplained. The Catholic population was notoriously poor, yet built a large number of schools that had to be staffed and furnished according to standards set by the states. There was a constant need for teachers, preferably religious women, and for money. To obtain teachers, bishops invited sisters from Europe while they established educational programs to stimulate vocations within their dioceses.

It is thought that this continually growing system, built with limited resources, in general lagged behind the public system in academic quality. Exceptions were the private Catholic secondary schools run by religious orders, which offered classical European education for upper-class, often non-Catholic, families in the United States. But during the nineteenth century, parish and diocesan schools made progress as Catholic colleges inaugurated programs to professionalize the religious teachers, modernize curricula, and improve textbooks (Gleason, 1995).

Catholic Schools and the Catholic Population

From their inception, Catholic schools served multiple functions. They socialized children into the Catholic faith, while they provided basic academic skills, with some advocates claiming that these two functions were inseparable because a religious outlook permeated all subject matter. Some schools also consciously preserved ethnic traditions, but at the same time they promoted socialization for American citizenship. This last function was encouraged, in part, in reaction to the continuing concern that Catholics owed loyalty to a foreign power in Rome. This charge, which caused tension at several moments in history, was allayed especially during times of war when Catholic citizens explicitly attempted to serve their country as dutifully as their Protestant brethren. For example, during the Civil War, nuns opened their hospitals to nurse injured soldiers on both sides of the conflict. Further, by the time of the Spanish-American War, Catholics had used the military as a means of upward mobility and had come to constitute the majority of U.S. military officers. During World War I, Catholic colleges started ROTC programs on their campuses, Catholics served in the military, and the U.S. bishops organized a national committee in support of the nation's military effort against Germany (Gleason, 1995; Morris, 1997).

World War II was yet another watershed. Returning Catholic veterans availed themselves of the GI bill to secure higher and professional education. These veterans made a generational leap in status beyond the working class of their immigrant forebears. Catholics rose to managerial and professional positions that enabled them to leave their ethnic neighborhoods and develop broadened interests in the culture as well as a new taste for their children's education. This shift was abetted by racial tension in cities as Blacks moved into the old ethnic neighborhoods, altering the parishes and communities in which the immigrants originally had settled (McGreevy, 1996).

The election of John F. Kennedy frequently is cited as the symbol of a fundamental change for American Catholics. Having attained this seat of power, Catholics were no longer perceived as fixed in the working class or of questionable loyalty to the nation. Although Kennedy was not a product of Catholic schools—his sisters were—his political attainment symbolized the distance that had been traveled since Irish Catholics came to the United States in 1850 to escape famine.

Perhaps more important to the 1960s was the Second Vatican Council, which presented a new paradigm for Catholicism. Catholicism had been known for creating distinctions between itself and other religions. But Vatican II encouraged unity with other faiths and a determined embracing of the modern world where religion was to be expressed in the work of creating a more just society.

The full consequences of Vatican II are still to be discerned. It surely altered the meaning of Catholic identity in America and decisively changed the role Catholic schools played in shaping it. As noted at the beginning of this chapter, school enrollment reached its peak in 1965, when the Council ended. In the very next year, enrollment started to plunge, while teaching sisters began a dramatic exodus from the religious life. It was as if an inexorable path had been carved through a mountain and a whole population rushed to see the other side, leaving behind the old landscape forever.

To some Catholic intellectuals of that day, the closing of the schools was a sign of maturity that was to be applauded. Catholics no longer needed to defend their religious stance because they had moved into the middle of U.S. culture and were even reaching its upper echelons (Ryan, 1964). Catholics no longer had to segregate themselves in separate schools but could practice their beliefs with the confidence that they were essential to the culture and, in fact, participated in its construction (Morris, 1997).

The Catholic Versus Public School Controversy

How, in light of this rich and complex history, did Catholic schools come to be entangled in rhetorical competition with public schools on the achievement question, embroiled in a political battle about vouchers, made a cipher for altered Church–state relations, and given the burden of saving inner-city minority youth from dropping out and lives of crime? There are probably good reasons for all of these things, and ferreting them out is beyond the intent of this volume. Meanwhile, however, the system these schools constituted and the institutional structure they supported have undergone a radical transformation. Catholic schools that charge high tuition, place academic achievement first, are staffed by lay teachers, and have significant non-Catholic enrollment resemble only vaguely the system of Catholic schooling that developed over the past 150 years.

The question of educating inner-city minority populations is too important to be conflated with political agendas or veiled attacks on teacher unions. That is why we have designed the second part of this volume to review the status of these schools, looked at more widely than through achievement alone. Indeed, from the perspective of some African American scholars, losing these schools would be a serious loss of human and spiritual capital (Irvine & Foster, 1996). But these schools are at risk for closing and new initiatives are needed if they are to be kept afloat. At the same time, the larger system that gave these schools their advantageous character in which education is a mission, not just a job, is in jeopardy.

It is our view that any serious reflection on Catholic schools must begin by acknowledging that, at this moment, they are at a crossroad. Only then can one proceed to ask meaningful questions that lead to intelligent policy. To reduce Catholic schools to issues, say, of vouchers or Church–state separation, with all that that implies, is intellectually inadequate to the historical legacy of these schools. As was noted, there are several kinds of Catholic schools and perhaps the future of this system of education is in allowing this diversity to flourish as long as parents want it to and performance justifies it. Our aim in this book is to encourage researchers to study these schools, not just from a historical perspective, but in their very diversity, their vulnerabilities, and their potential contributions to education in the future. The system of education that took root in the nineteenth century and reached its quantitative peak in 1965 is unlikely ever to be reconstituted. That system produced results that have been of obvious worth to the Catholic Church and the nation at large. There are still many contributions this system can make. But to ensure that they will be made, Catholic schools must be viewed in the context of significant issues in the Church and the nation. Only then can reasonable options be considered realistically from educational, social, and religious perspectives.

REFERENCES

Alexander, K. A., & Pallas, A. M. (1983). Private schools and public policy: New evidence on cognitive achievement in public and private schools. *Sociology of Education, 56*, 115–127.

Baker, D. (1993). The politics of American Catholic school expansion, 1870–1920. In B. Fuller & R. Rubinson (Eds.), *The political construction of education*. New York: Praeger.

Bryk, A. S., Lee, V. E., & Holland, P. B. (1993). *Catholic schools and the common good*. Cambridge, MA: Harvard University Press.

Coleman, J. S., & Hoffer, T. (1987). *Public and private high schools: The impact of communities*. New York: Basic Books.

Gleason, P. (1995). *Contending with modernity: Catholic higher education in the twentieth century*. New York: Oxford University Press.

Greeley, A. M. (1982). *Catholic schools and minority students*. New Brunswick, NJ: Transaction Books.

Guerra, M. J. (1999). *CHS 2000: A first look*. Washington, DC: National Catholic Educational Association.

Irvine, J. J., & Foster, M. (Eds.). (1996). *Growing up African American in Catholic schools*. New York: Teachers College Press.

Leahy, W. P. (1991). *Adapting to America: Catholics, Jesuits, and higher education in the twentieth century*. Washington, DC: Georgetown University Press.

McGreevy, J. T. (1996). *Parish boundaries: The Catholic encounter with race in the twentieth-century urban north*. Chicago: University of Chicago Press.

McLaughlin, T., O'Keefe, J., & O'Keefe, B. (Eds.). (1996). *The contemporary Catholic school: Context, identity, and diversity*. London: Falmer Press.

McLellan, J. A., Youniss, J., & Convey, J. (Eds.). (in press). *The Catholic character of Catholic schools*. Notre Dame, IN: University of Notre Dame Press.

Morris, C. R. (1997). *American Catholic: The saints and sinners who built America's most powerful church*. New York: Times Books.

Mueller, F. C. (in press). Sponsorship of Catholic schools: Preserving the tradition. In J. A. McLellan, J. Youniss, & J. Convey (Eds.), *The Catholic character of Catholic schools*. Notre Dame, IN: University of Notre Dame Press.

Ravitch, D. (1974). *The great school wars, New York City, 1805–1973*. New York: Basic Books.

Ryan, M. P. (1964). *Are parochial schools the answer? Catholic education in light of the council*. New York: Holt, Rinehart & Winston.

Smith, T. L. (1957). *Revivalism and social reform in mid-nineteenth-century America*. New York: Abingdon.

Walch, T. (1996). *Parish school: American Catholic parochial education from colonial times to the present*. New York: Crossroad.

Wittberg, P. (1994). *The rise and decline of Catholic religious orders: A social movement perspective*. Albany: State University of New York Press.

PART I

Operational Characteristics of Catholic Schools

THE CHAPTERS IN THIS PART provide fresh material about the operational features of Catholic schools. In Chapter 1, Jeffrey McLellan reviews trends in Catholic elementary school enrollment from 1940 through 1995. Rather than giving national totals, he focuses on the 20 largest diocesan school systems, which constitute over one-half of the total Catholic school population. The obvious conclusion from the data is that even before Vatican II, Catholic schools began losing their share of the market of potential students. This trend has continued through the 1990s, even as the raw decrease in enrollment has leveled off.

McLellan further explores several factors that might account for the declining market share. Guided by plausible hypotheses offered by experts, he checked the role of various factors such as the loss of religious teachers and the replacement of White Catholics by African American non-Catholics in the urban centers of these dioceses. This work offers new evidence about enrollment and opens the path that productive future research might take in pursuing this issue further.

In Chapter 2, Cornelius Riordan presents a novel synthesis of national data sets to establish trends in secondary school enrollment over the past 25 years. He uses the National Longitudinal Study (1972), High School and Beyond (1980), and the National Education Longitudinal Study (1992) to establish trends over time. These data provide nationally representative samples that give a comprehensive view of the Catholic secondary school population.

The results are clear on three points. During the period of time studied, these secondary schools have enrolled more economically elite, more non-Catholic, and more minority students. A fourth finding is that these schools now enroll more female students than they did 25 years ago. These findings fit results reported in Chapter 3 regarding increasing costs and rising tuition in Catholic schools. They also present a challenge to the traditional depiction of Catholic schools as serving primarily up-wardly mobile constituents. Historically, these schools were designed to educate the Catholic population, who were mainly recent immigrants and from the urban working class. This depiction is now only partially correct as about one-half of today's students are from the upper-quartile in socioeconomic standing.

In Chapter 3, Joseph Harris presents recent trends in costs and in-comes of Catholic schools. Historically, the Catholic Church has not re-ported openly on its financial status. In recent years, this fact has begun to change, and Harris has been one of the leaders in garnering and re-porting such data. The present report is especially important because it offers a comprehensive picture that coordinates parish income with school costs and tuition charges.

It used to be that parishes supported most of the costs for mainte-nance, staff, and materials. This is no longer the case. Harris demon-strates that in seeking other sources of income, schools have had to raise tuition. As was noted, this finding meshes with Riordan's results and probably also plays a role in McLellan's finding regarding declining market share.

In Chapter 4, Maryellen Schaub reviews a national data set on the teaching and administrative staff of Catholic schools. As McLellan noted, staffing is a critical factor in the changing character of Catholic schools. The change from religious to lay teachers is one of the central features that marks the period from Vatican II to the present. Hence, data on teachers and administrators are of core importance in understanding these schools.

Schaub compares teachers in Catholic schools with teachers in pub-lic schools on a number of relevant dimensions. She presents interesting puzzles to ponder by showing, for example, that Catholic school teachers on average earn less and have fewer benefits, but are more satisfied with their jobs, than public school teachers. Another puzzle builds off the satisfaction finding. Teachers in Catholic schools, who are more satisfied, claim to have less of a role in decision making and leave more decisions in the hands of the principal than do teachers in public schools.

In the last chapter in this part, Thomas Hoffer presents a meta-anal-ysis of studies that have compared achievement test scores of students in Catholic and public high schools. This topic has been the focus of much acrimony, as was noted in the Introduction to this book. Hope-fully, Hoffer's present analysis will quiet the troubled waters and allow objective observers to see in which areas and to what degree compara-tive differences exist.

More important, Hoffer carefully reviews data that bear on possible reasons for differences between these kinds of schools. Too much of the public debate has been centered on achievement test scores as outcomes, while too little effort has been directed to the processes that could account for differences. Hoffer's contribution is in articulating hypotheses and assessing them insofar as the data allow. No definitive conclusion is reached but productive leads for future research are clearly delineated.

CHAPTER 1

Rise, Fall, and Reasons Why: U.S. Catholic Elementary Education, 1940–1995

JEFFREY A. McLELLAN

RECENT STUDIES OF CATHOLIC EDUCATION that have captured attention and generated controversy have focused on secondary schooling (e.g., Bryk, Lee, & Holland, 1993; Coleman & Hoffer, 1987; Hoffer, Chapter 5, this volume). However, relatively little research has been devoted to Catholic elementary education. This is true despite the fact that the large majority of students (77% in 1996–97) (National Catholic Educational Association, 1997) in Catholic schools are enrolled in elementary schools. These schools overwhelmingly are run by single parishes (82%), with schools shared by more than one parish constituting the next largest group at 12%, and diocesan and private schools combining to account for only 6% of the total. These numbers reflect the historical roots of elementary education as a basic function of the American Catholic parish. Even today, in rapidly growing suburban areas such as Fairfax County, Virginia, when new parishes are established, the school building sometimes is constructed before the church building.

Over the past 60 years, Catholic elementary schools have expanded and then retreated in terms of number and enrollment. These changes have been cause for a great deal of commentary on the part of Catholics and others over the past 30 years. Some commentators have extolled the unique benefits of the parish school and bemoaned its demise. Others have questioned the need for these institutions in a "modern Church." A review of this literature reveals that speculation about the nature of this "rise and fall" could be informed by quantitative data. Specifically, it would be helpful for researchers and advocates to know how the Catholic elementary system changed over this time period, using the best available numbers. In addition, it would be useful to bring some quantitative information to bear on the question of why the number of schools and their enrollment started to shrink in the 1960s.

The best review of the "rise and fall" data is that of John Convey (1992). In a chapter on the demography of Catholic schools, Convey brought together the extant research on the topic, which, at that time, did not extend to the period prior to the 1960s. The first section of this chapter will attempt to address this gap through original analysis of data from U.S. Census, U.S. Department of Education, and Church sources. This review will show that there was a substantial increase in Catholic elementary enrollment from 1940 to 1960, followed by a dramatic decrease starting in the late 1960s. The data also will show that the system has continued to lose market share through the mid-1990s.

This fall in enrollment was of great contemporary concern to commentators and educators 30 years ago, inspiring leaders to produce books with titles like *S.O.S. for Catholic Schools* (Koob & Shaw, 1970) and *Can Catholic Schools Survive?* (Brown & Greeley, 1970), and it has continued to inspire speculation as to its cause. Clearly, some changes must have taken place that have brought about this decline in Catholic parochial schooling. Some of these reasons can be classified as attitudinal or theological in nature, including the following:

1. *The influence of the Church hierarchy.* Andrew Greeley's "Afterword" to his research collaboration *Catholic Schools in a Declining Church* (Greeley, McCready, & McCourt, 1976) is the most polemical critique of how the Church hierarchy handled the schools. Greeley claimed that the U.S. bishops were unwilling to take adequate steps to support the schools: "Changes in the administration and financing of Catholic education would be absolutely imperative to making such funds available, but there is so much caution and fear and mediocrity in the leadership of the American church that it seems much easier to close schools down or refuse to build new ones than to risk innovative techniques of administering and funding Catholic schools" (p. 324). The main remedy, according to Greeley, would be control of the schools by the laity instead of the clergy.
2. *The attitudes of Catholic parents toward enrolling their children in the schools.* Other reasons have to do with changes in the perceptions of Catholic parents during this period concerning the value, utility, and necessity of Catholic schooling for their children. These changes may be seen in terms of the post–World War II generation of Catholic par-

ents joining the American economic and cultural mainstream. The putative consequence of this shift was that parents no longer wanted to segregate their children in parochial schools to keep them away from "modern" influences. Also, it is possible that parents came to see Catholic schools as academically inferior to public schools and therefore harmful to the career prospects of their children. Two areas of greatest concern were overcrowded classrooms and insufficient teacher preparation relative to the public schools. Byrne (1990) writes of nuns trying to fulfill the need for "sisters for schools, at any cost" (p. 123). In reference to the 1930s, she notes that there were "insuperable limitations on sisters' capacity to obtain pre-service training. Those with patent ability were likely to find themselves in front of a classroom within days of entering the convent" (p. 123). McCluskey (1969) discusses the problems of overcrowded classrooms and inadequate staffing as being the subject of "horror stories" in the "country-club circuit" (p. 107).

Another point made by contemporary critics was the lack of input on the part of parents as to how the schools would be run. Koob and Shaw (1970) complained that the paternalistic approach of management by clergy, which worked with a relatively uneducated immigrant Catholic population, was no longer viable: "People accustomed to having control of their own affairs in other areas of life are not likely to acquiesce in unilateral decisions by an authority—whether bishop, pastor or religious" (p. 46). In a somewhat contradictory addition to the commentary on parent support of the schools, Greeley and his colleagues (1976) presented survey data showing that 80% of Catholics in 1974 would be willing to increase their Church contributions to keep a hypothetical parish school from closing.

3. *Theological shifts.* Walch's history *Parish School* (1996) includes a chapter titled "A Generation of Crises," which describes post-Vatican II doubts among Catholic intellectuals about parochial schooling. The most notable example of this position was Mary Perkins Ryan's 1964 book *Are Parochial Schools the Answer?* She believed not. Ryan's critique of the system was multifaceted. She complained that Catholic schools were an artifact of an outdated "siege mentality" among U.S. Catholics who developed the schools to counter an anti-Catholicism prevalent in earlier years. Like Greeley, she was against clerical domination of the schools, but her solution was to abolish them rather than put them under lay control. Ryan was particularly critical of the schools' focus on younger children rather than older youth and parents, whom she saw as more ready to "penetrate more deeply into the Christian meaning of life and to find that meaning in their own

lives" (p. 77). Her answer was that the money currently being spent on the schools be used instead on nonschool-based catechetical efforts such as classes for children who attended public schools, classes for adults, and enhanced liturgical celebration in church and home. Indeed, she saw the abolishment of the schools as freeing up female and male religious to do other work such as pastoral care and social service.

As previously noted, the first three potential reasons for the decline of parochial schooling are attitudinal or theological in nature. The data analyses in this chapter are not intended to address these issues. However, the next two potential reasons are organizational or demographic in nature and will be addressed in the second section of this chapter. The first reason was staffing changes due to the sharp decline in the availability of women religious to teach in the schools (Convey, 1992; Wittberg, 1994) and the consequent cost increases as the schools had to hire lay replacements at the "going rate." The second was the demographic shift of Catholics to the suburbs and non-Catholics to the cities. The idea here is that urban Catholics left their parish educational infrastructure behind and did not develop a new infrastructure when they arrived in the suburbs. A corollary of this reason is that the migration of Black non-Catholics to the cities left the schools with fewer students and the parishes with fewer members and resources. This phenomenon is discussed most extensively in McGreevy (1996).

RISE AND FALL IN ENROLLMENT, 1940–1995

Any examination of change in the size of the Catholic school system quickly reduces to the question of "market share." A market-share analysis controls for fluctuations in the size of the pool of consumers. This type of analysis relates the enrollment and number of Catholic schools to the number of potential students, thus giving the position of Catholic schools relative to other educational alternatives. Various methods have been used to calculate market share. One approach is to estimate the number of Catholic children of elementary school age in a given year and then compare the result with the number of children enrolled in Catholic schools. This approach has been used by Neuwien (1966), Thompson and Hemrick (1982), Harris (1989), and Schaub and Baker (1993) to calculate the proportion of Catholic children attending Catholic elementary schools. Table 1.1 summarizes their findings.

The percentages presented in this table suggest either unusual fluc-

Table 1.1. Estimated Percentage of Catholic Children Attending U.S. Catholic Elementary Schools in Certain Years

Year	Catholic children in Catholic elementary schools (%)	Source
1962	52	Neuwien (1966)
1965	47	Thompson & Hemrick (1982)
1979	33	Harris (1989)
1980	23	Thompson & Hemrick (1982)
1985	30	Harris (1989)
1986	23	Schaub & Baker (1993)
1987	27	Harris (1989)
1991	20	Schaub & Baker (1993)

Source: Adapted from Convey, 1992.

tuations in the Catholic school market share over the past 35 years or varying results due to methodological differences among the four research teams. For example, a comparison of Harris's 33% figure for 1979 with Thompson and Hemrick's findings of 23% for 1980 indicates either a precipitous enrollment decline among Catholic children or calculation differences. A calculation difference is more likely, given that Harris's figure for 1985 is 30%. The technical appendix to Schaub and Baker (1993) gives a detailed discussion of the variety of reasons for inconsistent estimates, including different sources of baptismal records, considerations of mortality and handicaps that would prevent school attendance by some children, and concerns of residential mobility and immigration. Approaches to estimation likely differ across the authors cited, depending on how they handled these issues.

Another way of looking at market share is to calculate the proportion of total elementary enrollment accounted for by Catholic elementary schools. This method avoids the perils of estimating the size of the elementary school-aged Catholic population, as noted by Schaub and Baker. It also has two other advantages. The first is that, unlike the studies cited above, it uses a consistent method covering a period of 55 years. The second is that it treats non-Catholic children as potential consumers of Catholic education. National Catholic Educational Association (NCEA) figures for the 1996–97 school year indicate that about 12% of Catholic elementary school students nationwide are non-Catholic.

Figure 1.1 compares overall and Catholic elementary enrollment in the period 1940 to 1995. The data reveal that since 1960, Catholic elementary schools have captured a shrinking share of U.S. elementary enrollment. This is particularly true for the so-called "echo boom" increase in elementary school students entering the system starting in the late 1980s. Table 1.2 presents the data in detail. From 1940 to 1960, Catholic elementary schools captured an increasing share of U.S. enrollment at the same time as enrollment was increasing. Thus, by 1960, Catholic elementary schools enrolled approximately 13.5% of the 32.4 million children in all U.S. elementary schools. This was the largest market share the schools were to achieve. By the 1964 school year when Catholic elementary schools reached their largest enrollment at 4.5 million students (Convey, 1992), the schools were already beginning to lose market share at 13.1%.

As discussed above, the precipitous drop in enrollment after 1965 was cause for considerable alarm at the time among Catholic educators and researchers. By the fall of 1974, Catholic enrollment was down 42% (2,602,000) from 10 years earlier (Ganley, 1979), while the U.S. total number of elementary pupils was virtually unchanged (34,564,000 in 1964 versus 34,378,000 in 1974) (U.S. Bureau of the Census, 1995). Thus, the number of potential consumers for Catholic schools did not change but enrollment nevertheless plummeted. This suggests that the answer must be found in something other than overall shifts in the elementary school-

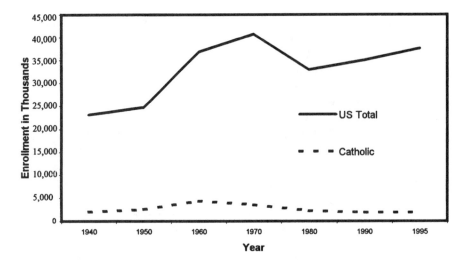

Figure 1.1. Elementary school enrollment, 1940–1995.

Table 1.2. The "Market Share" of U.S. Catholic Elementary Schools, 1940–1995

School year beginning:	Total U.S. enrollment (in thousands)	Elementary enrollment (in thousands)		Percentage of total		Catholic percentage of private
		Catholic	All private	Catholic	All private	
1940	21,127	2,035	—	9.63	—	—
1950	22,207	2,560	—	11.53	—	—
1960	32,441	4,373	4,936	13.48	15.22	88.59
1970	37,133	3,607	4,485	9.71	12.08	80.42
1980	30,625	2,269	3,537	7.41	11.55	64.15
1990	33,164	1,884	3,241	5.68	9.77	58.13
1995	35,665	1,884	4,135	5.28	11.59	45.56

Sources: Total U.S. enrollment and private school enrollment, 1960–1995 totals: U.S. Census Current Population Report Table A-1 "School Enrollment of Persons 3 to 34 Years Old, by Level and Control of School, Race, and Hispanic Origin: October 1955 to 1995"; URL: http://www.census.gov/population/socdemo/school/report95/taba-1. 1940–1950 totals: U.S. Census Statistical Abstract of the United States: 1970, p. 104. Catholic elementary school enrollment: U.S. Department of Education Digest of Education Statistics, 1997; Table 62 "Summary Statistics on Catholic Elementary and Secondary Schools, by Level: 1919–20 to 1996–97"; URL: http://nces01.ed.gov/pubs/digest97/d97t062.html.

aged population. One possibility is some change in the share of the private schooling market commanded by Catholic schools.

Table 1.2 shows that the private school share of the total enrollment reached 15% in 1960 and has fluctuated close to this number since, with not a great deal of variation. However, the Catholic sector of private schooling has been shrinking since 1970, dropping from 80% in that year to 46% in 1995. This means that new non-Catholic private schooling capacity has been added. Data from the National Center for Education Statistics (McLaughlin & Broughman, 1997) suggest that conservative Christian Protestant schools are providing an increasing share of private education. While only 5% of the Catholic schools in existence in 1993 were founded in the preceding 20 years, 79% of conservative Christian schools were started during that period.

REASONS FOR ENROLLMENT DECLINE

This section will present an empirical examination of organizational/ demographic changes that may have contributed to the decline in Catholic enrollment. Part of this analysis will focus on data from the top 20 dioceses in terms of Catholic school enrollment in 1940. [Note that the diocesan-level analyses reported here derive from analyses of the SCRIP data set compiled at Catholic University by Schaub and Baker (1993).] Table 1.3 lists the dioceses and their elementary school enrollment from 1940 to 1990. It also includes the proportion of the national total Catholic elementary enrollment accounted for by the "Top 20" over time. Two things are notable about these dioceses. The first is that they correspond to the 1940 distribution of the Catholic population, being located mostly in northern and eastern states. The second is that they typically include large urban centers.

In 1940, the "Top 20" contained nearly two-thirds of the Catholic elementary enrollment. This number steadily declined to only 42% in 1990. The most significant decline in the "Top 20" share of the national total took place between 1940 and 1960. A probable cause of this drop was the suburbanization of the Catholic population and population growth in western and southern states. The suburbanization phenomenon is reflected in some of the diocese "splitting" that has been taking place since 1940.

Table 1.4 shows the formation of new dioceses out of component counties of the "Top 20." The decades during which each of the new dioceses was created from counties that were originally part of the parent diocese of 1940 are indicated by the column headings. Fourteen of the 20 dioceses split during the 50-year period covered by the table. An examination of the splitting that has taken place suggests three patterns. The most common is the formation of a "daughter" diocese around another urban center within the parent diocese. Examples include the creation of the Baton Rouge and Madison dioceses out of parts of the New Orleans and Milwaukee dioceses, respectively. Another means of making a daughter diocese is by allocating to it the suburban counties of the central city (e.g., Joliet from Chicago and Rockville Centre from Brooklyn). In addition, a few daughter dioceses appear to have been formed from largely rural counties (e.g., New Ulm from St. Paul–Minneapolis).

A consideration of the splitting phenomenon is crucial to any examination of enrollment changes within dioceses over time. For example, when Rockville Centre was formed in 1957 out of suburbs of the Brooklyn diocese, 64 parishes with their schools were removed from urban dioceses and placed in the new diocese (*Official Catholic Directory*, 1957).

Table 1.3. Enrollment in "Top 20" Dioceses, 1940–1990

Diocese	1940	1950	1960	1970	1980	1990
Chicago	152,894	177,013	275,879	210,158	133,440	105,220
Philadelphia	115,121	127,791	222,607	182,218	117,514	96,600
Brooklyn	113,227	146,317	176,156	160,397	90,526	55,544
New York	94,273	110,469	160,678	145,085	96,088	75,185
Boston	91,306	90,172	114,660	81,705	45,489	35,724
Detroit	88,084	91,016	145,502	105,019	57,606	42,690
Pittsburgh	78,512	77,452	108,108	72,205	38,122	30,069
Newark	65,311	74,402	124,487	100,087	58,186	42,366
Cleveland	59,481	58,329	109,718	90,284	62,650	50,717
Milwaukee	49,346	54,305	93,928	59,830	43,893	33,536
Buffalo	48,381	46,311	77,882	56,319	32,358	22,084
St. Louis	47,062	58,076	82,554	66,328	48,220	45,746
Hartford	46,503	48,935	35,847	35,372	23,257	17,141
Springfield	37,683	18,137	24,444	18,106	10,261	9,037
Cincinnati	36,843	41,529	71,020	60,714	41,620	39,002
St. Paul–Minneapolis	34,150	43,478	72,105	48,597	31,265	25,469
New Orleans	31,680	45,831	68,603	52,706	43,281	37,298
Providence	27,572	29,481	38,845	26,310	17,415	12,193
Scranton	24,428	21,425	29,407	20,838	14,487	13,076
Fort Wayne–South Bend	24,152	25,141	22,495	15,834	11,787	10,332
Total	1,266,009	1,385,610	2,054,925	1,608,112	1,017,465	799,029
Proportion of Catholic enrollment nationally	62%	54%	47%	46%	45%	42%

Source: System for Catholic Research, Information, and Planning (SCRIP), Life Cycle Institute, Catholic University of America, Washington, DC. Data originally compiled by M. Schaub and D. Baker.

Table 1.4. Diocese "Splitting"

Diocese	1940s	1950s	1960s	1970s
Chicago	Joliet			
Philadelphia			Allentown	
Brooklyn		Rockville Centre		
New York				
Boston				
Detroit				Lansing
Pittsburgh		Greensburg		
Newark				
Cleveland	Youngstown			
Milwaukee	Madison			
Buffalo				
St. Louis		Jefferson City & Springfield		
		Cape–Girardeau		
Hartford		Norwich & Bridgeport		
Springfield	Worcester			
Cincinnati	Columbus			
St. Paul–Minneapolis		New Ulm		
New Orleans			Baton Rouge	Houma–Thibodeaux
Providence				
Scranton				
Fort Wayne–South Bend	Lafayette	Gary		

Source: System for Catholic Research, Information, and Planning (SCRIP), Life Cycle Institute, Catholic University of America, Washington, DC. Data originally compiled by M. Schaub and D. Baker.

Note: The Lansing and Columbus dioceses were extant dioceses that apparently were allocated constituent counties of "Top 20" dioceses during this period. Since they were not created at that time, these dioceses and their parent dioceses are omitted from analyses in Table 1.5.

This is why an examination of enrollment over time in the "Top 20" dioceses needs to account for the 18 dioceses that were created from the 1940 originals. The percentages reported in Table 1.5 take splitting into consideration by summing total enrollments for parent and daughter dioceses to cover the same set of counties over time.

Another approach to the measurement difficulties associated with

Table 1.5. Potential Factors in Decline of Parishes with Schools and Enrollment, 1960–1990

Potential factor	Mean decline in the percentage of parishes with elementary schools	Mean decline in enrollment from 1960 to 1990 in "Top 20" dioceses
Proportion of population living in an urban area, 1990		
Lowest quartile	17	58
Highest quartile	13	65
Growth in the proportion of the population that is Catholic, 1950–1990		
Lowest quartile	22	—
Highest quartile	21	—
Decline in percentage White of population of main city of diocese, 1950–1970		
Lowest quartile	19	55
Highest quartile	20	64
Increase in the proportion of teachers who are lay, 1960–1990		
Lowest quartile	23	54
Highest quartile	17	65

Sources: System for Catholic Research, Information, and Planning (SCRIP), Life Cycle Institute, Catholic University of America, Washington, DC. Data originally compiled by M. Schaub and D. Baker. Percentage White of population of main city of diocese calculated from U.S. Census data compiled into the County and City Data Book [United States] Consolidated Data File City Data 1944–1977, ICPSR.

Note: "Top 20" dioceses are as of 1940.

diocesan splitting over time is to develop a schooling index that is independent of the number of counties covered by a diocese. One such index is the proportion of regular parishes in the diocese that have parochial elementary schools. Such an index is conceptually salient given the centrality of the parish school to Catholic education. The second column of Table 1.5 uses this index.

Table 1.5 presents the results of analyses done to examine the potential influence of factors that may have caused the enrollment decline observed nationally from the 1960s to the 1990s. The rationale behind the comparisons presented is that if a factor helped speed the decline of the schools, then dioceses that experienced relatively high levels of this factor should show relatively high levels of decline when compared with those that experienced relatively low levels of this factor. These analyses contrast indicators from the highest quartile of dioceses on a given measure with those from the lowest quartile. The first indicator in these analyses is the change from 1960 to 1990 in the percentage of parishes in each diocese with an elementary school. The second indicator is the change from 1960 to 1990 in elementary enrollment in 18 of the "Top 20" dioceses.

Three of the four potential factors considered are demographic in nature. The first is the urbanicity of the diocese. The suburbanization theory discussed above would lead one to expect the more urban dioceses to have a greater decline in Catholic schooling than the less urban dioceses. Similarly, one would expect that dioceses where the Catholic population grew rapidly would have less decline in schooling than dioceses where this was not the case. A third demographic factor is the change in the proportion of the population of the central city of a diocese that was White, given the greater probability of Catholics to be White. This shift was the focus of McGreevy's (1996) study entitled *Parish Boundaries: The Catholic Encounter with Race in the Twentieth-Century Urban North*. A reading of McGreevy would suggest that in the "Top 20" dioceses where there was a greater shift from White to Black in the population of the central city, there should be greater decline in Catholic elementary schooling.

The fourth factor is the relative influence of the "laicization" of the teaching staffs of Catholic elementary schools over the past few decades. Overall, these schools have gone from being staffed largely by women religious to being staffed largely by lay teachers (see also Schaub, Chapter 4, this volume). Previous analyses by McLellan (1997) indicate that the decline in women religious teachers was precipitous, with the proportion of lay teachers skyrocketing from 22% in 1960 to 89% in 1990.

Summary of Findings

Differences in the decline of Catholic elementary schooling as they relate to factors of urbanization, change in number of Catholics, decline of White share of central-city population, and increased numbers of lay teachers include the following:

1. Overall, the more urban dioceses seemed to be more successful in stemming the decline in the proportion of parishes with schools. Dioceses within the highest quartile on urbanization lost an average of 13% of their parish schools from 1960 to 1990 versus dioceses within the bottom quartile, which lost 17% of their schools. However, the more urban dioceses of the "Top 20" suffered a greater decline in enrollment than did the less urban dioceses. From 1960 to 1990 the most urban quarter of the "Top 20" lost 65% of their enrollment as opposed to the least urban quarter, which lost only 58% of their enrollment.

2. Growth in the Catholic proportion of the population from 1950 to 1990 did not seem to influence the proportion of parishes with schools. The top quarter of dioceses in terms of Catholic population growth lost an average of 21% of their parish schools from 1960 to 1990, while the bottom quarter lost a nearly identical 22%. (For technical reasons this could not be calculated for the "Top 20" enrollment analysis.)

3. The decline in the White share of the population of the central cities of the dioceses made no difference in the proportion of parishes with schools but was associated with greater enrollment decline in the "Top 20." Dioceses with the highest rate of decline of White population in their central cities between 1950 and 1970 lost an average of 20% of their parish schools, while those with the lowest rate of decline lost 19%. However, when "Top 20" enrollment declines from 1960 to 1990 were related to White population declines in the central cities of the dioceses, differences did arise. The dioceses that lost the most Whites from their central cities lost an average of 64% of their enrollment over 30 years, while those that lost the fewest Whites lost only 55%.

4. Dioceses where the increase in lay teachers was lowest tended to have a greater decline in the proportion of parishes with schools, but the opposite trend was true for "Top 20" enrollment. The quartile of dioceses with the most "laicization" lost an average of 17% of their parish schools, while those with the least "laicization" lost 23% of theirs.

Meanwhile, the "Top 20" dioceses with the greatest increase in lay teachers lost an average of 65% of their enrollment, while those with the smallest increase lost only 54%.

It is evident that the schooling indices used in this analysis do not operate in the same direction when related to the four factors considered. It appears that in the two instances where proportion differences were observed in parishes with schools, an opposite effect was observed on enrollment. Enrollment is probably the better indicator of the two in these cases because it is an absolute number. Proportion of parishes with schools is a measure that can be affected by two factors. The first is how many schools there are in the diocese; the second, how many parishes there are. One way for a diocese to achieve a relatively high proportion is to close parishes that do not have schools. Thus, this is probably a less meaningful number than enrollment changes over time, including "daughter" dioceses.

CONCLUSION

Through the use of newly constructed indicators of historical change, this study supports many of the findings of previous reports on Catholic schooling. Thus, the national market share of Catholic elementary schools did indeed rise from 1940 to 1960 and did indeed decline sharply starting in the mid-1960s. What this study adds, however, is that the Catholic share of both total U.S. enrollment and total private enrollment in elementary schools continued to decline through the mid-1990s. This decline suggests reason for present-day concern about the future of parochial schooling. Although the current enrollment decline is not so dramatic as that of 25 years ago, it appears to be part of the same unbroken trend.

Since the 1960s, there has been a substantial literature speculating about the causes of this decline. Some of the causes posited are philosophical or theological in nature and are not amenable to quantification. Nevertheless, three standard reasons given for the decline are supported by the limited quantitative analyses reported here. These are the suburbanization of the Catholic population, racial population shifts in the central cities, and the virtual disappearance of women religious teachers.

Acknowledgment. I wish to thank David Baker for suggestions inspiring the "market share" analyses contained herein.

REFERENCES

Brown, W. E., & Greeley, A. M. (1970). *Can Catholic schools survive?* New York: Sheed & Ward.

Bryk, A. S., Lee, V. E., & Holland, P. B. (1993). *Catholic schools and the common good.* Cambridge, MA: Harvard University Press.

Byrne, P. (1990). *Transforming parish ministry.* New York: Crossroad.

Coleman, J. S., & Hoffer, T. (1987). *Public and private high schools: The impact of communities.* New York: Basic Books.

Convey, J. J. (1992). *Catholic schools make a difference. Twenty-five years of research.* Washington, DC: National Catholic Educational Association.

Ganley, W. (1979). *NCEA/Ganley's Catholic schools in America.* Englewood, CO: Fisher.

Greeley, A. M., McCready, W. C., & McCourt, K. (1976). *Catholic schools in a declining church.* Kansas City: Sheed & Ward.

Harris, J. C. (1989). *The enrollment patterns in Catholic schools: The past and the future, 1979–1992.* Washington, DC: National Catholic Educational Association.

Koob, C. A., & Shaw, R. (1970). *S.O.S. for Catholic schools.* New York: Holt, Rinehart & Winston.

McCluskey, N. G. (1969). *Catholic education faces its future.* Garden City, NY: Doubleday.

McGreevy, J. T. (1996). *Parish boundaries: The Catholic encounter with race in the twentieth-century urban north.* Chicago: University of Chicago Press.

McLaughlin, D. H., & Broughman, S. (1997). *Private schools in the United States: A statistical profile, 1993–94.* Washington, DC: U.S. Department of Education, National Center for Education Statistics.

McLellan, J. A. (1997, May). *Enrollment and organizational trends in Catholic elementary and secondary schools: 1940–1995.* Paper presented at the Conference on the Future of Catholic Education, Catholic University, Washington, DC.

National Catholic Educational Association. (1997). *Catholic schools in America: Elementary/secondary.* Silverthorne, CO: Fisher.

Neuwien, R. (Ed.). (1966). *Catholic schools in action.* Notre Dame, IN: University of Notre Dame Press.

Official Catholic Directory. (1957). New York: P.J. Kenedy.

Ryan, M. P. (1964). *Are parochial schools the answer? Catholic education in the light of the council.* New York: Holt, Rinehart & Winston.

Schaub, M., & Baker, D. (1993). *Serving American Catholic children and youth: A diocesan level study of PREP and Catholic school enrollments and unserved children.* Prepared for the U.S. Catholic Conference Department of Education, Washington, DC.

Thompson, A. D., & Hemrick, E. (1982). *The last fifteen years: A statistical survey of Catholic elementary and secondary formal religious education 1965–1980.* Washington, DC: United States Catholic Conference.

U.S. Bureau of the Census. (1970). *Statistical abstract of the United States*. Washington, DC: U.S. Government Printing Office.

U.S. Bureau of the Census. (1979). *County and city data book* [United States] consolidated data file, city data 1944–1977. Ann Arbor, MI: Inter-university Consortium for Political and Social Research.

U.S. Bureau of the Census. (1995). *Current population report* [on-line document], Table A-1 "School enrollment of persons 3 to 34 years old, by level and control of school, race, and Hispanic origin: October 1955 to 1995"; URL: www.census.gov/population/socdemo/school/report95/taba-1

U.S. Department of Education. (1997). *Digest of Education Statistics* [on-line document], Table 62 "Summary statistics on Catholic elementary and secondary schools, by level: 1919–20 to 1996–97"; URL: http://nces01.ed.gov/pubs/digest97/d97t062.html

Walch, T. (1996). *Parish school: American Catholic parochial education from colonial times to the present*. New York: Crossroad.

Wittberg, P. (1994). *The rise and decline of Catholic religious orders: A social movement perspective*. Albany: State University of New York Press.

CHAPTER 2

Trends in Student Demography in Catholic Secondary Schools, 1972–1992

CORNELIUS RIORDAN

IN THIS CHAPTER, I WILL PROVIDE a summary of demographic trends that have occurred among students in Catholic secondary schools during the period 1972–1992. These two decades cover a period of history with notable changes affecting all educational institutions. Historically, during this time, we endured the end of the Vietnam War and Watergate, the Iran crises, and the dissolution of the Soviet Union. During this time there were major changes in family structure, family work patterns, and the locus of child care; there were geographic shifts in population and significant changes in the demographic population of the schools; there was a significant increase in poverty, and especially children in poverty. During the 1980s, in particular, there was an extensive evaluation of the entire educational industry, leading to numerous recommendations for reform.

During this time Catholic schools declined in numbers (schools and students) and then (more recently) began to rise slightly again, and they received positive evaluations compared with public schools in the form of several social science studies (Coleman & Hoffer, 1987; Bryk, Lee, & Holland, 1993). The high points for Catholic school enrollments are the early 1960s for elementary school children and the later 1960s for secondary school students (National Center for Education Statistics, 1992). Since that time, however, enrollments declined by 50% (57% decline in elementary schools and 44% in secondary schools). Although there have been some years showing a small increase, the overall pattern is clearly and alarmingly downward. These downward trends in enrollments are troubling, especially when coupled with positive reports regarding the high quality of education provided in Catholic schools.

A long-standing critique of Catholic schools is that they are socially divisive and elitist. Bryk, Lee, and Holland (1993) make this point in their book *Catholic Schools and the Common Good*. Historically, concern has always existed that the schools were divisive both in terms of religion and racial/ethnic background. Until the 1960s, Catholic schools were homogeneous social institutions—they were Catholic and White, often of a single ethnic group (e.g., Irish). Although this divisiveness may have been true historically, it appeared to Coleman, Hoffer, and Kilgore (1982), Greeley (1982), and Coleman and Hoffer (1987) that this was no longer true, at least as of 1982. During the last decades of the twentieth century, Catholic schools had become increasingly non-Catholic and non-White, leading to the view advanced by all of the above researchers that the Catholic schools have replaced the public schools as America's common schools, that is, the schools that take all comers and especially the disadvantaged. This much publicized finding led all of these researchers to justifiably conclude that Catholic schools, rather than public schools, should be viewed as providing the ideal of the "common school."

Moreover, the above-cited researchers argued and demonstrated that Catholic schools are more effective than public schools in terms of increasing academic achievement, especially among minority and/or disadvantaged students (see also Hoffer, Chapter 5, this volume). Among students from homes of high or middle socioeconomic status, the difference between Catholic schools and public schools is quite small or null in terms of academic outcomes (a finding that is intuitively and reasonably obvious; for a broader review of studies, see Riordan, 1997a). Coleman and colleagues (Coleman & Hoffer, 1987; Coleman, Hoffer, & Kilgore, 1982; Greeley, 1982; Hoffer, Greeley, & Coleman, 1985) concluded that Catholic schools provided *greater equality and greater achievement* than public schools among comparable students (see also Bryk, Lee, & Holland, 1993; for a critique of this conclusion, see Alexander & Pallas, 1983, 1985; Willms, 1985).

This conclusion has played a large role in proposals to reform the public schools over the past 15 years. In fact, the outcome of the Catholic–public school comparisons has been focused almost entirely on what the public school can learn from the Catholic school. This occurred despite the cautions and protestations of those who were critical of the basic findings as well as the policy implications of the findings (see Alexander & Pallas, 1983, 1985; Heyns, 1981; Murnane, 1981). The common school idea was institutionalized in American educational ideology as an egalitarian ideal. By this dictum, public schools were established to provide equal educational opportunity for all comers; this was especially true of the urban public school systems developed in the early nineteenth century. Students from the great diversity of society would attend school side by side and the results would be greater equality among them. However, the above research discovered that this was not the case in the 1980s. Student performance was higher and was more equal in Catholic schools. It is important to note that this higher student performance in Catholic schools was never found to be of a great magnitude, typically being only about .10 of a standard deviation or less (see Jencks, 1985; Hoffer, Chapter 5, this volume).

The news of greater Catholic school effectiveness provided parents with the opportunity to "choose" a good school for their children. Thus, the situation provides an opportunity to examine the results of school choice as a school reform strategy. What has happened to the demographic composition of Catholic schools during the period 1972 to 1992? Is there evidence that the schools have maintained their demographic diversity, as the research claimed existed in the early 1980s, or have they become more elitist, responding to the demands of a market searching for good schools?

In this chapter, I will show that indeed Catholic secondary schools increasingly are serving a non-Catholic, non-White, and nonreligious population. However, I also will demonstrate that this religious and racial diversity is at the same time increasingly selective in terms of socioeconomic status (SES). In effect, I will demonstrate that Catholic secondary schools are no longer serving a disadvantaged population, even in urban areas. In the end, I will argue that these social transformations will soon bring Catholic schools to a crossroad with regard to their mission and their identity, and that at the same time these findings should raise a cautionary flag for supporters of privatization and vouchers in the public sector.

SOME METHODOLOGICAL CONSIDERATIONS

I draw upon data from three national surveys of high school students conducted by the National Center for Education Statistics (NCES). These data sets are the National Longitudinal Study (NLS 1972), High School and Beyond (HSB 1980), and the National Educational Longitudinal Study (NELS 1992). These surveys represent, respectively, the graduating high school classes of 1972, 1980, and 1992 (see Appendix 2.1 for details). The strength of these data sets is longitudinal research. They were designed essentially with this in mind. However, the data can be used to make cross-sectional comparisons over time. With some modifications to NELS, we can compare the NLS 1972 seniors, the HSB 1980 seniors (not the HSB 1982 seniors, whose data are far more complicated), and the NELS 1992 seniors (after excluding dropouts, early graduates, and any students who were not twelfth graders in the spring of 1992). The methodological problems of doing such a cross-sectional statistical analysis are detailed in several NCES reports (Green, Dugoni, Ingels, & Quinn, 1995).

For each data set, I have employed one or more flags or variables to remove transfers and dropouts from the analysis. Insofar as is possible, we wish to know the changing background characteristics of students in Catholic schools who attended for a full 3 or 4 years of high school. I have employed this restriction throughout the analyses. Appendix 2.2 identifies the variables and flags used to accomplish this in each case. Limiting the analysis in this way to those students who attended the same school produces results that in some cases may differ from NCES reports and/or other studies that do not flag students in this manner. This restriction provides a more stable portrait of both the demographics and student outcomes. Of course, this restriction does not allow us to estimate the patterns of transfers and dropouts and how these might change the demographic patterns and the outcomes, and it does underestimate the number of minorities and non-Catholics attending Catholic schools. A listing of all other variables for each data set is provided in Appendix 2.3.

In all of the tables in this chapter, I have employed the appropriate sample weights and corrections for design effects associated with the two-stage stratified sampling process that was used to gather the data. Specifically, the NELS results for students in Catholic schools were multiplied by a factor of 1.5, and the results for students in public school by a factor of 1.7 (these are actually mean root design effects). For the results among racial or gender subgroups within each school sector, the design effect factor was reduced by .5 (see Chapter 3 in Ingels et al., 1994). For NLS 1972, the same mean root design effects were employed as in NELS. Tourangeau and colleagues (1987) researched the design effects associated with NLS and concluded that it was reasonable to use the average mean root design effect of 1.61 for both subgroup analyses and for analyses involving all respondents. Although they do not provide specific subgroup design effects for public and Catholic schools, I have used 1.5 for Catholic schools and 1.7 for public schools. This is not only consistent with NELS, but it is also reasonable. For the base-year

HSB 1980 data, guidelines are less specific, and researchers are advised to use 1.5 as a general approximation (Sebring et al., 1987). I decided to use 1.5 for Catholic schools and 1.7 for public schools for the sake of consistency. Design effects for subgroup analyses were reduced by .5 as in NELS and NLS.

In an earlier report (Riordan, 1997b), I provided an estimate of two times the standard error for each percentage or mean multiplied by a design effect correction. This allowed the reader to quickly construct a 95% confidence interval around each percentage. This sampling error estimate (i.e., a 95% confidence interval) turns out to be plus or minus 1% for public schools, and usually plus or minus 3 or 4% for Catholic schools. In this chapter, I have removed these standard errors from the tables for the sake of simplicity, but the reader should always apply them for a fuller understanding of each table.

NON-WHITE AND NON-CATHOLIC ENROLLMENTS

In this section, I examine demographic indicators of student population—the percentage of students who are Catholic and the percentage who are minority. Over the past 20 years Catholic secondary schools have become increasingly non-Catholic and non-White in their student composition. In NELS, I used a composite of two measures of religion in the data (F1S81 and F2N22). Only students who were consistently Catholic or Non-Catholic on both measures were used in the analysis. Table 2.1 shows that in 1992, 21% of seniors in Catholic secondary schools were non-Catholic—nearly three times as many non-Catholic students as in 1980 and 10 times as many as in 1972. These estimates are confirmed by the data obtained by the National Catholic Educational Association (NCEA, 1973, 1995).

To a large degree, however, the total estimates in Table 2.1 conceal the reality of the change in student composition. A somewhat different picture emerges if we control the results by racial background of the

Table 2.1. Percentage of Non-Catholic Student Enrollments in Catholic Secondary Schools, 1972–1992

	1972	*1980*	*1992*
Percent non-Catholic	1.8	7.0	21.1
Number of cases	(912)	(2,415)	(764)

Table 2.2. Percentage of Non-Catholic Student Enrollments in Catholic Secondary Schools by Race, 1972–1992

	1972	*1980*	*1992*
Whites	1.0	5.0	14.1
Number of cases	(841)	(1,832)	(584)
Non-Whites	13.9	24.0	43.7
Number of cases	(69)	(571)	(180)

students as shown. Table 2.2 shows that by 1992 both White and non-White students in Catholic schools were, in fact, more likely to be non-Catholic than in either 1980 or 1972. *White students were at least 10 times more likely to be non-Catholic in 1992 as they were in 1972.* By 1992, 14% of White students were non-Catholic. *Fully 44% of the non-White students identified themselves as non-Catholic.* This is not at all surprising since most African Americans and Asian Americans are not Catholic nor are some Hispanic Americans. Thus, it appears that there was a significant transformation in the religious composition of Catholic schools and that the change was *not* limited to non-White students. However, nearly half of the minority students in Catholic secondary schools are non-Catholic. What has the trend been in minority enrollments over the past 20 years?

The NCEA (1973, 1995) reported that the percentage of non-White students attending Catholic secondary schools increased from 11% in 1972 to 17% in 1982 and to 24% in 1993. Our analysis of the NCES data resonates with these results. Table 2.3 shows the trend in minority enrollments in Catholic and public secondary schools from 1972 to 1992. I have

Table 2.3. Minority Enrollment in Catholic and Public Secondary Schools, 1972–1992

| | *1972* | | *1980* | | *1992* | |
	Catholic	*Public*	*Catholic*	*Public*	*Catholic*	*Public*
Percentage non-White	5.9	14.6	10.8	18.2	25.0	25.9
Number of cases	(916)	(11,914)	(2,484)	(21,297)	(799)	(11,903)

Note: Estimates for 1980 differ slightly from those computed by Coleman, Hoffer, and Kilgore (1982, Table 3-1), using exactly the same data. The discrepancy is due to slight differences in the coding of the race variable and the elimination of transfers from the analysis.

included both Catholic and public schools here to examine the extent to which the racial composition of Catholic schools is becoming more like that of public schools. Quite remarkably, the percentage of non-White students in Catholic secondary schools has increased dramatically over the past 20 years to a point where the racial demography of Catholic and public schools is now virtually the same. In 1972, only 6% of the students in Catholic schools were non-White compared with 15% in public schools. This difference may appear smaller than one might have thought, but the relatively low percentage of non-White students in public schools in 1972 is supported by the independent analyses of Green and colleagues (1995). These data, of course, are for graduating seniors. In any event, by 1992 the proportion of minority students in Catholic and public schools had increased dramatically. In *both* school sectors, minorities constituted about 25% of the graduating student body. The percentage of minorities attending public schools would increase if we excluded rural schools. For example, with rural schools excluded in 1992, minorities constituted 30% of graduating public school seniors compared with 25% for their counterparts in Catholic schools.

SOCIAL CLASS

How does this transformation of the racial demography of Catholic schools compare with the socioeconomic composition of the schools? Given the increase of minority students attending Catholic schools, one might assume that the schools have become socioeconomically more diverse as well. This assumption, however, turns out to be incorrect. One of the strengths of the NCES data sets is the measure for socioeconomic status. The measure is a composite of parental educational and occupational status, parental income, and a set of household items. It is extremely valid and reliable and can be used to compare across the cohorts. Table 2.4 shows the percentage of students from each school sector in both the lowest and highest quartiles of the socioeconomic scale as well as the average SES scores (the scale has an overall mean of zero and a standard deviation of 1).

In 1972, a slightly greater percentage of students in Catholic schools (30%) came from homes in the highest SES quartile than did students in public schools (24%). Similarly, more students in public schools (25%) came from the lowest SES quartile than did students in Catholic schools (12%). This difference in the social class composition of the schools also can be seen in the average scores. This social class demographic portrait in 1972 reflects a taken-for-granted image of Catholic schools serving a

Table 2.4. Socioeconomic Status (SES) Composition of Catholic and Public Secondary Schools, 1972–1992

	1972		1980		1992	
	Catholic	Public	Catholic	Public	Catholic	Public
% lowest quartile	12.3	24.6	15.2	29.0	5.5	20.2
% highest quartile	29.7	24.2	35.5	22.0	45.8	27.4
Number of cases	(918)	(11,903)	(2,465)	(21,040)	(798)	(11,863)
Average score	.16	−.01	.23	−.08	.39	.00

Note: The average SES score has a mean of zero and a standard deviation of 1.0. The public school average is zero (slightly lower in 1980).

substantial number of students from poor and working-class backgrounds.

Table 2.4 shows, however, that over the 20-year period from 1972 to 1992 Catholic schools became significantly and dramatically more selective and less diverse in terms of socioeconomic status. The difference between the mean scores doubled, the percentage of lowest-quartile-SES students in Catholic schools was cut in half, and the number of highest-quartile-SES students in Catholic schools nearly doubled. Thus, Catholic schools on average have become more selective and are no longer serving primarily the disadvantaged or even the working class, despite the fact that a goodly number of minority students now attend Catholic schools. This social transformation of student composition in Catholic schools intensified between 1982 and 1992.

Not surprisingly, this transformation in the SES of students attending Catholic schools has been accompanied by a persistent and substantial increase in the average tuition at Catholic schools during this same period. In 1972, average annual tuition at Catholic secondary schools was approximately $500 (NCEA, 1973) compared with $2,800 in 1992 (Guerra, 1995). This increase is at least twice the rate of other educational cost inflation (public teacher salaries, college professor salaries, and so forth) during this same time period (National Center for Education Statistics, 1992). Moreover, the tuition increase occurred at both the elementary and the secondary school levels (see Harris, Chapter 3, this volume).

This increase in tuition is due, in no small measure, to the accompanying transformation of the teaching faculty of Catholic schools. In 1970, lay faculty accounted for 48% of Catholic secondary school teachers, but this had increased to 83% by 1990 (see Schaub, Chapter 4, this volume). Of course, it is possible that this transformation in the socioeconomic context of Catholic schools is limited to White students. In further analysis of these data, however, I have determined that the basic results shown in Table 2.4 are not changed in any significant way when the results are broken down by race, gender, or urbanization.

In 1992, fully 40% of minorities in Catholic schools came from upper-income homes compared with only 15% of minorities attending public schools (see Table 2.5). In Catholic schools, minorities and Whites differed only slightly in their SES background, whereas in public schools minority and White students differed significantly according to socioeconomic status. By contrast, we observe that in 1972, there were fewer Whites *and* minorities in Catholic schools who came from high-SES homes. Even allowing for the high sampling error among the low number of minorities in the NLS survey, there can be no doubt that Catholic schools in 1972 were serving an entirely different population.

If we examine the average SES scores for Whites and minorities separately (Table 2.5), we see that the average score for Whites attending Catholic schools increased (from .18 to .45) and the average score for minorities increased to an even greater degree (from −.04 to .23). Throughout the 20 years, the socioeconomic demographics of public schools have remained relatively constant for both Whites and non-Whites. The slight increase in public school SES in 1992 (both White and non-White) may be due in part to the fact that dropouts in 1990–92 were twice as likely to come from poverty-based homes as in 1980–82 (Kaufman, McMillen, & Sweet, 1996). Recall that in this analysis we consider only graduating seniors who remained in the same school for their high school career.

Conceivably, the increase in non-Catholic White students might account for some of this increasingly SES selectivity. In fact, however, this is not the case—the SES of White Catholics is .45 compared with .43 for White non-Catholics. Among minorities, the SES levels are higher for Catholics (.35) than for non-Catholics (.14). All of this suggests that parents of above-average SES increasingly have come to select Catholic schools regardless of their race or their religious identification.

To pursue the matter one step further, we can ask if this SES selection process is constrained or conditioned by gender. To examine this, I conducted an analysis of student socioeconomic status by school type controlling for both race and gender. I limited the analysis here to just the raw SES score with its mean of zero. Table 2.6 shows the now familiar pattern for students in the public schools—no change in SES among any of the race-by-gender subgroups. In Catholic schools, however, we note an interesting set of exceptions to the pattern shown previously in

Table 2.5. Socioeconomic Status (SES) Composition of Catholic and Public Secondary Schools by Race, 1972–1992

| | Catholic | | | | | | Public | | | | | |
| | Minority | | | White | | | Minority | | | White | | |
	1972	1980	1992	1972	1980	1992	1972	1980	1992	1972	1980	1992
% lowest quartile	20.4	29.2	10.8	11.8	13.5	3.7	54.1	54.4	38.4	19.7	23.5	13.9
% highest quartile	20.6	29.8	39.4	30.0	36.1	48.0	8.7	8.9	14.8	26.8	25.8	31.7
Number of cases	(70)	(594)	(199)	(846)	(1,849)	(599)	(2,350)	(4,552)	(3,513)	(9,525)	(16,247)	(8,336)
Average score	−.04	.05	.23	.18	.26	.45	−.46	−.51	−.36	.06	.01	.13

Notes: The average SES score has a mean of zero and a standard deviation of 1.0. The public school average is zero (slightly lower in 1980). African and Hispanic Americans score below average, and this appears as a negative number.

Table 2.6. Average Socioeconomic Status (SES) of Catholic and Public
Secondary Schools by Race and Gender

	Catholic Schools				Public Schools			
	Male		Female		Male		Female	
	Minority	White	Minority	White	Minority	White	Minority	White
1972	.04	.28	−.04	.07	−.43	.09	−.49	.04
1980	.06	.33	.05	.19	−.44	.06	−.57	−.03
1992	.48	.48	−.04	.40	−.33	.14	−.39	.11

Notes: The average SES score has a mean of zero and a standard deviation of 1.0. The public
school average is zero (slightly lower in 1980). African and Hispanic Americans score below average, and this appears as a negative number.

Table 2.5. *Specifically, the increase in SES is actually much greater than pre-*
viously noted for minority males and White females. In 1972, only White
males scored significantly above average on the SES composite—White
females and minority males and females came from average (poor or
working-class homes). Over the 20-year period, however, the social class
background of White females and minority males attending Catholic
schools rose dramatically (along with that of White males). In fact, in
1992 the average SES of minority males was exactly equal to the average
SES of White males in Catholic schools, followed closely by that of White
females. Among minority females, there was no appreciable increase in
SES selectivity whatsoever from 1972 to 1992.

   In 1992, it was minority males and White males (and White females)
in Catholic schools who came from predominantly middle-class homes.
An increasing number of middle-class families in these three race-by-
gender subgroups were selecting Catholic schools, probably responding
to the publicized greater effectiveness of these schools. Middle-class minority families were not making the same choice for their daughters. In
contrast, in 1972, middle-class White families followed exactly the same
pattern of gender differentiation between their sons and daughters. It
would be interesting to examine these male/female results according to
whether the schools were coeducational or single gender, but there are
not enough cases in 1972 to do this and maintain the racial breakdown.

   In my research, I also examined the extent to which these socioeconomic demographics might differ according to whether or not the
schools were in urban, suburban, or rural areas. This investigation (not
shown in tabular form here) turned up several interesting discoveries.
First, the vast majority (81%) of Catholic secondary school students in
the NELS 1992 sample were located in urban centers. There are very few

Catholic secondary schools in rural areas (see Coleman et al., 1982, Table 2-4). Indeed, there were actually no students attending Catholic secondary schools in the 1992 NELS sample in rural areas. The absence of Catholic schools in rural areas is in contrast to public secondary schools in NELS, where 35% of students attend schools in rural areas.

In any event, in 1992 the SES distribution of students remained constant in Catholic schools regardless of urbanization. The SES of students in public schools, however, changed significantly. Suburban public schools were clearly more selective (34% high SES in the suburbs compared with 26% in the cities). Remarkably, the socioeconomic status of students attending Catholic schools was the same regardless of whether they attended in the cities (46% high SES) or in the suburbs (44% high SES). The SES of public school students, however, was significantly higher in the suburban schools than in the urban schools and was very low in rural schools. It is important to note, however, that for Catholic schools the urban/suburban pattern shown for 1992 is dissimilar to what existed in 1972. At that time students in suburban Catholic schools came from homes of higher socioeconomic status (38%) than in the urban areas (28%). For public schools, however, the urban/suburban two-tiered system existed in both 1972 and 1992 (see also "Quality Counts," 1998). As we have noted, however, by 1992 urban and suburban Catholic schools were not differentiated by social class. This indicates that Catholic urban schools especially were becoming more selective in terms of the socioeconomic status of their students.

Finally, this discussion of the increase in the socioeconomic status of students attending Catholic schools prompts us to ask how these SES levels compare with those of students attending other private schools. In the NELS 1992 data, there are two other private school types with a sufficient case base: other religious private and other nonreligious private. In NLS 1972 and HSB 1980, there are an insufficient number of non-Catholic private schools so the following analysis is confined to the NELS 1992 data. Table 2.7 repeats the now familiar finding from Table 2.4 for public and Catholic schools and adds the results for the other two private school types. It is immediately clear that the SES level of students attending Catholic schools (.39) is not close to the degree of SES selectivity among students in other religious private schools (.72) or in nonreligious private schools (.98), despite the trend that we have described in the previous tables. However, Table 2.7 lacks the capacity to show the trends for the other private schools. Quite possibly, the other private schools have remained stable over the past 20 years, leading to the conclusion that Catholic schools are becoming more like these other private schools in their student SES composition. Or perhaps the other private

Table 2.7. Socioeconomic Status (SES) Composition of Catholic, Public, and Other Private Secondary Schools in 1992

	Public	*Catholic*	*Private, other religion*	*Private, nonreligious*
% lowest quartile	20.2	5.5	0.9	0.7
% highest quartile	27.4	45.8	65.2	80.7
Number of cases	(11,863)	(798)	(381)	(871)
Average score	.00	.39	.72	.98

Note: Design effect for other private schools is 2.6.

schools also have increased their degree of elitism over the past 20 years, suggesting a more widespread exodus on the part of high-SES families from the public schools.

RELIGIOUS DEMOGRAPHY

What evidence exists concerning the effectiveness of Catholic schools in promoting religiosity and/or in the selection of religiously oriented students? Church attendance may vary considerably from denomination to denomination. Weekly church attendance has been promoted by the Catholic church for centuries. Some previous studies have examined church attendance between Catholic and public school students, considering only Catholics. Here we consider all students in each sector. We treat church attendance in the same way we treat religiosity; that is, it is an indicator of religiosity. We really are asking how religious students are who attend Catholic and public schools, regardless of their religion. To some degree, this may bias a favorable response in the direction of Catholic schools. However, if we consider only Catholic students, we cannot obtain a measure and feeling for the religious context of the schools, which is how we frame the question here. Moreover, in the effect analysis, we actually control for religion (Catholic and other). Questions regarding religiosity were not asked in the NLS 1972 survey and thus the following analysis is confined to HSB 1980 and NELS 1992.

Considering the 1992 results, Catholic school students were significantly less likely than public school students to rarely or never attend church. Table 2.8 shows that this difference is on the order of 20 percentage points and it remains a significant effect even after background controls are added, as shown in the effect size analysis. Moreover, this 20% point gap existed in 1980 as well. It is important to note, however, that

Table 2.8. Percentage of All Students Who Rarely or Never Attend Church

	1980		1992	
	Catholic	*Public*	*Catholic*	*Public*
% Rarely/Never	20.1	41.5	24.9	45.5
Number of cases	(2,413)	(20,231)	(720)	(10,911)
Catholic/public effect size diff.				
Uncontrolled		.44		.36*
Controlled		.29		.26*

Notes: Catholic/public effect sizes are differences between two means divided by the pooled standard deviation of these means. This standardizes the effect across the years and allows for comparisons that are not possible using the actual mean scores. In cases where this type of analysis is employed, a set of home background variables are used as controls for "selection bias." These controls are limited to those variables that are available in exactly the same measured form in each of the data sets (see Appendix 2.3). The table is composed of students of all religions.

* Significant at less than .01 after applying 2 × SE × DE. Controlled for background variables shown in Appendix 2.2. For the regression analysis, the dependent variable is coded 1–6.

the percentage of students who rarely or never attend church *increased slightly in both sectors from 1980 to 1992.*

The results are not altered substantially when we control for either race or SES separately. Minorities in Catholic schools are only slightly more likely (by only 2%) not to attend church. Low-SES students in Catholic schools are 10% more likely to not attend, and this shows up in the controlled analysis where the effect is reduced from .36 to .26 in 1992, with similar results in 1980. In this controlled analysis, church attendance was coded 1 (more than once a week) to 6 (not at all).

Similarly, Catholic school students in 1992 were more likely to consider themselves religious than were public school students. This is true even after controlling for the background variables. The choices on this question are Yes, very religious; Yes, somewhat; and No, not at all. Of these, only the two extreme categories are meaningful, conveying clear images of the degree of religiosity. As it turns out, the differences on "very religious" do not differ among students in Catholic and public schools in 1992 (17.9 for Catholic and 14.1 for public). Thus, Table 2.9 presents the results for those who reported that they were not at all religious. It is notable that there is no difference by school type among minority students in the degree of religiosity. Thus, the differences shown in Table 2.9 really hold only for White students.

There has been a significant increase in nonreligious students in

Table 2.9. Percentage of Students Responding "No, Not at All" to Whether They Think of Themselves as a Religious Person

	1980		1992	
	Catholic	*Public*	*Catholic*	*Public*
% No, Not at all	10.7	21.7	21.8	30.9
Number of cases	(2,418)	(20,322)	(722)	(10,215)
Catholic/public effect size diff.				
Uncontrolled		.17*		.19*
Controlled		.17*		.16*

Notes: Effect sizes are differences between two means divided by the pooled standard deviation of these means. This standardizes the effect across the years and allows for comparisons that are not possible using the actual mean scores. In cases where this type of analysis is employed, a set of home background variables are used as controls for "selection bias." These controls are limited to those variables that are available in exactly the same measured form in each of the data sets (see Appendix 2.3). The table is composed of students of all religions.

* Significant at less than .01 after applying 2 × SE × DE. Controlled for background variables shown in Appendix 2.2. For the regression analysis, the dependent variable is coded 1–3.

both sectors since 1980. Among Catholic school students, the percentage doubled (from 11 to 22%), while the increase among public school students was similar (from 22 to 31%). I want to emphasize that this change in Catholic schools is not due to an increase in non-Catholics or in non-Whites or to an increase in higher-SES students (low-SES students are less religious). In fact, the similarities in the increase between the two sectors may be part of larger societal forces. However, this increased secularization contains more probative implications for Catholic schools in terms of identity and mission.

CONCLUSIONS

During the period from 1972 to 1992, Catholic secondary schools and the students attending the schools underwent a substantial demographic transformation. In 1992, a larger percentage of students attending the schools were non-White and non-Catholic compared with 20 years earlier. The racial makeup of Catholic schools in 1992 was virtually identical to that in public schools (25% non-White), and about 20% of the students were non-Catholic. Despite this change in the direction of diversity, however, Catholic secondary schools actually have become significantly more selective in terms of socioeconomic status. Nearly 50% of the students attending and graduating from Catholic secondary schools in 1992 come from upper-middle-class homes (upper quartile). This transformation also existed in Catholic elementary schools, where Hafner, Ingels, Schneider, and Stevenson (1990) found that over one-third of students came from upper-middle-class homes. Figure 2.1 summarizes these trend patterns for social class, religion, and race in Catholic secondary schools.

Historically, Catholic schools have served the disadvantaged. This is not to say that the schools were attended mostly by lower-SES students, but only that they have always contained a substantial proportion of low-SES and working-class children. Moreover, research has found that Catholic schools are more effective than public schools and possibly even more effective than other private schools, but that this greater effectiveness is more pronounced with low-SES and otherwise disadvantaged students (see Bryk, Lee, & Holland, 1993; Coleman & Hoffer, 1987; Coleman, Hoffer, & Kilgore, 1982; Greeley, 1982). Furthermore, following the message of Vatican II, Catholic schools rededicated themselves to intensifying and expanding educational service to the disadvantaged. Within the context of Vatican II and Christian ministry, "deserting the poor and serving a more affluent clientele would be counter witness to the gospel" (Bryk, Lee, & Holland, 1993, p. 52).

Taken as a whole, the argument has been advanced that Catholic

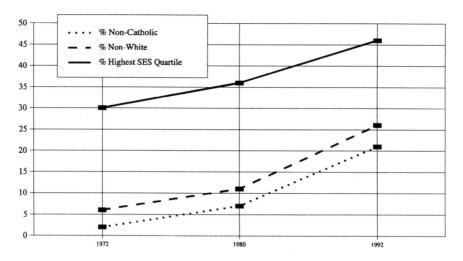

Figure 2.1. Demographic characteristics of Catholic secondary school students.

schools are better able than public schools to produce both equality and achievement. This argument rests on the demonstrated empirical fact that minorities and students of low cognitive ability and low SES make greater academic gains in Catholic schools, thereby closing the gap between advantaged and disadvantaged students. Quite possibly, this meritorious characteristic can persist despite the increase in selectivity that is occurring in Catholic schools. Yet, the change should be examined carefully not only in terms of effectiveness but also with consideration to who shall be served. Schiller (in press) has, in fact, discovered that the Catholic/public school academic advantage "decreased at least 25 percent between the early 1980s and the 1990s."

In sum, it would appear that Catholic schools are at a critical crossroad. They have established an excellent record by increasing academic achievement, religious and racial diversity, and equality. That is the good news. The bad news is that enrollments have decreased substantially since the early 1980s, and the schools also have become more selective in terms of social class (regardless of race or religion or urbanization) and they have become less Catholic and less religious. These latter social transformations will, if continued, call into question the traditional identity and mission of Catholic schools. Moreover, they ultimately will constrain the previously demonstrated capacity of the schools to provide both equality and achievement.

This set of divergent trends presents a conundrum for the future of Catholic schools. It appears that the high quality and the increasingly high cost of education in Catholic schools is causing students with average to scarce economic resources to go elsewhere for their schooling. With each passing year, there are fewer students attending Catholic schools, and those who do attend are increasingly non-White, non-Catholic, nonreligious, and yet from homes of high socioeconomic status. Students who are nonreligious, non-Catholic, or non-White were not deterred from attending Catholic schools in 1992, but students of low SES were excluded. This current state of affairs is a 180-degree turnaround from all previous decades in the twentieth century. In those times, the schools were affordable, and consequently attended by students from all social classes. Of course, in those times past, the schools were also all-White, all-Catholic, and consensually more religious.

The bottom line is this: Students in Catholic schools choose and accept a pro-academic environment—this creates a highly selective student body, as evidenced in this chapter by the increasingly higher socioeconomic status of students, regardless of race. Although not shown here (and it is very difficult to demonstrate), there are surely other intangible factors that make most students who choose Catholic schools academically unique. These two forces work in concert with one another. Catholic schools provide a demanding, high-quality education, and only high-quality students are willing to enroll in these schools. The schools are increasingly expensive and hence available only to those who can afford the price of admission. This process will quickly (if it has not already) remove Catholic schools from the business of providing greater equality of educational opportunity. In the end, they will have to relinquish the short-lived but much-loved definition of "common school" that was bestowed on them in the 1980s.

APPENDIX 2.1
DATA SETS USED IN THE ANALYSIS

National Longitudinal Study (NLS)

NLS is a two-stage probability sample, with schools as first-stage units and students as second-stage units. The base-year questionnaire was administered in the spring of 1972 to 16,683 twelfth-grade high school students who were enrolled in 1,070 public, private, and church-affiliated schools in the United States. Of these, 74 were Catholic schools. A total of 1,027 students were obtained in the Catholic school sample. The analysis, however, was limited to those students who had not transferred into the school after ninth grade. The NLS survey conducted follow-ups in 1973, 1974, 1976, 1979, and 1986. All of the variables in the analyses are drawn from the base year except for family composition, which actually was gathered retrospectively in the 1986 follow-up.

High School and Beyond (HSB)

HSB is also a two-stage probability sample, with schools as first-stage units and students as second-stage units. The base-year questionnaire was administered in 1980 to 58,270 students in 1,015 public, private, and church-related schools. The sample included a sophomore and senior cohort. In this chapter, only the senior cohort was employed since the sophomore cohort was no longer a representative sample at the senior year (see Green et al., 1995). The senior cohort was composed of 28,240 students of whom 2,687 attended 84 Catholic schools. Follow-up surveys were conducted on the HSB senior cohort in 1982, 1984, and 1986, but all of the variables used in this analysis were part of the 1980 base-year survey.

National Educational Longitudinal Study (NELS)

NELS is a two-stage probability sample, with schools as first-stage sampling units and students as second-stage units. The base-year questionnaire was administered in the spring of 1988 to 24,599 eighth graders who were enrolled in 1,052 public and private schools in the United States. Of these, 104 were Catholic schools. On average, each of the participating schools was represented by 23 student participants. In the first follow-up administered in the spring of 1990, most respondents had changed schools between the eighth and tenth grade. Thus, at this point, there were 21,474 student participants, including 1,229 "freshened" sample students who attended 3,967 schools. A total of 17,424 students completed the survey in both the base and first follow-up. For the second follow-up in spring 1992, NCES decided to follow with certainty all those students who were members of the first follow-up, along with 1,126 "freshened" sample senior-year students. This yielded 16,114 students who completed the senior year questionnaire (not all of these have eighth- and/or tenth-grade data available).

APPENDIX 2.2
SAMPLE SIZES, WEIGHTS, AND FLAGS
USED IN THE ANALYSES

	NLS 1972	*HSB 1980*	*NELS 1992*
Total sample size	16,683	28,240	16,114
Catholic sample size	1,027	2,687	840
Weight for seniors	W1	DESIGNWT	F2QWT
Flag for seniors	—	Grade = 2	F2SEQFLG = 0
Flag for "in same school"	SRFQ3	EB010	F2f1SCFL
Same-school sample size	13,391	24,182	14,219
Same-school Catholic sample size	918	2,510	799

Flags for the same school (to exclude transfers) are not consistent across the three data sets. In NLS 1972, the variable is from the school record (did student transfer to this school from another school?). In HSB 1980, the variable is from the student record (in what grade did you begin to attend this school?). In NELS 1992, the variable is a composite using all three waves of data (1988, 1990, 1992). All values are for seniors.

APPENDIX 2.3
VARIABLES USED IN ANALYSES OF PUBLIC
AND CATHOLIC SCHOOL STUDENTS

National Longitudinal Study, 1992

F2SES1   Socioeconomic status of student (mean = 0, sd = 1)
F2RACE1   Student's racial identity (White = 1; minority = 0)
RELIGION   Composite of measures on religion in 1990 and in
                1992 (for the freshened members of the sample)
                (Catholic = 1, all others = 0)
G12CTRL   School type (Catholic and public)
SCHQ40   Degree of urbanization (urban, suburban, rural) (not
                used in 1980 analyses)

High School and Beyond, 1980

BBSESRAW   Socioeconomic status of student (mean = 0, sd = 1)
BB089   Student's racial identity (White = 1; minority = 0)
BB091   Student's religion in 1972 (Catholic = 1, all others = 0)
SCHLTYPE   School type (Catholic and public)
SCHQ40   Degree of urbanization (urban, suburban, rural)

National Educational Longitudinal Study, 1972

SESRAW   Socioeconomic status of student (mean = 0, sd = 1)
CRACE   Student's racial identity (White = 1; minority = 0)
BQ92   Student's religion in 1972 (Catholic = 1, all others = 0)
PUBPRIV   School type (Catholic and public)
SCHQ40   Degree of urbanization (urban, suburban, rural)

Acknowledgments. I am grateful to the following people who assisted me in one way or another during the research and the writing of this paper: Jeffrey Owings, Dennis Carrol, and Aurora D'Amico at the National Center for Educational Statistics; David Baker at Pennsylvania State University; Barbara Keebler at the National Catholic Educational Association; Manolis Kaparakis, Marcia Battle, Julie Riordan, and David Perda at Providence College.

REFERENCES

Alexander, K. A., & Pallas A. M. (1983). Private schools and public policy: New evidence on cognitive achievement in public and private schools. *Sociology of Education, 56,* 115–127.

Alexander, K. A., & Pallas, A. M. (1985). School sector and cognitive performance. *Sociology of Education, 58,* 115–127.

Bryk, A. S., Lee, V. E., & Holland, P. B. (1993). *Catholic schools and the common good.* Cambridge, MA: Harvard University Press.

Coleman, J. S., & Hoffer, T. (1987). *Public and private schools: The impact of communities.* New York: Basic Books.

Coleman, J. S., Hoffer, T., & Kilgore, S. B. (1982). *High school achievement: Public, Catholic, and private schools compared.* New York: Basic Books.

Greeley, A. M. (1982). *Catholic schools and minority students.* New Brunswick, NJ: Transaction Books.

Green, P. J., Dugoni, B. L., Ingels, S. J., & Quinn, P. (1995). *Trends among high school seniors 1972–1992.* Washington, DC: U.S. Department of Education, Office of Educational Research and Improvement, NCES 95-380.

Guerra, M. J. (1995). *Dollars and sense: Catholic high schools and their finances.* Washington, DC: National Catholic Educational Association.

Hafner, A., Ingels, S., Schneider, B., & Stevenson, D. (1990). *A profile of the American eighth grader: NELS:88 student descriptive summary.* Washington, DC: National Center for Education Statistics.

Heyns, B. L. (1981). Policy implications of the public and private school debates. *Harvard Educational Review, 51,* 519–525.

Hoffer, T. B., Greeley, A. M., & Coleman, J. S. (1985). Achievement growth in public and Catholic Schools. *Sociology of Education, 58,* 74–97.

Ingels, S. J., Dowd, K. L., Baldridge, J. D., Stipe, J. L., Bartot, V. H., Frankel, M. R., & Quinn, P. (1994). *Second follow-up: Student component data file user's manual* (NELS). Washington, DC: U. S. Department of Education.

Jencks, C. (1985). How much do high school students learn? *Sociology of Education, 58,* 128–135.

Kaufman, P., McMillen, M. M., & Sweet, D. (1996). *A comparison of high school dropout rates in 1982 and 1992.* Washington, DC: U.S. Department of Education.

Murnane, R. J. (1981). Evidence, analysis, and unanswered questions. *Harvard Educational Review, 51,* 483–489.

National Catholic Educational Association. (1973). *United States Catholic schools 1972–1973.* Washington, DC: Author.

National Catholic Educational Association. (1995). *United States Catholic elementary and secondary schools 1995–1996.* Washington, DC: Author.

National Center for Education Statistics. (1992). *Digest of education statistics.* Washington, DC: U.S. Department of Education.

National Center for Education Statistics. (1994). *Second follow-up: Student component data file user's manual.* Washington, DC: U.S. Department of Education.

Quality counts. (1998, January 8). *Education Week* [Entire issue].

Riordan, C. (1997a). *Equality and achievement: An introduction to the sociology of education.* New York: Addison Wesley Longman.

Riordan, C. (1997b). *Trends in student demography, attitudes, and behavior in Catholic secondary schools: 1972–1992.* Paper commissioned by the Future of Catholic Schools Project. Washington, DC: Catholic University of America.

Schiller, K. S. (in press). The Catholic school advantage: A continuing debate. In J. G. Cibulka (Ed.), *Educational choice: Lessons from public and private schools.*

Sebring, P., Campbell, B., Glusberg, M., Spencer, B., Singleton, M., Turner, M., & Carroll, C. D. (1987). *High school and beyond 1980 senior cohort.* Washington, DC: National Center for Education Statistics.

Tourangeau, R., Sebring, P., Campbell, B., Glusberg, M., Spencer, B., & Singleton, M. (1987). *The national longitudinal study of the high school class of 1972 (NLS-72) fifth follow-up (1986) data file user's manual.* Washington, DC: National Center for Education Statistics.

Willms, D. J. (1985). Catholic-school effects on academic achievement: New evidence from the High School and Beyond follow-up study. *Sociology of Education, 58,* 98–114.

CHAPTER 3

The Funding Dilemma Facing Catholic Elementary and Secondary Schools

JOSEPH CLAUDE HARRIS

THE PRESENT METHOD OF FINDING the cash to pay Catholic school bills contributes to a situation where schools enroll diminishing proportions of the Catholic student population. Andrew Greeley (1989) described the problem this way: "Catholic schools seem to be entering a twilight—not facing immediate extinction, perhaps, but slipping slowly into darkness" (p. 106). The current school funding model can best be described by eavesdropping on the regular December school commission meeting for St. Sample parish in Somewheresville, USA. The task of constructing a budget for the subsequent school year usually starts when the commission chair quizzes the head of the parents' club, "How much money can you raise next year?" The answer to that question leads to a second inquiry asked of the group at large, "How much subsidy can we hope for from the parish?" Such informal survey results provide the basis for designing the elastic element of the budget process, the next year's tuition schedule. Should subsidy be static or perhaps even shrinking and fund raising stagnant, then parents must fund teacher salary increases or new science textbooks by increasing tuition rates. The problem with the present system is that it works well when parents can afford to pick up the tab; otherwise, schools simply close. Some of each has been happening over the past 40 years.

Data describing enrollment and funding patterns illustrate the development of Catholic school structures since the early 1960s. Catholic schools registered about 47% of a Catholic school-age population of

11.447 million in 1962 (Neuwien, 1966). When the National Catholic Educational Association first surveyed elementary school finances in 1969, parishes paid 63% of elementary school costs (Bredeweg, 1980). In the intervening 3 decades, the proportion of Catholics enrolled in Catholic schools plummeted to 18% of a school-age population of 11.754 million in 1991 (Schaub & Baker, 1993). Similar change affected parish support, which paid for 25% of elementary school costs for 1994.[1] Catholic schools have evolved from a Church-funded endeavor managed by professed religious to a system of largely parent-funded programs for a diminishing portion of the Catholic school population.

Catholic educators have needed to charge substantial tuition because school costs have grown dramatically in the past decades. For example, parish elementary school budgets ballooned by an average annual rate of 9.4% between 1980 and 1989. (The cost of the average parish elementary school is estimated at $184,372 for 1980 and $420,230 for 1989.)[2] School costs grew at twice the rate of inflation during the 1980s.[3] School leaders coped with much larger school expenses by increasing tuition at an average annual rate of 12.4%. (Tuition revenue for the average school is estimated at $73,082 for 1980 and $208,515 for 1989.)[4] The current economic model of Catholic school funding suggests a declining market share (see McLellan, Chapter 1). Fewer Catholics will be able in the future to afford a program where user fees grow at triple the rate of inflation.

Catholic education has experienced a fiscal revolution. Parish programs once educated about half the Catholic population when the entire parish community paid the bill. These elementary schools now enroll one Catholic student in five, with parents and principals funding the bulk of the budget. Catholic secondary schools presently operate as independent businesses, with tuition and alumni-based fund raising providing virtually all required funds. Two questions need to be addressed. What factors have caused program costs to grow so dramatically? Why has Church fiscal support dwindled to such a small proportion of the budget?

PARISH ELEMENTARY SCHOOLS

What Has Happened to Elementary School Costs?

As already pointed out, elementary school costs have increased. The average elementary school required $450,144 to operate in 1990. This same average school budget likely grew to $589,865 by 1994–95. If costs continued to increase in a linear fashion, then the average elementary school budget should have been $687,273 for 1997–98. The troubling aspect of this pattern is not that the price of private education has risen. The cost of a pound of hamburger or the sticker price on a 747 probably increased also in recent years. The difficulty lies in the fact that parish elementary school costs grew at an average annual rate of 7% between 1990 and 1994. The growth rate is somewhat smaller than the average 9% increases experienced during the 1980s. The entire pattern, however, about doubled the rate of inflation since 1980. Since other funding sources did not increase at rates beyond inflation, participating parents needed to spend ever-increasing portions of their family budget to pay tuition bills. Two factors have contributed to the development of this pattern. Like all players in our economic system, school leaders paid the price of inflation; in addition, Catholic school administrators embarked on an ambitious program of curriculum revision. We will look now at the effect inflation had in the pattern of escalating school costs.

The Impact of Inflation. Isolating the impact of inflation entails a discussion of the notions of current and constant dollars. Current dollars are simple: Sum the program operating cost for a given period, and the total expenses represent current dollar cost for that period. Constant dollar accounting represents an estimate of cost as if inflation had not happened.

As noted earlier, the cost of operating an average school jumped from $450,144 in 1990 to $589,865 in 1994. The increase between 1990 and 1994 amounted to $139,721. About 43% of this growth, or $60,272, can be attributed to paying for inflation. The additional growth of $79,449 represents an investment in factors beyond the need to fund inflation.

Other Cost Factors. On average, Catholic school principals and parish boards invested $79,449 to fund program revisions and other expenses beyond inflation since 1990. This budget jump can be subdivided into costs associated with hiring more teachers and all other costs. The category of all other amounted to about $37,793 or 27% of the budget growth. Many of these cost increases were undoubtedly unavoidable. If the school heat bill unexpectedly jumped 10%, the principal did not have the option to stop buying that particular product.

All staffing increases totaled 30% of the new costs or about $41,657. The fact that the average elementary school enrolled an additional 17 students between 1990 and 1994 probably added about $16,186 to the school budget. The remainder of the new money purchased a lower pupil–teacher ratio. School administrators elected to lower the pupil–

teacher ratio from 18.3 to 17.2. This particular change may not sound dramatic for the entire country, but it cost $126 million to accomplish. Also, this program revision means much more than a given teacher having one less paper to correct.

First, some definitions: Pupil–teacher ratio and class size do not mean the same thing. Class size refers to the total number of students sitting in front of a classroom teacher on a given day. For Holy Rosary school, where our two youngest children spend much of their time, the class size ranges from 26 in the primary grades to 30 in the junior high program. The pupil–teacher ratio at Holy Rosary is 20.5. The difference lies in the definition of pupil–teacher ratio. Teacher numbers are reported in full-time equivalents (FTEs), which are computed by dividing the amount of time employed in instruction by the time normally required of a full-time position. The elementary school scene is no longer one where a classroom teacher instructs a class in all subjects in the same classroom. Not too many years ago, eight teachers, a principal, and a secretary staffed many schools. The secretary frequently subbed as principal because the principal often replaced absent instructors. This world has changed, as evidenced by the data in Table 3.1.

Both enrollment and the number of teachers have grown since 1990. FTE staffing has increased by 8,822, while enrollment has grown by 36,860. Obviously school administrators did not need to hire 8,000 plus new teachers to take care of the new students. Maintaining a constant pupil–teacher ratio would have required only 2,012 additional teachers. It is likely, rather, that the number of course offerings staffed by specialists have multiplied. Classes in computers and music no longer qualify as electives or simply nice ideas to be implemented when surplus funds somehow appear in the budget. For most schools, a librarian is at least

Table 3.1. Staff Size and Pupil–Teacher Ratio in Catholic Elementary Schools

	1990–91		1993–94	
	Staff size	*Pupil–teacher ratio*	*Staff size*	*Pupil–teacher ratio*
Religious	13,100		10,564	
Lay teachers	95,300		106,658	
Total staff	108,400	18.31	117,222	17.24

Notes: The National Catholic Educational Association incorporated the concept of FTE teacher for the first time in 1991. FTE teacher data for 1990–91 represent an estimate that fits the historical pattern of actual data collected between 1991 and 1994.

a part-time position, a much different approach from our youth when Sister stored an odd shelf of books behind her desk. Catholic schools have developed a broadened curriculum in search of quality education.

Summary. The cost to operate an average Catholic elementary school increased by $139,721 between 1990 and 1994. Inflation caused 43% of the budget growth. Somewhere in the neighborhood of 18% of the cost increase can be related to the lowering of the pupil–teacher ratio, while 12% can be associated with increased enrollment. The remaining 27% probably happened because of a long list of other factors, ranging from a need for new books to salary hikes beyond cost-of-living increases. These data do not point to a program struggling only to survive. Parish school boards would not have spent $126 million to purchase a much different curriculum if survival were a paramount issue. Catholic schools thrive when they serve populations of parents who can afford the tuition; the dilemma arises when the service cannot be offered to a growing Catholic student population.

The Problem of Parish Subsidy

The present situation of parish financial support for Catholic elementary schools seems to make no sense. Catholic schools work, and yet parishes provide progressively less fiscal support, a decline from 63% of program cost to 28% between 1969 and 1994. Less financial support means that parents must make up the financial difference. Perhaps one result of the increased burden for parents can be found in the fact that a net total of 823 elementary schools closed between 1983 and 1993 (Brigham, 1994). Catholic Church managers seem to be abandoning a most successful religious education program. Why? Is it a question of a lack of resolve or a situation of dwindling parish resources? We will look first at the recent pattern of parish subsidy and then at the questions of organizational commitment and also the nature of the burden that subsidy places on parish resources.

A typical parish provided a school subsidy of $152,814 in 1990. This 1990 amount represents a 69% increase over the 1980 subsidy estimate of $90,228. Inflation consumed most of the buying power of the increased subsidy. The additional subsidy amounted to only about 7% after subtracting the effect of inflation.

Subsidy increased from $152,814 to $162,211 for the average parish school between 1990 and 1994. If this pattern continued in a linear fashion, subsidy should have grown to an average of $167,619 for the 1997 school year. The increase in subsidy in recent years actually represented a drop in buying power. If we discount for the effect of inflation, parish subsidy in both 1994 and 1980 was identical. This means that the parish maintained a constant level of support in terms of buying power. The problem arises when we realize that the cost of operating an average school grew, after subtracting for inflation, by $258,265. Principals needed to raise this additional quarter of a million dollars.

Church Policy. The pattern of diminishing parish support has not been caused by a change in stated Church policy regarding schools. The leaders of the American Catholic Church originally intended the Catholic school program to be an effort of the entire congregation when in 1884 they directed every parish to build and maintain a school in perpetuum. In November 1990, the American bishops affirmed their commitment to schools in the pastoral letter, *In Support of Catholic Elementary and Secondary Schools.* The bishops asked that new initiatives be launched to secure sufficient financial assistance from both private and public sectors for Catholic parents to avail themselves of the opportunity to send their children to Catholic schools. Obviously, the declining impact of parish support on the school budget does not stem from a change in the formal program plans of the Church. We will look next at the state of giving in the Catholic Church to measure the capability of the parish to provide subsidy to a parish school.

A Picture of Parish Revenue. Diocesan fiscal managers representing 1,957 parishes provided data that are the basis for this discussion of elementary school finances. This response group reported that total revenue for the average parish increased from $337,674 in 1990 to $402,800 in 1994 (see Table 3.2), indicating an average annual growth rate of 4.4%.

One pattern stands out. Small parishes do not sponsor schools. Revenue for a school parish averaged $659,871 in 1994, while a nonschool parish operated with average revenue of $263,500. Average household contributions in a school parish tend to be somewhat higher than average—about 6%. While these higher donations make some difference in revenue totals, the bulk of the variation relates to more registered house-

Table 3.2. Estimate of Average Parish Revenue for Catholic Parishes in the United States, 1990–1994 (dollars)

Year	Average parish	School parish	Nonschool parish
1990	337,674	510,497	240,401
1992	368,424	583,694	250,674
1994	402,800	659,871	263,500

holds in school parishes. A typical school parish involves about 1,650 families, while nonschool parishes register approximately 730 households. The one-third of parishes in the United States that do sponsor schools include about 55% of all registered Catholic households.

The elementary school structure has evolved along economic lines. School subsidy averaged $162,211 for 1994. This program commitment represented about 25% of revenue for a school parish. A nonschool parish would have spent 62% of revenue on subsidy in 1994. The fact that average school subsidy is beyond the means of smaller parishes is reflected in elementary school closure data. The number of rural schools declined by 449 between 1983 and 1995. In addition, a net of 623 elementary schools closed their doors in urban situations, where parish size has been declining for many years (National Catholic Educational Association, 1996).

Revenue data for larger parishes that could afford to sponsor an elementary school differed from the average for all parishes. School parish income grew at an average annual rate of 6.6%. The average school parish received an additional $149,374 in revenue between 1990 and 1994. Parishes probably increased school subsidy by $9,397 for the same time period. These data suggest that subsidy actually declined as a burden to a typical school parish from 30% of revenue in 1990 to about 25% in 1994. Had school parishes maintained the level of 30% support for schools, subsidy for 1994 would have been $197,961. The difference between what probably happened and what might have happened is $35,750.

A quick look back at school cost data underscores the revolution that has occurred in the school funding model. The cost of operating an average elementary school grew by $139,721 between 1990 and 1994—an average annual increase of 7%. Parishes probably provided $9,397 of the new needs in increased subsidy. Had the average school parish maintained a consistent commitment of 30% of revenue as subsidy, then an average school would have received an additional $35,700. Even under these relatively optimistic circumstances, school managers would have had to find an additional $94,574 to pay for all additional program costs between 1990 and 1994. The average school now costs about as much to operate as the sponsoring parish. The historical model of a parish financially sponsoring a school wore out many years ago. Present fiscal realities suggest a need for radical new funding approaches.

The Future of Fund Raising

Fund raising for Catholic elementary schools no longer stops with an occasional bake sale to buy some new books for the library. The bake sales still happen, but current programs now include sophisticated auctions that often net in excess of $50,000. A recent innovation called "SCRIP" allows schools to realize revenue by training parents to buy groceries and just about everything else with discounted gift certificates. "SCRIP" may sound tame, but 200 families buy a lot of groceries from a chain that gives 5% of the proceeds to the school.

All other funding beyond tuition and subsidy grew from $67,756 in 1990 to $88,476 in 1994, an increase of $20,720. If this growth pattern continued in a linear fashion, other funding should have reached $102,882 for the 1997–98 school year. What is truly startling about elementary-level fund raising is the fact that all other revenue totaled only $21,062 for 1980. Fund-raising revenue quadrupled between 1980 and 1994. The increased revenue grew from 11% of the 1980 school budget to about 15% of school cost for 1994.

Tuition—How Long Will It Last?

As previously noted, the cost of operating an average Catholic elementary school grew by $139,721 between 1990 and 1994. Administrators paid these new bills with a modest contribution from the parish ($9,397), some additional fund raising ($20,720), and a hefty tuition hike of $109,605. The great advantage to just charging more tuition is that it is simple and easily executable. The customer audience—parents—is well defined and presently purchasing the product. As long as at least some parents continue to feel a strong need for Catholic elementary education and can afford the rapidly rising tuition bills, then passing the new costs directly along to the consumer offers a quick solution to the need to find new money.

But I raise the question of how long the present patterns might persist. To answer that inquiry, I will first examine present tuition payment patterns and then look at the burden these requirements place on an average family. Finally, I will discuss the feasibility of charging tuition to pay for an extensive educational effort.

The data in Table 3.3 illustrate the pattern of tuition growth in both current and constant dollars. The constant dollar information displays cost information after discounting for the impact of inflation. Tuition increased a total of $109,605 between 1990 and 1994. Approximately 28%, or $30,739, of this increase can be attributed to the effect of inflation. Most of the tuition growth exceeded the pace of inflation. As a result, the average school household needed to take money from some other family fiscal priority to pay tuition bills.

We can estimate the tuition burden on parents by comparing tuition

Table 3.3. Annual Tuition for an Average Catholic Elementary School (current and constant dollars)

Year	Current dollars	Index	Constant dollars	Index
1990	229,573	100	260,312	100
1991	250,919	109	273,026	105
1992	279,008	122	294,718	113
1993	305,651	133	313,477	120
1994	339,178	148	339,178	130

as a proportion of household income in 1980 and 1993. In 1980–81 the average elementary school had 283 students and cost $184,372 to operate. Tuition income amounted to $73,082. It involved approximately 149 households.[5] The tuition payment averaged $490 per household. If Catholic household income in 1980 equaled the average income for all households, then tuition represented 2.3% of gross household income (U.S. Bureau of the Census, 1984, P60-142).

In 1993–94 the average school enrolled 280 students and operated with a budget of $547,751. Tuition income totaled $305,651. The average school might typically involve approximately 192 households. The average household tuition would be $1,591. If Catholic household income was about $41,000 in 1993, then tuition for elementary schools could be estimated at 3.9% of gross household income (U.S. Bureau of the Census, 1995). The burden that elementary tuition placed on an average Catholic family increased by 70% between 1980 and 1993.

A final question to consider is the practicality of using tuition as the primary funding source for parish elementary schools. A look at the general structure of educational finances suggests that the American system of universal public education depends on the willingness of the community to tax all households to pay school bills. For example, expenditures for public K–12 programs totaled $253 billion in 1992 (National Center for Education Statistics, 1995). If we distribute this burden to each of the 95 million American households for that year, then public education cost each household $2,653 or about 7% of an average household income of $39,000 (Rawlings, 1993). If, on the other hand, only the 24.8 million households with school-aged children paid for elementary and secondary programs, then the per household cost would have been $10,228 or 27% of average household income. These data confirm what many might accept as common sense. Most parents could not possibly afford to pay the cost of educating their children. The present public education model of universal education exists because it receives the monetary support of the entire community.

Catholic educators came to rely on tuition as a primary source of new dollars for obvious reasons. Budgets have grown at twice the rate of inflation since 1990. Administrators paid for inflation—$60,272 between 1990 and 1994 for the average school—and substantial program revisions—a total of $79,499 for all costs beyond inflation. Lowering the pupil–teacher ratio by adding instructional specialists in computers, art, music, and so on, contributed about $28,000 to the growing fiscal structure. Principals and school boards needed lots of cash, and parents represented an available source for these needed funds.

The strategy of relying on tuition has worked in many situations. While the enrollment increase of 36,000 students between 1990 and 1994 did not keep pace with population growth, this expansion represents positive numbers in a context where enrollment dropped by 50% since the 1960s. The negative side to the tuition program is that it limits participation to those who can afford to pay the bills. The economics of education suggest that universal education requires extensive community fiscal support. If only parents of school-aged children paid for public K–12 programs, the bill would increase by a factor of four from about $2,500 per household to $10,000.

CATHOLIC SECONDARY SCHOOLS

Independent Businesses

At the turn of the twentieth century, Catholic secondary schools existed for those few who could afford the cost. In 1900, a total of 183 Catholic colleges operated secondary schools as preparatory departments. Communities of women religious maintained approximately 500 academies for girls (McCluskey, 1969). The situation changed when American educators began to promote the concept of universal education extending to the twelfth grade. The Catholic Educational Association in 1911 strongly urged that parochial and diocesan school programs be expanded to include secondary education. A broadened Catholic secondary school effort began at that time.

One critical policy difference determined the eventual fiscal structure of Catholic elementary and secondary schools. Bishops intended that the entire Catholic community pay for parish elementary schools. For many years, pastors totally subsidized parish programs. The need to charge tuition arose in more recent years when school costs grew to a point where parish managers could no longer pay all the costs of operating an elementary school. While parents paid the majority of elementary school costs, the entire parish community still provided about one-fourth of the program cost during 1994.

Catholic secondary schools, on the other hand, evolved into a program for the general population at the recommendation of the Catholic Educational Association. The Catholic community received no episcopal injunction to subsidize schools. Catholic high schools flourished initially because communities of women and men religious contributed teaching and management services. In some situations, parishes or groups of parishes undertook sponsorship of a secondary school. In later years, many dioceses constructed secondary schools and staffed these programs with religious and diocesan clergy. Normally, formal program subsidy from the general Catholic community never entered into the financial picture. Later developments led to the present system of tuition-supported programs. From 1911 to the present, however, the responsibility for funding a secondary school normally rested with the principal and the parents and extended families of the student body.

We will first investigate secondary school cost increases between 1990 and 1994 to isolate the impact of inflation from program changes. We can then describe revenue sources to outline how principals and boards paid the escalating bills.

A Secondary School Budget

The estimated cost of operating an average Catholic secondary school topped $2 million for the first time in 1993 and grew to $2.169 million in 1994.[6] Secondary school costs are presented in both current and constant dollars. The current dollar cost increase for secondary programs was $435,288 between 1990 and 1994. Program costs grew at an average annual rate of 5.8%; inflation increased for the same period at an annual rate of 3.2%. The total dollar increase was divided about equally between inflation ($232,140) and the cost of other program revisions ($203,148).

Costs Beyond Inflation. Catholic secondary school principals and parent boards spent $203,148 beyond inflation between 1990 and 1994. This budget increase can be divided into costs related to hiring additional teachers and "all other" costs. The category of "all other" amounted to about $45,842 or 11% of budget growth. The remainder of the new costs can be attributed to additional staffing.

All increases in the number of teachers for secondary schools totaled

36% of the new program costs or \$157,306. The major portion of new staffing costs happened because the average secondary school enrolled an additional 40 students. The average faculty grew by 4.96 FTE instructors. A small portion of this growth, .78 FTE instructors, occurred because of a drop in the pupil–teacher ratio. Secondary enrollment and staffing data are described in Table 3.4.

As indicated, the cost to operate an average Catholic secondary school increased by \$435,288 between 1990 and 1994. If this pattern continued, the cost of a typical secondary school should have increased to \$2.486 million by 1997. Inflation caused 53% of this secondary budget growth. About 6% of the increase can be related to lower pupil–teacher ratios, while 30% can be associated with increased enrollment. The remaining 11% happened for a wide variety of reasons. These data suggest a picture of a program coping successfully with significant cost increases.

Revenue Estimates. Any discovery that Catholic secondary school leaders must fend for their fiscal selves would come as no surprise to a principal or school board member. The situation of a secondary school principal resembles the lot of a parish pastor. The first task of any principal is always to find a way to pay the bills. In 1990 the average secondary school generated 90% of its revenue from school-sponsored sources. This proportion increased slightly to 92% for 1994. Any diocesan subsidy that a high school receives is likely to be in the form of limited scholarships and/or some direct allocations from chanceries to schools that actually are owned by various dioceses.

Funding for an average secondary school came from four sources: Tuition, fund raising, subsidy, and other revenue. The great majority of new dollars, 79%, came from increased tuition. Fund raising accounted for 9% of the increased dollars. Other revenue accounted for the remain-

Table 3.4. Staff Size and Pupil–Teacher Ratio in Catholic Secondary Schools

	1990–91		1993–94	
	Staff size	*Pupil–teacher ratio*	*Staff size*	*Pupil–teacher ratio*
Religious	7,550		6,193	
Lay teachers	34,800		40,406	
Total staff	42,350		46,599	
Enrollment	591,533	13.97	614,571	13.19

ing 4% of school-sponsored revenue, while subsidy funded an average of 8% of the school budget.

Tuition. Tuition increased for the average school between 1990 and 1994. If these patterns continued, it is likely that tuition increased to around $1,860,558 by 1997. The constant dollar growth beyond the impact of inflation was $174,928 (see Table 3.5).

Since most secondary schools rely on tuition, it would be helpful to estimate the relationship between tuition and Catholic household income. In 1994–95, the average secondary school enrolled 496 students. Tuition income amounted to $1,607,826. If we assume that secondary school tuition is collected on a per pupil basis, then household tuition for a single student was $3,241 in 1994. If we assume that Catholic household income equaled average income for all American households, then this sum is 7.4% of estimated Catholic household income for 1994 (U.S. Bureau of the Census, 1996).

Catholic secondary schools differ from elementary schools in that they have never received extensive subsidy. Catholic secondary school managers resorted to significant tuition charges to survive in the face of the massive changes experienced by the groups of professed religious who sponsored high schools and contributed their teaching. Lay teachers and administrators now fill 87% of secondary school faculty positions. Religious who still teach can no longer afford to contribute their services without pay. Many religious organizations presently struggle to support growing numbers of retired members. One result of the need to charge fees to support high schools was discussed by Thomas Bier (1990), who described the effects of suburban migration on the Catholic Church in Cleveland as follows:

> When children reach school age, many families move out of the city because of unwillingness to use public schools. The critical point seems to be at the

Table 3.5. Annual Tuition for an Average Catholic Secondary School (current and constant dollars)

Year	Current dollars	Index	Constant dollars	Index
1990	1,123,696	100	1,432,898	100
1991	1,368,794	108	1,489,392	104
1992	1,449,079	115	1,530,674	107
1993	1,529,488	121	1,568,651	109
1994	1,607,826	127	1,607,826	112

transition from elementary to high school. Many parents send their children to parochial elementary schools but then want to send them to a public high school (possibly because of the cost of a parochial high school). They will not do that in Cleveland so they leave the city. . . . Cleveland's parochial school parishes are being severely undermined by the unwillingness of residents to send their children to a Cleveland public high school after sending them to a parochial elementary school. (p. 10)

Catholic secondary schools work well for the portion of the population who can pay the tuition charges (see Hoffer, Chapter 5, this volume). The dilemma of Catholic secondary schools is simply that the present funding model forces Catholics to make choices like migration to the suburbs to avoid unworkable public programs or unaffordable but effective Catholic secondary efforts.

PAYING FUTURE SCHOOL BILLS

Catholics migrated to America with few possessions beyond the clothes they wore. Worried about the hostile Protestant atmosphere in public schools, pastors and bishops directed their poor flock to build a system of parish schools. They managed to operate an ever-expanding system of schools using the one economic resource the American Catholic Church possessed in abundance—women and men religious who taught classes of 40 and 50 students for room and board and a modest stipend to support the Motherhouse. But that world dissolved in the mid-1960s. At present about 10% of the 163,000 Catholic school teachers belong to religious societies and orders. In the near future Catholic schools will likely be completely lay-staffed and lay-managed.

The transformation to a lay-staffed program has changed the fiscal relationship of parishes to schools. At one time pastors could pay all elementary school costs from receipts received in the Sunday collection. For 1994, however, the average parish elementary school operated on a budget of $589,865. The sponsoring parish provided a subsidy of $162,211, which amounted to about 25% of parish revenue. Had parish leaders somehow managed to allocate 50% of parish revenue as subsidy—$329,935—schools would still have needed to raise $259,930. It probably isn't realistic to imagine a scenario where parishes will ever again pay all the school bills.

Catholic school administrators coped with increasing costs by charging whatever tuition was needed to balance the budget. For example, the cost of operating an average Catholic elementary school grew by

$139,722 between 1990 and 1994. Administrators paid these new bills with increased subsidy ($9,397), additional fund raising ($20,720), and a tuition hike of $109,605. Such tuition increases likely represent a growing burden on the resources of Catholic families. We earlier estimated that elementary tuition grew from 2.3% to 3.9% of average household income between 1980 and 1993. Tuition for a single secondary student for 1994 was $3,241 or 7.4% of household income. The tuition burden for an average Catholic household with one elementary student and one secondary student likely exceeds 11% of household income.

The economic model of a Catholic school system supported by collections and contributed services began to vanish in the mid-1960s. The current system relies on tuition and fund raising to pay the increased costs involved in operating a lay-staffed educational system. Catholic schools succeed for the proportion of the population that can afford the escalating tuition charges. The dilemma lies in the fact that a diminishing portion of the Catholic population can participate in the program.

NOTES

1. This statistic is part of the research I prepared for this chapter and is my responsibility. In general, all statistics referring to elementary and secondary school costs and revenue for the period 1987–1997 are estimates I prepared.

2. The average annual rate of change is calculated as follows: (($420,230/$184,372) ^ (.1111)) − 1.

3. Inflation growth is estimated according to the CPI U at 124 for 1989 and 82.4 for 1980. The average annual rate of inflation is calculated as follows: ((124/82.4) ^ (.1111)) − 1.

4. The average annual rate of tuition increase is calculated as follows: (($208,515/$73,082) ^ (.1111)) − 1.

5. The calculation of 149 households is determined by dividing the enrollment total of 283 students by 1.9 elementary students per household. The factor of 1.9 is derived from an analysis of enrollment data from the National Center for Educational Statistics (1995) and family data from the Census Bureau. Reference is made to the NES publication, *Projections of Educational Statistics to 2003*, for the enrollment data. Family data come from two census publications, *Current Population Reports*, which give the number of households involved in private schools for 1987 and 1993. The estimate of households for 1980 is derived from a linear estimate of the 1987–1993 data. It was necessary to estimate 1980 data because the Census Bureau began publishing estimates of numbers of households involved in private education in 1987. The 1993 data are taken from the Series P-20, No. 474, publication. The calculation for 1993 is 280 students divided by 1.5 elementary students per household.

6. Data describing the fiscal patterns of secondary schools published by the

National Catholic Educational Association (Guerra, 1991, 1993, 1995) provide the foundation for these estimates. Since the NCEA data are likely not typical of average-sized schools, the published cost data have been adjusted to provide estimates for more typical schools.

REFERENCES

Bier, T. (1990). *Sellers of Cleveland homes.* Cleveland: Ohio State University, Urban Center.

Bredeweg, F., C.S.B. (1980). *Catholic elementary schools and their finances—1979.* Washington, DC: National Catholic Educational Association.

Brigham, F. (1994). *United States Catholic elementary and secondary schools 1993–1994.* Washington, DC: National Catholic Educational Association.

Greeley, A. (1989, February 11). Catholic schools: A golden twilight? *America,* p. 106.

Guerra, M. (1991). *Catholic high schools and their finances—1990.* Washington, DC: National Catholic Educational Association.

Guerra, M. (1993). *Dollars and sense: Catholic high schools and their finances—1992.* Washington, DC: National Catholic Educational Association.

Guerra, M. (1995). *Dollars and sense: Catholic high schools and their finances—1994.* Washington, DC: National Catholic Educational Association.

McCluskey, N. G. (1969). *Catholic education faces its future.* Garden City, NY: Doubleday.

National Catholic Educational Association. (1996). *United States Catholic elementary and secondary schools 1995–1996.* Washington, DC: Author.

National Center for Education Statistics. (1995). *Digest of educational statistics.* U.S. Department of Education, Office of Educational Research & Improvement, NCES 95-029, Table 158, p. 155.

Neuwien, R. (Ed.) (1966). *Catholic schools in action.* Notre Dame, IN: University of Notre Dame Press.

Rawlings, S. (1993). *Household and family characteristics: March 1992.* U.S. Bureau of the Census, Current population reports, Series P20-467, Washington, DC: U.S. Government Printing Office.

Schaub, M., & Baker, D. (1993). *Serving American Catholic children and youth.* Washington, DC: Department of Education, United States Catholic Conference.

U.S. Bureau of the Census. (1984). *Current population reports, Series P60-142, Money income of households, families, and persons in the United States: 1982.* Washington, DC: U.S. Government Printing Office.

U.S. Bureau of the Census. (1993). *Current population reports, Series P60-184, Money income of households, families, and persons in the United States: 1992.* Washington, DC: U.S. Government Printing Office.

U.S. Bureau of the Census. (1995). *Current population reports, Series P60-188, Income, poverty, and valuation of noncash benefits: 1993*. Washington, DC: U.S. Government Printing Office.

U.S. Bureau of the Census. (1996). *Current population reports, Series P60-189, Income, poverty, and valuation of noncash benefits: 1994*. Washington, DC: U.S. Government Printing Office.

CHAPTER 4

A Faculty at a Crossroads: A Profile of American Catholic School Teachers

MARYELLEN SCHAUB

A SCHOOL'S FACULTY IS BOTH its most valuable asset and its biggest expenditure. The national debate about educational quality has come full circle to embrace the idea that quality teaching matters in developing effective elementary and secondary schooling (e.g., National Commission on Teaching and America's Future, 1996). At the same time, teacher compensation is the largest operational cost in running schools. Currently there are some 3 million teachers in the country, making teaching the largest occupation in the nation. Their joint annual salaries and benefits of some $100 billion represent one of the largest social costs in American society. Given this, employing high-quality people to be teachers and retaining them throughout a productive career are of major importance to the quality of education throughout the nation. This is true for public schools and private schools alike.

Recruiting and retaining high-quality teachers is a large administrative undertaking by schools and is a particularly challenging task faced by all types of private schools. At the beginning of the 1990s 12% of all teachers worked in private schools and 5% of these teachers worked in Catholic schools. This means that among private school teachers about 4 out of 10 teach in a Catholic school. This chapter describes those 150,000 Catholic school teachers, their training and professionalization, their compensation packages, their working environment in schools, and their satisfaction with the job. This description is a statistical profile of the national condition of Catholic school teachers, and is meant to parallel several recent national reports documenting the condition of all U.S. teachers (Choy et al., 1993; National Commission on Teaching and America's Future, 1996).

Six trends about full-time Catholic school teachers are presented here: (1) the transition to a lay faculty; (2) the kinds of people now teaching in Catholic schools; (3) their compensation packages; (4) the professionalization of the faculty; (5) teachers' attitudes about the schools and teaching; and (6) on-the-job conditions. To put these trends into perspective, comparisons are made where possible with both public school teachers and other private school teachers.

The main source of information for this chapter comes from the U.S. Department of Education's survey on teachers and schools known as the "Schools and Staffing Survey" (hereafter referred to as SASS). The survey, last done in the academic year 1993–94, collects basic information about teachers and their schools from a nationally representative sample of 58,000 teachers across the country teaching in some 8,000 schools. Within the survey is a fully representative sample of private school teachers that can be broken down by school affiliation. This means that the information reported here comes from a nationally representative sample of Catholic elementary and secondary school teachers. Also, as is presented here, Catholic school teachers can be directly compared with public school and all other private school teachers. Additionally, the Catholic sample can be broken down by "parochial, diocesan, and religious-order schools." Other information comes from recent federal reports on teaching, and some data come from the System for Catholic Research, Information, and Planning (SCRIP) (1993).

Although among all private schools, Catholic schools have the highest rate (85%) of full-time teachers, it is just below the almost 90% rate in public schools (McLaughlin, O'Donnell, & Ries, 1995). Other religious schools, for example, have on average only 77% full-time teachers. Perhaps the most dramatic trend to occur in the past 20 years among Catholic school teachers is the decline in religious teachers (i.e., sisters and brothers from religious orders). Catholic schools were staffed almost solely by religious men and women during the historical enrollment peaks of the 1930s and 1940s. Since then the numbers of religious teachers have declined dramatically. By 1970, the percentage of lay faculty in Catholic elementary and secondary schools was 53% and 48%, respectively. In 1980 this had increased to 75% and 70%, and by 1990, to 88% and 83%, respectively.[1] Many aspects of Catholic schooling have undergone extreme change in the past 25 years, but none as financially transforming as who is staffing these schools (Baker & Riordan, 1998). Therefore, in a 50-year period, what was once a fully religious teaching faculty has been replaced almost completely by lay teachers.

If this trend continues, and current estimates of the overall decline of people in religious orders strongly suggest that it will (Hoge & Davidson, 1989), by the early 2000s a significant proportion of Catholic schools will operate without any religious teachers at all. Unfortunately, there are no national estimates of the proportion of lay faculty who are Catholic, but many other trends in Catholic schooling toward less emphasis on religious education, as well as the greater involvement of non-Catholic families, suggest that the non-Catholic segment of the teaching force may be increasing too.

WHO ARE THE TEACHERS?

Given this major shift toward a lay teaching force, what kind of people now teach in these schools and how different are they from teachers in other types of schools? Table 4.1 presents a general demographic profile of elementary and secondary teachers in public, Catholic, and other private schools. There are some notable similarities among them, as well as some dramatic differences. For example, compared with public school teachers, Catholic school teachers are, on average, less educated and less

Table 4.1. Demographic Profile of Teachers, 1993–94

	Public		Catholic		Other private	
	Elem.	*Sec.*	*Elem.*	*Sec.*	*Elem.*	*Sec.*
% female	84	54	91	53	83	65
% minority	10	8	5	3	7	4
Mean age	42.9	43.5	41.9	42.9	41.4	40.9
% married	73	74	64	59	73	76
% bachelor's	99	98	96	99	91	91
% master's	44	50	24	51	27	37
% Ph.D.	1	1	0	3	1	3
% certified in main field	92	92	67	64	51	45
% certified in any field	94	95	71	67	60	54
Mean years' experience	14.8	15.9	12.4	14.4	11.1	11.7
Mean teaching salary ($)	33,116	34,387	17,926	25,089	19,451	21,105

likely to be certified in either their main or any other teaching field. Almost one-fourth of Catholic and 27% of other private elementary school teachers have a master's degree, as compared with 44% of public elementary school teachers.[2]

Certification is a state-sanctioned credential attesting that a teacher has obtained a minimum number of college credit hours and student teaching has been successfully completed. While lack of certification does not necessarily mean these requirements have not been completed, certification is a commonly used indicator for potential employment and teacher quality. Sixty-seven percent of Catholic elementary school teachers are certified in their main teaching field and 71% in any field, compared with over a 90% certification rate for public elementary school teachers. Similar trends are seen among the certification rates of Catholic secondary school teachers as compared with public secondary school teachers. However, the average teacher in all three types of schools has at least a bachelor's degree and 10 years of teaching experience.

TEACHER COMPENSATION PACKAGE

Salary

Relatively low teacher salaries among Catholic school teachers is a commonly cited problem, and this clearly will be a challenge to Catholic schools in the future. As with all occupations, different salary levels attract different types of people to jobs, and higher salaries generally buy a better educated and more qualified staff.

The extent of Catholic school teachers' underpayment is illustrated in Table 4.1. For example, the average Catholic elementary school teacher makes slightly less than $18,000 per year, while the average public elementary school teacher makes slightly more than $33,000 per year. Similarly, the average Catholic secondary school teacher makes $25,000 per year as compared with $34,400 for the average public school counterpart. Although secondary school teachers in each type of school make more than their elementary counterparts, this difference is over $7,000 among Catholic school teachers. This is a much larger difference than, for example, for public secondary school teachers, who earn, on average, only a little more than $1,000 more than their elementary school counterparts.

These figures are averages of individual teacher salaries, but SASS also contains school-wide salary schedules for new and experienced teachers. These data show standard teacher salaries paid by schools and avoid the effects of idiocratic differences between individual teachers.

They also eliminate what can be considerable differences between lay and religious teacher salaries within Catholic schools. Average school schedules presented in Table 4.2 further illustrate the disparity between Catholic and public school teachers. Across all types, Catholic school faculty are paid significantly less than public school faculty, but a little more than other private school faculty.

Note the disparity in standard pay for the most experienced teachers. Salary differences between Catholic and public school teachers are largest for the most experienced teachers. Catholic elementary schools pay their most experienced teachers almost $16,000 less than public elementary schools. This is true even for generally higher-paying, religious-order elementary schools, where teachers are paid on average about $14,500 less than their public school counterparts. Secondary schools show the same trends, but the differences are less dramatic. Again the disparity in pay between Catholic and public school teachers increases with the number of years of teaching experience. Experienced Catholic secondary school teachers average approximately $6,500 less than their public school counterparts, and teachers in religious-order secondary schools average approximately $3,500 less than their public school counterparts.

Over the course of their teaching careers, the Catholic elementary

Table 4.2. School-Level Mean of Teacher Salary Schedules, 1993–94 (dollars)

	Normal yearly base salary for a teacher with BA/BS degree and no experience	Highest possible step on the salary schedule for experienced teachers
Elementary		
Public	22,659	42,984
Total Catholic	16,042	27,036
Parochial	15,860	26,657
Diocesan	16,373	27,878
Religious order	17,293	28,320
Other private	15,252	24,442
Secondary		
Public	22,017	40,751
Total Catholic	18,249	34,129
Parochial	16,166	28,523
Diocesan	18,139	33,618
Religious order	19,281	37,115
Other private	14,419	24,618

school teacher becomes increasingly underpaid in comparison to her public school counterpart. The Catholic school teacher starts a career receiving about 40% less than if she were in a public school and by the time she reaches the highest step her salary is almost 60% less than that of a comparable public school teacher. On the other hand, the initial pay disparity between Catholic and public secondary school teachers of about 22% remains about the same throughout a career. The overall range in salaries among Catholic school teachers is considerably smaller than that found in public schools, particularly for the highest salaries in schools (Baker, Han, & Keil, 1996).

Catholic school teachers clearly make significant financial sacrifices to teach in these schools. As the faculty moves toward a fully lay corps of teachers, there is a range of implications of these salary levels for sustaining high-quality personnel. Teacher recruitment and retention may become significantly more difficult in the face of large salary disparities. Most important, teacher quality could be diminished as the most qualified and experienced teachers are attracted to higher-paying jobs.

Benefits

Benefits are part of an overall compensation package. Almost all parochial, diocesan, and religious-order secondary schools (100%, 98%, and 95%, respectively) offer some type of medical insurance, as do most public secondary schools (95%) (Baker et al., 1996).[3] As for teachers' pensions, 71%, 88%, and 70%, respectively, of Catholic parochial, diocesan, and religious-order secondary schools report offering some type of pension contribution as compared with 67% of public secondary schools. Ingersoll, Quinn, and Bobbitt (1997) report similar findings in terms of average number of benefits by calculating an average number of medical, dental, pension, and life insurance benefits offered by each school. They found that the average Catholic school offered 3.0, while the average public school offered 3.1. Thus, although teachers in the Catholic sector suffer large pay deficits, their benefits are similar to those of teachers in public schools. However, the SASS data include only the type of benefit and not its cash value, so we cannot tell whether Catholic school benefits are of lesser value than public school benefits.

TEACHER PROFESSIONALIZATION

Although numerous initiatives have attempted to enhance the professional status of teaching, it often is considered to be an occupation with only a "semiprofessional" status (e.g., Lortie, 1969, 1975). Nevertheless, in recent years much emphasis has been placed on enhancing professionalization within teaching (e.g., National Commission on Teaching and America's Future, 1996). For example, the National Commission on Excellence in Education (1983) renewed interest in the education, preparation, and training requirements for teachers. Enhancing factors include professional development such as participation in professional activities and inservice programs, as well as credentials requirements. These topics are crucial to sustaining teacher quality since a teacher's professional credentials and development influence both subject knowledge and teaching skills, which in turn influence student learning.

In general, Catholic schools have fewer professional requirements for teachers and less participation in professional activities by their teachers. However, Catholic and public school teachers show similar trends in participation in some specific areas, such as mentor programs and continuing education.

The SASS data contain information on teacher professionalization, but far too many individual indicators to report them separately here, so for clarity I report some condensed measures that have been developed by U.S. Department of Education studies of teacher quality.[4] Tables 4.3 and 4.4 display measures of professionalization for elementary and secondary school teachers, respectively. "Credentials" is a composite of four

Table 4.3. Measures of Average Elementary Teachers' Professionalization, 1993–94

	Total public	Total Catholic	Paro- chial	Dioce- san	Religious order
Credentials					
Mean number professional requirements	2.93	2.23	2.23	2.25	2.00
Induction					
% participation in mentor program	27	26	26	27	26
Professional development					
% receiving continuing education support	20	18	18	19	12
% participation in professional activities	74	64	62	67	76
Mean effectiveness	2.38	2.39	2.40	2.37	2.32
Management school environment					
% with influential principal	78	97	97	97	96
% with influential faculty	37	28	27	29	54

Note: "Effectiveness" is a self-rating of one's own teaching impact.

Table 4.4. Measures of Average Secondary Teachers' Professionalization, 1993-94

	Total public	*Total Catholic*	*Parochial*	*Diocesan*	*Religious order*
Credentials					
Mean number professional requirements	2.91	1.89	2.37	1.88	1.77
Induction					
% participation in mentor program	26	29	25	31	29
Professional development					
% receiving continuing education support	21	25	25	20	28
% participation in professional activities	66	57	54	62	54
Mean effectiveness	2.50	2.43	2.64	2.44	2.37
Specialization					
% in-field teaching	84	83	79	84	84
Management school environment					
% with influential principal	81	99	97	98	100
% with influential faculty	36	44	31	35	55

indicators of teacher's level of professionalization including the following:

1. Full standard state certification for the field to be taught
2. Graduation from a state-approved teacher education program
3. College major or minor in the field to be taught
4. Passage of a national, state, or local teachers' examination, as reported by school administrators

These objective indicators of professional training commonly are used by schools in hiring teachers. As seen in the tables, Catholic schools require their teachers to have a lower number of professional credentials than do public schools. This is true for both elementary and secondary schools, and interestingly, given their overall academic reputation, Catholic religious-order schools require the least number of professional credentials.

Participation in professional activities, such as inservice training and professional development programs, is an avenue for teachers to stay up-to-date in a specific field, as well as in pedagogy in general. A school average was constructed using teachers' responses about how often they participated in types of professional activities and training. A school was deemed as having annual participation in professional activities if the average teacher in the school participated in professional activities at least "once or twice a year" (Ingersoll et al., 1997). Approximately 10% fewer Catholic elementary and secondary schools than public schools have annual participation in professional activities. For elementary schools, 64% of Catholic and 74% of public schools were defined as having annual participation, while for secondary schools 57% of the Catholic and 66% of the public schools were defined as having annual participation. Interestingly, similar proportions of teachers in Catholic and public schools felt the professional activities they participated in had beneficial impact on their professional development. Although overall teachers saw a general positive effect, neither group felt these programs had an overwhelmingly positive impact on their professional development.

Three other indicators of teacher professionalization show little variation between Catholic and public school teachers. Slightly more than one-quarter of teachers from both Catholic and public schools participated in a mentor program during their first year of teaching. Similarly, 25% or less receive some type of continuing education support, in addition to normal salaries, as a job benefit.[5] Lastly, within secondary schools, Catholic and public teachers have similar rates of teaching within area of specialization. More than 80% of teachers' instruction time in both Catholic and public secondary schools is spent teaching in an area of their expertise—an area in which the teacher has at least a college minor.

MANAGEMENT OF THE SCHOOL ENVIRONMENT

Tables 4.3 and 4.4 also include indicators of the managerial environment of the school in terms of the principal's and teachers' influence over school policy making. Many recent educational reforms have called for more school-based management in public schools, and in some respects Catholic schools often are considered prototypes of this type of environment. Schools in which principals and teachers make decisions about important policy, instead of the district or other central administration, are considered to have school-based management.

SASS sampled school principals' responses to a series of questions about school decisions in terms of how much actual influence the principal and faculty have on a series of school management issues.

Almost all Catholic school teachers work in a school with a principal who manages the school environment and has significant influence in decisions on curriculum, teacher hiring, student discipline, budget expenditures, content of inservice programs, and teacher evaluations. Public school teachers tend to work in a similar managerial environment but to a lesser degree. At the same time, the average Catholic school teacher has less influence in school management than her public school counterpart, with the exception of religious-order-run Catholic schools.

Although Catholic schools have strong principal leadership, the teachers have a less influential role. This style of school-based management may diminish the influence of teachers because principals have such an influential role.

TEACHER ATTITUDES

Teachers' views of the working conditions in their schools are presented in Tables 4.5 and 4.6. Teachers were asked to respond to the following statements (phrases at the end of each are used in Tables 4.5 and 4.6):

1. I am satisfied with my teaching salary (Salary satisfaction).
2. I receive a great deal of support from parents for the work I do (Parental support).
3. Necessary materials are available as needed by the staff (Materials available).
4. Most of my colleagues share my beliefs and values about what the central mission of the school should be (Share colleagues' views).

Table 4.5. Selected Attitudes of Elementary School Teachers on Teaching Conditions, 1993–94 (percent agreeing)

	Total public	Total Catholic	Parochial	Diocesan	Religious order	Other private
Salary satisfaction	44	26	27	23	35	46
Parental support	58	85	86	85	77	84
Materials available	74	79	79	79	79	90
Share colleagues' views	87	95	96	96	85	95
Clear communication from principal	83	88	89	88	75	89
Conflict with school rules	22	18	17	17	24	13
Best effort useless	23	13	12	15	14	11

Table 4.6. Selected Attitudes of Secondary School Teachers on Teaching
Conditions, 1993–94 (percent agreeing)

	Total public	Total Catholic	Paro-chial	Dioce-san	Religious order	Other private
Salary satisfaction	47	42	39	39	45	51
Parental support	43	83	75	83	85	84
Materials available	73	85	84	80	90	88
Share colleagues' views	79	90	88	90	90	92
Clear communication from principal	77	86	86	83	88	90
Conflict with school rules	27	16	16	19	14	14
Best effort useless	32	15	26	16	12	15

5. The principal knows what kind of school he/she wants and has
   communicated it to the staff (Clear communication from principal).
6. I have to follow rules in this school that conflict with my best
   professional judgment (Conflict with school rules).
7. I sometimes feel it is a waste of my time to try to do my best as
   a teacher (Best effort useless).

Working conditions commonly are associated with teacher quality
and retention. With the exception of teaching salary, Catholic school
teachers in both elementary and secondary schools seem far more satisfied with their working conditions. The most dramatic difference between Catholic and public school teachers is perceived parental support
for teaching activities. Eighty-five and 83%, respectively, of Catholic elementary and secondary school teachers agreed with the statement "I receive a great deal of support from parents for the work I do." However,
only 58% and 43%, respectively, of public elementary and secondary
school teachers agreed. Significant differences also are seen in responses
to "I sometimes feel it is a waste of my time to try to do my best as a
teacher." Only 13–15% of Catholic school teachers agreed with this statement, compared with 23–32% of public school teachers. However, public
school teachers were more likely to agree with the statement "I am satisfied with my teaching salary." Catholic elementary school teachers (26%)
are the least satisfied with their teaching salaries. In addition, within
Catholic elementary and secondary schools, teachers in parochial and

diocesan schools are less satisfied with their salary than teachers in religious-order schools.

As shown in Table 4.7, Catholic school teachers are generally more satisfied with their jobs than public school teachers. Teachers responded to the question "If you could go back to your college days and start over again, would you become a teacher or not?" Almost 8 out of 10 Catholic school teachers said they would most likely become a teacher again, but less than 7 out of 10 public elementary school teachers responded positively, and public secondary school teachers were the least likely to become a teacher again (6 out of 10). Therefore, although Catholic school teachers are less satisfied with their teaching salary, they are more satisfied with their working conditions and jobs.

COMPARABILITY OF SCHOOLS

The above analysis suggests that Catholic school teachers are happier with their work environments than public teachers. This is an important finding with obvious positive implications for teacher retention, so it warrants some further exploration. Is this still true if Catholic teachers are compared with public teachers from similar schools? Recent analyses have suggested that Catholic schools currently are enrolling more students from wealthier families than ever before, particularly when compared with the average public school (Riordan, Chapter 2, this volume). Since teaching in schools with more advantaged students can add positively to the work environment of teachers, I analyzed SASS Catholic and public schools with a similar, low percentage (8% or less) of poor students approved for the federal subsidy of the free lunch program. Doing this yields a comparison between approximately 50% of Catholic schools and 14% of public schools. Mostly this more restricted analysis finds the same patterns as in the preceding comparisons.

Table 4.7. Teachers Responding That They Would Become a Teacher Again, 1993–94 (percent)

	Total public	*Total Catholic*	*Parochial*	*Diocesan*	*Religious order*	*Other private*
Elementary	67	78	79	76	76	83
Secondary	60	77	76	78	76	78

CONCLUSIONS AND IMPLICATIONS

This statistical profile of Catholic school teachers finds that there are both positive and negative aspects of the overall condition of the faculty nationwide. To the positive, Catholic school teachers are more satisfied than public school teachers with their working conditions and jobs, on average. And this is true when only schools with similar numbers of advantaged students are compared. Further, the average Catholic teacher is likely to work in a locally managed school and have a principal who has a major influence on school policy. To the negative, Catholic school teachers are paid less, are less educated, and are less certified than their public school counterparts. In addition, Catholic schools demand fewer professional requirements of their teachers and their teachers participate in fewer professional activities.

The condition of teachers in Catholic schools is mixed. In many significant ways the average Catholic school is a good place to teach; there is strong support from parents, and usually there is a principal who is a strong leader within the school. It is easy to see how so many Catholic school teachers become committed to Catholic education. But at the same time, these teachers sacrifice some important things to teach in these schools. Their salaries and opportunities for professional development are comparatively low, and this is particularly of concern as Catholic schools increasingly must rely on lay teachers. This mixed condition presents a unique challenge to Catholic school leaders—how to retain what is positive about teaching in Catholic schools and reduce the negative. If specific solutions cannot be found, the negative aspects could start to jeopardize the recruitment and retention of high-quality teachers in the very near future.

Enrollments in both public and private schools are expected to continue to increase, and the U.S. Department of Education predicts we will need half a million new teachers by 2002 (Choy et al., 1993). This potential enrollment increase, along with the dramatic increase in lay faculty and comparatively lower salaries, has important implications for future staffing needs of Catholic schools.

There are a number of crucial policy questions about how Catholic schools will enhance conditions for their teachers over the next several decades. For example, how long can a good place to work be a substitute for higher salaries elsewhere? To keep qualified teachers in a time of expanding education, will Catholic schools have to greatly increase tuition? Can Catholic schools continue to maintain a high-quality teaching force as they enroll wealthier students, who often have very high educational expectations? Will the mission of Catholic schools be compromised without the presence of religious faculty, as well as high numbers of non-Catholic students? Will parishes, dioceses, and religious orders all continue to operate schools with separate faculties? The challenges that will be faced by Catholic schools with respect to staffing issues will have effects on the whole system. Future school closings as well as enrollments are closely tied to these issues of staffing and largely dependent on quality and availability of teaching staff.

NOTES

1. Number of male religious and priests in Catholic elementary and secondary schools is reported as a combined figure for all three time periods. This number was added to the secondary faculty figure. Therefore, the percentage of lay teachers in elementary schools could be slightly smaller, and the percentage of lay teachers in secondary schools could be slightly greater.

2. Since SASS is collected from a sample, these are estimates of the proportion in the total population of Catholic school teachers. I mention only relevant differences that are large enough to be statistically significant.

3. Baker et al. (1996) define secondary school slightly differently than I do here. In addition, these figures are not based on cash values, which could be dramatically different.

4. For further details on how this and other composite measures in this chapter were originally developed, see Ingersoll et al. (1997).

5. These figures reflect teachers taking advantage of a benefit and cannot indicate the percentage of schools offering tuition and course fee reimbursement.

REFERENCES

Baker, D. P., Han, M., & Keil, C. (1996). *How different, how similar? Comparing key organizational qualities of American public and private secondary schools* (NCES Publication No. 96-322). Washington, DC: U.S. Department of Education.

Baker, D. P., & Riordan, C. (1998). The "eliting" of the common American Catholic school and the national education crisis. *Phi Delta Kappan, 80* (1), 16–23.

Choy, S., Bobbitt, S., Henke, R., Medrich, E., Horn, L., & Lieberman, J. (1993). *America's teachers: Profile of a profession* (NCES Publication No. 93-025). Washington, DC: U.S. Department of Education.

Hoge, D., & Davidson, J. (1989). *American Catholic laity in a changing church.* Kansas City: Sheed & Ward.

Ingersoll, R. M., Quinn, P., & Bobbitt, S. (1997). *The status of teaching as a profession: 1990–91* (NCES Publication No. 97-104). Washington, DC: U.S. Department of Education.

Lortie, D. (1969). The balance of control and autonomy in elementary school teaching. In A. Etzioni (Ed.), *The semi-professions and their organizations: Teachers, nurses and social workers* (pp. 1–53). New York: Free Press.

Lortie, D. (1975). *School teacher*. Chicago: University of Chicago Press.

McLaughlin, D., O'Donnell, C., & Ries, L. (1995). *Private schools in the United States: A statistical profile, 1990–91* (NCES Publication No. 95-330). Washington, DC: U.S. Department of Education.

National Commission on Excellence in Education. (1983). *A nation at risk: The imperative of educational reform*. Washington, DC: U.S. Government Printing Office.

National Commission on Teaching and America's Future. (1996). *What matters most: Teaching for America's future*. New York: Author.

System for Catholic Research, Information, and Planning (SCRIP). (1993). Life Cycle Institute, Washington, DC: Catholic University of America.

CHAPTER 5

Catholic School Attendance and Student Achievement: A Review and Extension of Research

THOMAS B. HOFFER

SCHOOLS ARE EXPECTED TO HAVE many effects on their students, ranging from the inculcation of relatively diffuse attitudes and norms to quite specific cognitive skills. How well schools achieve all of their various goals is currently a matter of great public concern, but the concern is greatest with respect to the cognitive goals of schooling. The symbolic watershed event in the current era of reform is the 1983 report *A Nation at Risk* (National Commission on Excellence in Education). The report lamented a "rising tide of mediocrity" and sounded alarms about declines in national security and the standard of living to galvanize support for raising performance standards and outcomes.

The main themes of the report were based on evidence of college-entrance examination scores that had been declining since the mid-1970s. Responding to that growing evidence, the U.S. government began to collect comparable data on the academic outcomes of public and Catholic school students in the early 1980s. Researchers interested in finding evidence of effective alternatives to the structures and practices of the public schools eagerly turned to these new databases for clues. Much of the large volume of research comparing the two sectors reflects an interest in identifying ways to improve American education generally, both public and private.

This chapter summarizes and critiques research comparing public and Catholic school student achievement scores in verbal skills, mathematics, science, and social studies. Findings from three national studies are reviewed: the National Assessment of Educational Progress (NAEP), High School and Beyond (HS&B), and the National Education Longitudinal Study of 1988 (NELS:88). The chapter is divided into three main sections: a review of theoretical arguments about the nature and size of sector effects, a review of the empirical results from the national surveys, and a conclusion discussing the strengths and weaknesses of research done to date and how future work might improve upon it.

SECTOR DIFFERENCES AND THE THEORETICAL ARGUMENTS FOR SECTOR EFFECTS

Theory and data are always closely bound together, and the more exacting the connections, the better the theory one formulates and the better the data one collects. Where one steps into the circle of evidence and theory inevitably has at least an element of the arbitrary. For present purposes, I take as a point of departure a range of empirical evidence from national surveys showing that Catholic school students score significantly higher on standardized achievement tests than their public school counterparts. These data do not, however, necessarily indicate that Catholic schools are more effective than public schools, for that is an issue that must be resolved through analysis of the overall sector differences. The first theoretical issue is how to account for the overall achievement differences. Before considering the alternative explanations, it is useful to review the basic evidence.

Overview of Sector Differences in Achievement

The National Assessment of Educational Progress data are the best source for national estimates of public and Catholic school student achievement differences and for historical trends in those differences. This is because NAEP uses large samples of schools and students and administers a much larger set of items in each subject area than other studies. Furthermore, NAEP includes national samples of students at three age and grade levels (ages 9, 13, and 17; grades 4, 8, and 12), whereas the national longitudinal studies start with eighth graders (the National Education Longitudinal Study of 1988) or tenth graders (High School and Beyond). The NAEP study is designed especially for estimating average scores and charting historical trends in those averages for the three age–grade populations and major subpopulations within them, but is relatively useless for analyzing the scores in terms of factors predicting the average differences. For that purpose, one must turn to the national longitudinal studies, HS&B and NELS:88.

Results are reported here for only mathematics, reading, and writing, despite the fact that NAEP also assesses achievement in science, history, and geography. Public–Catholic breakdowns were not available at the time of this writing for the latter subject areas, although the U.S. Department of Education indicates (personal communication) that those data will be available in the near future.

The NAEP data presented in Table 5.1 show that, on average, Catholic school students in grades 4, 8, and 12 perform at levels significantly above their public school counterparts in the areas of mathematics, reading comprehension, and writing skills. Although the differences are slightly smaller in grade 4, they are, overall, very large in all cases. The NAEP scores are reported on a scale that ranges from 0 to 500. This scale is itself completely arbitrary, and one must define some standard against

Table 5.1. Average NAEP Test Scores for Public and Catholic School Students, 1992

Test, grade level, and full sample SD	Public	Catholic	Difference[a]	Effect size[b]
Mathematics				
Grade 4 (SD = 33.1)	217.3 (0.8)	226.6 (1.2)	9.3 (1.4)	.28
Grade 8 (SD = 30.9)	266.1 (1.0)	277.2 (2.1)	11.1 (2.3)	.36
Grade 12 (SD = 30.1)	296.6 (1.0)	310.4 (2.5)	13.8 (2.7)	.46
Reading comprehension				
Grade 4 (SD = 40.3)	215.9 (1.1)	230.2 (2.2)	14.3 (2.5)	.35
Grade 8 (SD = 39.4)	258.1 (1.0)	275.4 (1.9)	17.3 (2.1)	.44
Grade 12 (SD = 43.0)	288.7 (0.7)	306.3 (1.5)	17.6 (1.7)	.41
Writing skills				
Grade 4 (SD = 38.2)	220.1 (1.3)	233.5 (2.3)	13.5 (2.6)	.35
Grade 8 (SD = 36.3)	259.9 (1.2)	274.4 (2.4)	14.5 (2.7)	.40
Grade 12 (SD = 32.0)	283.3 (1.0)	304.8 (1.6)	21.5 (1.9)	.67

Sources: National Center for Education Statistics (1994); *NAEP Data on Disk: 1992 Almanac Viewer* (Washington, DC: US Department of Education). Full sample standard deviations are taken from the Data Appendix of Campbell, Reese, O'Sullivan, and Dossey (1996).

Note: Numbers in parentheses are standard errors.

[a]Catholic-minus-public differences. Standard errors of the differences are calculated by taking the square root of the sum of squared standard errors for the separate public and Catholic means.
[b]Effect sizes are calculated by dividing the Catholic-minus-public difference by the total sample standard deviation. These estimates are not adjusted for social background or other differences among public and Catholic school students.

which to interpret any differences of interest. One minimal standard is statistical significance, that is, the likelihood that a given difference could occur by chance, through "the luck of the draw" (sampling error) in a sample survey. The differences in Table 5.1 are all sufficiently large that one can dismiss chance as an explanation: Even the smallest of these differences are less likely than one in one thousand to arise from sampling error.

The main standard that NAEP provides in its reports is a set of five "performance levels" that are defined for discrete 50-point ranges of the 0–500 scale scores. The performance levels are defined, first, by identifying specific test items that students achieving at each level are, on average, likely to answer correctly and incorrectly. Subject-matter specialists then scrutinize these item sets to identify the kinds of skills and knowledge needed to answer the benchmark items correctly. NAEP reports these scores as percentages of students achieving at each level of performance. These scores are attractive since they indicate the extent to which students have attained relatively specific competencies in each subject area. Unfortunately, the NAEP reporting mechanisms do not include breakdowns by public and Catholic school attendance, and these scores are thus unavailable to the research public.

An alternative standard that is available is to use a conventional "effect size" metric to express the sector differences. Often used to compare results across studies in meta-analyses, the effect size metric expresses group differences as fractions of the full sample standard deviation for the achievement score (Glass, McGaw, & Smith, 1981). Generally, effect sizes equal to or greater than 0.10 are considered substantial, but one must consider the time frame during which the effect was generated. The longer the time period in which students are exposed to a "treatment," the larger will be the effect estimate. The effect size estimates reported in the last column of Table 5.1 are much greater than the 0.10 minimum standard and indeed indicate very large achievement differences between public and Catholic school students. But these differences do not control for social background differences among public and Catholic school students, and they are differences that represent the accumulation of learning differences across not only the current grade levels listed, but also all prior grades.

How do the NAEP data compare with the national longitudinal studies? Direct comparisons are not possible, since the test scores are expressed in different metrics in each study. Nonetheless, it is possible to standardize the public–Catholic differences into the conventional effect size metric and to compare effect sizes across studies. The standardization selected here is again to express the sector differences as proportions of the respective full-sample standard deviations. These are presented in Table 5.2.

These comparisons indicate that the overall achievement differences between public and Catholic school students are fairly consistent across studies and subject areas. Among twelfth graders, the differences in mathematics and reading comprehension estimated from NELS:88 are somewhat larger than those from NAEP and the 1982 High School and Beyond study. The NELS:88 gaps are also greater than the HS&B sector differences in tenth grade. The NELS:88 sector differences among eighth graders, however, are smaller than the 1992 NAEP data show. The sector differences are largest in reading and mathematics across the studies, and smallest in science.

The main points from Tables 5.1 and 5.2 are that (1) contemporary national studies with independent samples of schools and students, but using similar broad-range achievement tests, are consistent with respect to the presence and size of large achievement differences favoring Catholic school students; and (2) the limited historical record shows that the higher scores of Catholic school students found in the most recent data also were found in the early 1980s. Again, it is important to emphasize that the effects shown in Tables 5.1 and 5.2 are simply the average sector

Table 5.2. Average Achievement Test Score Differences Between Public and Catholic School Students by Grade and Subject, Selected Data Sets (percent of test score standard deviation)

	Catholic school effect sizes			
	Math	*Reading*	*Writing*	*Science*
12th graders				
NAEP 1992	.46	.41	.67	—
NELS:88 1992	.53	.49	—	.41
HS&B 1982	.48	.42	.46	.26
10th graders				
NELS:88 1990	.44	.47	—	.32
HS&B 1980	.40	.36	.42	.24
8th graders				
NAEP 1992	.36	.44	.40	—
NELS:88 1988	.21	.37	—	.16

Sources: NAEP data are from NCES (1994). High School and Beyond data are from Coleman and Hoffer (1987) pp. 64 and 65. NELS:88 data are original tabulations for this report. See Ingels et al. (1994) for complete information on the NELS:88 project and data files.

Note: Effect values are unadjusted.

differences at each grade level. Some, perhaps all, of the achievement differences may be due to social background differences between public and Catholic school students. Even the apparent trend toward larger differences at higher grade levels also may be selection effects, if, for example, Catholic schools tend to weed out weaker students through the high school years at a greater rate than public schools.

Theoretical Explanations of Sector Differences

What accounts for the sector differences shown in Tables 5.1 and 5.2? This question takes us to the center of a lively debate that began in the early 1980s and has continued to the present. The main poles of the debate are "no effects of Catholic school attendance on achievement" versus "positive effects of Catholic school attendance." Explanations of the latter claim divide into four distinct models of how Catholic school effects are generated. These competing explanations, in turn, carry quite different practical implications, and we will turn to those after reviewing the main arguments.

Individual Selection. The "null" explanation is that sector differences simply reflect differences in the kinds of individual students attending public and Catholic schools. According to this theory, achievement in Catholic schools is higher simply because Catholic school students are higher achievers to begin with or come from families that promote achievement more effectively. If public and Catholic school students with similar backgrounds and initial levels of achievement were compared, this theory predicts that no differences in final levels of achievement would be found.

In contrast to the selection-based explanation, other theories predict greater effectiveness for Catholic schools. In the next section, I identify four distinct hypotheses, or models, that have been articulated by different researchers over the past decade or so.

Aggregate Student Composition. The *aggregate-student composition hypothesis* has been best articulated in the public–Catholic school debate by McPartland and McDill (1982). This hypothesis asserts that Catholic schools have higher levels of achievement as a direct consequence of having a more selective student body. The key idea here is that a student will learn more if he or she has higher-achieving peers.

This "contextual" effect, over and above the individual effects of background, has been developed in two different directions in the sociology literature. The first conceives context as essentially a social-psychological, normative factor that affects the orientations and efforts of students and school staff. Aggregations of students along socially salient lines of stratification lead to certain kinds of "collective representations" or shared self-images that in turn shape norms of behavior and individuals' attitudes and actions. The indicators of composition most widely used are average student socioeconomic status and the proportions of students who are minorities (typically African American, but also Hispanic in some studies). McPartland and McDill (1982) emphasize this normative conception of school composition effects.

A second variant of the composition model can be derived from the sociological literature on ability grouping and tracking. Barr and Dreeben (1983) note that *classes* with initially higher average achievement tend to move at a more rapid pace than classes with lower average achievement. Students with the same level of initial achievement learn more in the faster classes than in the slower ones. While the composition of classes is the key variable in this conception, class composition is likely to be shaped in important ways by school-level student enrollment characteristics. As Barr and Dreeben (1983) argue, there is a whole "technology" of transforming school-level student "inputs" into instructional units of classrooms and groups within classes. By implication, we thus can note that the consequences of school inputs for instructional group composition are by no means automatic: Two schools with the same inputs can divide and allocate students to instructional contexts in very different ways, reflecting differences in other resources (e.g., the number and qualifications of the school's teachers, and the number and size of classrooms), goals (e.g., all graduating students must be prepared to succeed in college, versus half of the graduates must be prepared for college), and the theories linking resources to goals.

The first, social-psychological variant of the aggregate-student composition model leads to the same conclusion as the individual selection model, that Catholic schools do not do anything better than public schools. The higher achievement in Catholic schools is instead a simple result of higher and perhaps more homogeneous student inputs. The second variant, in contrast, points to a range of specific actions that school administrators and teachers take to transform school-level student enrollments into classes and, within classes, instructional groupings. One thus should not control for class-level inputs when trying to determine the effects of schools or, more properly, school sectors. The appropriate variable on which to control for both variants is school composition, instead of class-level compositional variables.

Competitive Market. The *market hypothesis* is given its most elaborate articulation in Chubb and Moe's *Politics, Markets, and America's Schools* (1989). The main argument they advance is that the competitive position of private schools (including Catholic and other private schools) essentially forces them to be more responsive and accountable to their constituencies, and that this leads to higher student achievement. Public schools are largely shielded from market forces, due to the barriers to parental choice that the state has constructed. These barriers include the tax code, which forces parents with children in private schools to pay taxes to support public schools and to pay the private school tuition. It also includes the system of democratic control over the public school system, which leads to bureaucratic standardization and a lack of responsiveness to parental demands.

Institutional Charter. The *institutional charter argument* is developed most acutely in Bryk, Lee, and Holland's *Catholic Schools and the Common Good* (1993). Their argument is that Catholic schools were originally developed, or "chartered," to teach a common academic curriculum to all students, and that this mission has been largely maintained up to the present. The academic tradition is rooted in and still invigorated to a significant degree by Catholic religious and social ideals. Although perhaps most pronounced in the schools of the Jesuit order, the ideas of literacy as a means of recovering the truths contained in sacred texts and commentaries, and the well-honed intellect as a tool to defend the faith, are still part of the Catholic school ideology. Another key element of Catholic ideology that affects schooling is the belief in the fundamental equality of all peoples under God. The linking of this idea of equality to an active faith in God gives the notion of equality more immediacy than the secular idea of equality rooted in the abstract idea of "citizen" that defines the public school ideal. Perhaps as a result, Catholic schools tend to expect all students to complete an academic curriculum, whereas public schools are only beginning to consider ways to bring more students into the academic program fold.

Although not developed by Bryk, Lee, and Holland, another dimension of the historical charter of Catholic schools, one discussed by Greeley in his 1982 book *Catholic High Schools and Minority Students*, also may continue to have an impact in the present day. This dimension is more of a reflection of American Catholics' struggle for social equality than of religious belief per se. Specifically, part of the motivation to maintain a common academic curriculum may be rooted in the upward-mobility orientation of the Catholic ethnic groups that many of the Catholic schools originally were built to serve. Discrimination from the Protestant establishment that controlled most local public school districts may well have had the effect of relegating the sons and daughters of Catholic immigrants to vocational or dead-end programs, had they stayed in the public system. Having their students outperform their public school counterparts may have been a goal of some Catholic educators and constituencies, for the prejudiced and unresponsive public schools would have limited the achievement and future life chances of Catholic youth. At present, this orientation would be concretely manifest in a competitive spirit among Catholic educators vis-à-vis their public education counterparts, and this competitive spirit would be independent of the market position of the Catholic schools.

Functional Community and Social Capital. The functional community hypothesis is articulated by Coleman and Hoffer in *Public and Private High Schools: The Impact of Communities* (1987). Coleman and Hoffer see Catholic school advantages as accruing in essentially accidental ways. Rather than emphasizing the force of institutionalized practice, however, they point instead to the immediate social structures in which the schools are embedded. Particularly important, they argue, is the greater likelihood of Catholic school parents to know one another through church participation and thus to be able to exchange information and establish norms about the conduct of their children's schooling. The social ties that are built on the basis of participation in Church (or other institutions, such as work) constitute a "functional community," which contrasts with a "value community" that is defined by shared values rather than concrete relations with face-to-face contacts. The ties among individuals in the functional community can be viewed as "social capital" that parents can draw upon to help steer their children in productive directions.

Like the aggregate-student composition model, this theory points to explanatory mechanisms that do not entail any greater effort, talent, or quality of organization on the part of Catholic school educators. Their greater effectiveness is rather due to the more fortunate circumstances of Catholic school students, particularly the greater social capital available to them from their parents' social networks. But it is important to emphasize that this social capital is constructed by parents through participation in a community, and thus contrasts with the aggregated human capital or emergent class consciousness of the composition model, which does not necessarily entail any social relations among parents. It is thus the mutually reinforcing fit of school and community that Coleman and Hoffer emphasize.

Theories of Catholic School Effects, Individual Decisions, and Social Policy

While there can be no argument over whether Catholic school students score higher on achievement tests than their public school counterparts, the different possible explanations carry significantly different connotations for both individual families and public policy. For individual families, the individual-selection effects model implies that Catholic schools produce no added value to their students' levels of achievement. If greater achievement is the parents' goal in enrolling their child in Catholic school, evidence supporting this theory would suggest the parents are wasting their money, at least in terms of enhancing their child's measured achievement. All of the other models, in contrast, do imply a positive effect of Catholic schools and support the notion that children learn more in Catholic schools than in the public alternatives.

Similarly, the different theories hold different implications for public policy. Policy arguments that favor reducing the financial constraints on parents of enrolling their children in Catholic schools are supported by images of more effective teachers, sounder curricula, and more astute administrators. In contrast, few would argue in favor of expanding access on the basis of individual or aggregate selection effects. These simply point to the power of segregating students rather than to superior effort or school organization.

This is obviously true for the individual selection model, but one could argue that aggregate-selection effects are still a positive effect of the Catholic schools. That is, by concentrating students from more advantaged backgrounds in a single Catholic school instead of a range of more heterogeneous public schools, Catholic schools are producing higher levels of achievement among those students than they otherwise would have realized. But what is missing from that argument is a balancing of the gains with the negative effect on students remaining in the public schools, which the concentration entails. The positive aggregation effects thus imply negative segregation effects, but the exact balance of the gains and losses is not known. The gains may exceed the losses, or gains and losses may balance in a "zero-sum" way, or the losses may exceed the gains. In any case, to the degree that aggregate selection effects are present, an expansion of the Catholic sector is not optimal in the classical Pareto formulation of at least some gains coupled with no losses.

The functional community hypothesis, in contrast, points to a Pareto-optimal condition. According to this hypothesis, Catholic schools achieve better results because of the match of the school with the community of families it serves. The ties among families are built through membership in the church and participation in Church-related activities. A school linked to that community will benefit from the strengths of the community. If the school a child attends is not linked to the community in which his or her families participates, then the benefit of the community dissipates and does not go elsewhere.

REVIEW OF EMPIRICAL RESEARCH

The point of departure for a review of national survey-based research is the comparisons of public and Catholic schools presented in Coleman, Hoffer, and Kilgore's *High School Achievement: Public, Catholic, and Private Schools Compared* (1982). Although the data they analyzed were cross-sectional (from the 1980 base year of the High School and Beyond survey), the definition of the research problem and the methods they used established standards that virtually all subsequent research has adopted. This is true of the several analyses of the High School and Beyond longitudinal data, as well as the analyses of the NELS:88 data that have appeared in the past few years. The key aspects of that approach are as follows:

1. A "Catholic school effect" on achievement (and other outcomes) consists of the unexplained difference between public and Catholic school students remaining after statistically controlling for differences in the students' backgrounds.
2. The presence and size of the Catholic school effect may depend on the background of the students. Coleman and colleagues claimed that Catholic schools were more effective for students from relatively disadvantaged social backgrounds, leading them to characterize Catholic schools as more closely approximating the "common school" ideal of American education than do their public school counterparts.
3. A complete explanation of the Catholic school effect would entail two levels of explanation. The first consists of identifying the specific mechanisms or ways in which public and Catholic schools differ, such that once those factors are statistically controlled, the Catholic school effect disappears. Beyond that statistical accounting, an adequate theory of sector effects would explain why public and Catholic schools differ on the mechanisms of interest. In other words, one might find that the Catholic school effect disappears when one compares the achievement of students taking rigorous college-preparatory programs of courses in high school. In one sense, the different academic

demands of public and Catholic schools may be regarded as an explanation of the achievement differences. But why do public and Catholic schools differ in the academic demands they make of students? An adequate explanation of sector effects would answer both of these questions.

This section assesses previous studies on these three points. Specifically, the questions posed of each study are (1) For each achievement outcome analyzed, what is the size of the estimated Catholic school effect? How was the analytic sample defined, which statistical methods were used, and which background variables were controlled and omitted in estimating the effects? (2) Were effects of Catholic school attendance estimated separately for different subpopulations, or were the effects assumed to be equal for all groups? (3) Did the authors attempt to account for Catholic school effects in terms of specific schooling variables and, if so, which were most important in explaining the Catholic school effects? How did the authors interpret their findings with respect to the larger theoretical models set forth earlier in the chapter?

Sector Effects on Average Achievement Scores

Findings from the 1980 Base Year of High School and Beyond. Almost all of the contemporary literature on Catholic school effects on academic achievement is tied, either directly or indirectly, to the Coleman, Hoffer, and Kilgore (1982) analysis of the 1980 High School and Beyond data. Those data were only the base year of HS&B and were thus cross-sectional. Coleman and colleagues used multiple regression to control for a large set of social background variables that were likely to be correlated both with being in a Catholic school versus public school and with the achievement outcomes. The control variables included a set that clearly is not affected by sector and a set that may be affected to some extent by sector. Variables that clearly are not influenced by the student's enrollment in a Catholic school included the following:

> Family income
> Mother's and father's education
> Race and Hispanic ethnicity
> Number of siblings
> Both parents present in the home
> Number of rooms in the home
> Mother's working before child was in elementary school
> Mother's working when child was in elementary school

Variables that may be affected by enrollment in a Catholic school, but which Coleman and colleagues also treated as controls, included the following:

Encyclopedia or other reference books in the home
More than 50 books in the home
Typewriter in the home
Pocket calculator in the home
How often student talks to parent about personal experiences
Whether mother thinks student should go to college after high school
Whether father thinks student should go to college after high school

When these variables were controlled for in the regression analyses, Coleman and colleagues found significant effects of Catholic school attendance on achievement among both the 1980 sophomores and 1980 seniors. The estimated Catholic school effects were about one-half to one-third the size of the unadjusted effects shown in Table 5.2. In the effect size metric of Tables 5.1 and 5.2, Coleman and colleagues estimated effects of Catholic school attendance on achievement scores of the 1980 sophomores to be 0.16 in reading, 0.20 in vocabulary, and 0.15 in mathematics. The effects for the 1980 seniors were similar: 0.12 in reading, 0.29 in vocabulary, and 0.14 in mathematics.

These results were quickly criticized in several journal articles (special editions of the *Harvard Educational Review* in 1981 and *Sociology of Education* in 1982 and 1983). The main criticism was that Coleman and colleagues did not adequately control for background differences among public and Catholic school students, especially the ability or initial level of high school achievement among students. Without randomized assignments of students to schools, one can never fully rule out the possibility of selection effects. Controlling for the effects of background variables associated with the type of school attended and the achievement outcomes is one strategy for approximating the experimental situation; using longitudinal data to compare changes on the outcome variables is another. Since the High School and Beyond project administered the same achievement tests to the 1980 sophomores 2 years later, when most were seniors, this method also became available to the research community.

When the HS&B first follow-up data were released in late 1984, several teams of researchers immediately began to assess the effects of Catholic schools on achievement gains over the 2-year period. The results largely confirmed the findings of the cross-sectional analyses, indicating significant positive effects of Catholic school attendance on test scores. The methodology was essentially the same as before, but with the added control for sophomore level of achievement. Adding the sophomore score to the model meant that the Catholic school effects would be confined to those occurring during the last 2 years of high school. The cross-sectional analysis, in contrast, does not yield effect estimates that are specifically tied to the high school years. The cross-sectional estimates are instead cumulative effects that have built up over the full span of schooling. A serious limitation of the Coleman, Hoffer, and Kilgore analyses was that it was not possible to determine when the Catholic schools had their effects. The effects could have been generated (1) in equal increments over the entire Catholic school (elementary and secondary) career of the student, or (2) only during some subset of that career. While the debate assumed that the high school years were the critical ones, this was not supported by data. Interestingly, the HS&B 1982 data do include retrospective self-reported indicators of whether the student was enrolled in a public, Catholic, or other private school at each elementary and secondary grade level, when those data would allow one to see whether the size of the sector effects depended on the duration and specific grades when a student was enrolled in Catholic school. This is addressed again shortly.

Sector Effects from the HS&B 1982 First Follow-up. In any case, the availability of the HS&B 1982 first follow-up data allowed researchers to compare growth rates of public and Catholic students from the end of sophomore year to the end of senior year. The first round of analyses were featured in a dedicated issue of *Sociology of Education* in the spring of 1985; Coleman and Hoffer published a monograph titled *Public and Private High Schools* (1987), which extended those analyses and analyzed other outcomes. The models for estimating the Catholic school effects on achievement included essentially the same set of background variables as the base-year analyses, plus controls for the sophomore achievement scores. Analyses by Hoffer, Greeley, and Coleman (1985), Willms (1985), and Alexander and Pallas (1985) converged on the finding that Catholic schools contribute from 0.03 to 0.04 additional standard deviation units during the junior and senior years of high school (Jencks, 1985, Table 2). This is an average across all six achievement tests in the HS&B battery: reading, vocabulary, mathematics, writing, science, and civics. The Catholic school effects were largest in writing, vocabulary, mathematics, and reading, but close to zero in science and civics.

These effects are small in absolute terms, but become quite large if cumulated over several years. The question is, From how far back do they cumulate? Jencks (1985) proposed one estimate, based on the students' reports of how many years they spent in Catholic schooling, which I mentioned earlier. From those data, it appears the average Catholic high school senior has spent about 9.5 years in Catholic schooling. As an estimate of the cumulative effect of Catholic schooling on achievement by the end of high school, Jencks used the predicted senior score difference (the average across the six tests) between public and Catholic students with average social backgrounds (restricted to SES and race-ethnicity). Those estimated cumulative sector effects range from only about 0.11 to 0.22 standard deviation units. When these are divided by the 9.5 average number of years, the average annual effect becomes only about 0.01 to 0.02 standard deviations per year.

These estimated effects are much smaller than those for the last 2 years of high school. Jencks notes three possible explanations for the difference: (1) the estimates may differ simply by chance, since the differences at the level of 1-year estimates probably are not statistically significant; (2) public and Catholic elementary schools may be equally effective, so that the only Catholic school effects on achievement are during the high school years; and (3) sector effects may decay over time, so that advantages of Catholic elementary school attendance may have been realized but then lost in later years. This last point is not clear, for Jencks's analogy of the decaying effects of compensatory educational program participation does not correspond to the sector comparisons. Decaying effects usually are conceptualized with respect to what happens after one leaves a treatment, but this was not the typical case for the Catholic high school students for whom the cumulative effects were estimated.

The aggregate-student composition hypothesis asserts that the effects of student background must be assessed at both the individual and school aggregate levels. None of the published analyses of the HS&B base-year data included measures of school-average or other aggregated student characteristics, but the hypothesis was addressed in two separate analyses of the HS&B first follow-up survey. Neither study found much support for the hypothesis. Willms (1985) included school-mean student SES, the proportion Black, and the proportion Hispanic in his models. Including these measures did not, however, substantially reduce the estimated Catholic sector effects for any of the achievement outcomes, and Willms thus dropped them from his final models.

Coleman and Hoffer (1987) augmented Willms's aggregate measures with school-average sophomore verbal and mathematics achievement scores, and the proportion of students in the school who reported (retrospectively, when they were sophomores) that when they were in ninth grade they planned to go to college. This set of variables thus provided a much more rigorous test of the hypotheses than Willms's set. The results showed that these added controls explained only about one-tenth of the Catholic school effect on verbal and mathematics achievement growth of Blacks and Hispanics, none of the Catholic school effect on White students' verbal score growth, and but about one-third of the Catholic school effect on math achievement growth of White students (Coleman & Hoffer, 1987, p. 147).

NELS:88 Analyses of Sector Effects. The next major data collection effort that would permit analyses of the effects of Catholic schooling on achievement scores was the National Education Longitudinal Study of 1988. In light of the numerous articles and books published on the subject with the High School and Beyond data, it is surprising that no comparable studies have yet appeared using the NELS:88 data. This database presently has test scores available for when the students were in grades 8, 10, and 12, and thus allows researchers both to attempt cross-validation with HS&B and, if effects are found, to gain a better picture of the timing of the effects.

The only published analysis of Catholic school effects on achievement growth using the NELS:88 data is an article by Gamoran (1996) analyzing the relative effectiveness of different kinds of high schools located in urban areas. His analysis is confined to the 1988–1990 period, when the NELS:88 students were in the spring of their eighth grade to the spring of their tenth grade (unless they dropped out or repeated a grade). Controlling for initial achievement and social background variables, Gamoran found no evidence of significant Catholic school effects on achievement growth in reading, science, or social studies compared with students in comprehensive public schools. He did, however, find evidence of a positive effect of Catholic schools on mathematics achievement of the same order of magnitude as the HS&B estimates: about .06 in the effect size metric for the 2-year span, or about .03 per year.

Schiller (1994) has analyzed the NELS:88 mathematics scores and found significant Catholic sector effects over the tenth- to twelfth-grade span. Controls used here included the previous cycle math score plus an extensive set of social background variables that compared closely with the set used by Coleman and colleagues and their critics in the HS&B analyses. These probably overestimate the Catholic sector effects, since the HS&B analyses showed that additional controls for the other achievement tests reduced the Catholic effect estimates (Jencks, 1985; Willms, 1985). Schiller does not provide information on the metric sizes of the Catholic sector effects or the test score standard deviations, and it is thus not possible to produce effect size estimates to compare with the HS&B estimates.

As an initial step toward filling out the picture of Catholic sector effects in the NELS:88 data, I have run ordinary least squares regressions of the 1992 test scores on dichotomous indicators of whether the student was enrolled in a Catholic or other private high school in 1992, the 1988 (eighth-grade) test scores, plus controls for SES, race, Hispanic ethnicity, and gender. A summary of the sector effect estimates is shown in Table 5.3. The results in Table 5.3 are rough estimates in the sense that they do not allow for interactions of sector with the control variables and do not include controls for school-aggregate student composition or for individual student family structure and functioning. The lack of sector interactions may diminish the Catholic sector effect estimates (that was a consequence of such an omission in the HS&B data), and the lack of controls for school-aggregate student composition and for individual family structure and functioning differences may increase the Catholic sector effect estimates. Past research suggests that the latter bias (overestimating the sector effects) is not likely to be large, since each regression controls for all 4 eighth-grade achievement tests.

Table 5.3. Estimated Effects of Catholic High School Attendance on Grades 8–12 Achievement Gains, Controlling for Grade 8 Achievement and Social Background

	b	*t-Value*	*1992 SD*	*Effect size*
Reading comprehension (*n* = 12,047)	1.29	4.33	10.10	.128
Mathematics (*n* = 12,045)	1.84	3.66	14.39	.128
Science (*n* = 11,972)	0.18	0.74 (n.s.)	6.21	.029
History/civics (*n* = 11,912)	0.83	3.48	5.40	.154

Source: NELS:88, 1992 second follow-up and 1988 base-year data.

Notes: Estimates were obtained from OLS regressions of 1992 test scores (expressed in what NELS:88 refers to as the "true score number of items correct" metric) on dichotomous indicator of whether the student was enrolled in a Catholic high school in 1992, whether the student was enrolled in another private high school in 1992, all four 1988 tests, plus family SES, 0–1 indicators of whether the student is Black, Hispanic, or Asian; and 0–1 indicator of whether student is female. The regressions were weighted with the second follow-up design weight. The standard errors used to calculate the *t*-values were estimated with the Taylor series method to include the design effect of the NELS:88 stratification and clustering (Shah, Barnwell, Hunt, & La Vange, 1992). The *t*-values are statistically significant for reading comprehension, mathematics, and history/civics. The standard deviations of the 1992 test scores are for the full sample of students. See Hoffer (1998) for more details.

At first glance, the Catholic school effects on reading, mathematics, and social studies appear to be much larger than the HS&B estimates, for which the comparable effect sizes ranged from 0.06 to 0.08. But it must be remembered that the results in Table 5.3 are for 4 years instead of 2. When the NELS:88 results are divided by four, the estimated annual effects for verbal skills and mathematics match the annual estimates from HS&B fairly closely (as reported earlier, Jencks, 1985, Table 2, shows an annual effect size estimate of about .03).

Sector Effects on Achievement Scores of Different Subpopulations

The results reviewed thus far pertain to an "average student," defined in terms of the background variables included as controls in the models of achievement. But what holds true on average may be very far from the mark for students from different backgrounds. Coleman and colleagues (1982) found that the overall impact of social background on achievement, as indexed by the R^2 statistic for the achievement-on-background regression equations, was weaker among Catholic school students than among public school students. Specifically, they found that (1) parental education and minority status had smaller effects on achievement among both the HS&B sophomores and seniors, and (2) the effects of parent education and race-ethnicity were smaller among Catholic school seniors than among Catholic school sophomores, whereas the opposite pattern was found among public school seniors and sophomores. Thus, social background effects were smaller and appeared to diminish as the students progressed in the Catholic schools. This led Coleman and colleagues to argue that the Catholic schools were closer to the "common school" ideal that animated the development of the public school system than were the public schools themselves. Andrew Greeley (1982) independently obtained similar results and made similar conclusions from his analysis of minority student academic outcomes, also using the HS&B base-year data.

Although these findings were essentially serendipitous, not pursued in relation to a prior theory, they attracted considerable interest and criticism. The main point from the HS&B base-year debates and reanalyses was that the observed pattern was consistent with either of two alternatives: (1) Catholic schools do a better job of promoting learning among traditionally less-advantaged youth; or (2) the nominally "less-advantaged" youth that Catholic schools enroll are an especially select group, with unmeasured background characteristics that lead to the higher levels of achievement remaining after controlling for measured background (Goldberger & Cain, 1982). While there was no evidence for the validity of (2), it could not be refuted, since the critical factor was not measured.

The common-school hypothesis about Catholic schooling also was re-examined with the HS&B 1982 follow-up data. Probably the best operationalization one could make of the Goldberger–Cain unmeasured selection hypothesis would be to control for the sophomore achievement scores in regressions of senior achievement on the background variables of interest. Regressing senior achievement on sophomore achievement plus SES, race, and Hispanic ethnicity, Hoffer, Greeley, and Coleman (1985, Table 2.4) found that the effects of sophomore achievement and the three social background variables were consistently smaller than the effects in the public schools. Across the six HS&B achievement tests, the effects of the four variables were closer to zero in the Catholic schools in 22 of 24 comparisons. However, only a few of the differences in coefficients proved to be statistically significant, and the results probably are best regarded as suggestive, rather than conclusive (Jencks, 1985, p. 134, makes this point).

In later work with the HS&B follow-up data, Coleman and Hoffer (1987, Chapter 5) examined relative effects of additional background factors on achievement in the two school sectors. They distinguished between measures of "traditional disadvantage," which include social class, gender, race, and ethnicity; and "deficiency," which include household structural and functional problems. Measures of deficiency they used in their analysis included whether there was a single parent head of household, whether the mother worked outside the home before the child started school, the extent to which the parent and child talked about personal issues, and whether the parents expected the child to go to college after high school. These are not particularly good measures of the constructs, but they were all the HS&B data had to offer, and all showed significant effects on achievement in the full sample. The results for the measures of deficiency indicated that they were much less related to verbal achievement in the Catholic schools than in the public, but only slightly less related in the Catholic schools to mathematics achievement.

I examined the 1988–1992 NELS:88 data to see whether the effects of social background on achievement gains differed for public and Catholic high school students (Hoffer, 1998). Social background variables included family SES, race/ethnicity, and gender. Achievement gains were measured in reading comprehension, mathematics, science, and social studies. The results generally give only weak support for the common-school hypothesis. The effects of SES in Catholic schools are lower on all four outcomes, but the public/Catholic difference is not statistically significant in any comparison. Similarly, the effects of race and Hispanic ethnicity on achievement gains also do not significantly differ among public and Catholic school students, and the effects are about as likely to be greater as smaller for Catholic students.

What Do Catholic School Students Do Differently?

The preceding two sections have described the basic findings on Catholic school effects on achievement outcomes. The results reviewed thus far indicate that Catholic high school attendance has positive effects on high school students' achievement in verbal skills and mathematics, but not in science or social studies. Moreover, Catholic school effects are greater for students from families with one or more structural or functional obstacles. The question now addressed concerns how Catholic schools produce these effects. The main explanations that have been advanced are couched at two levels: the within-school mechanisms that are affected by school sector and that affect student achievement, and the larger differences between schools that shape these internal schooling factors.

As Bidwell and Kasarda (1980) argue, differences in average achievement among schools are ultimately explained by differences in the specific kinds of schooling experiences students have within schools. In other words, if one wants to understand why school-level outcomes differ, one must look for differences in the outcome-producing processes internal to the schools. This points to a certain logical priority of the within-school factors, and the research in fact has developed accordingly. The first efforts to give an account of the Catholic school effects were undertaken by Coleman, Hoffer, and Kilgore (1982). The framework they used generally distinguished two sets of factors: disciplinary standards and academic standards.

The HS&B data contained several measures of individual students' conformity to school rules, including absenteeism, tardiness, and class cutting. Students also reported their perceptions of the disciplinary climate in the school. The measures of academic demands included hours of homework and coursework in academic areas.

When these were factored into the regression analysis of achievement outcomes, Coleman and colleagues (1982) found that discipline problems were much lower in the Catholic schools and had significant effects on achievement outcomes. The better discipline in Catholic schools accounted for most of the Catholic sophomores' higher achievement in reading and mathematics, compared with public school sophomores. In contrast, the measures of academic demands accounted for relatively little of the Catholic sophomore advantages. Catholic students did more homework than public students, and that accounted for a small but significant part of the achievement differences, but the coursework measures did not explain much at all. For the 1980 seniors, though, all of the Catholic advantage in mathematics was explained by the greater number of math courses completed by Catholic students. The different effect of the math coursework variable on the sophomore and senior achievement scores reflects the fact that the measures of math coursework were much better for the seniors.

The explanatory picture changed when the HS&B follow-up data were analyzed. Coleman and colleagues' base-year analyses of the schooling variables, like their analysis of achievement scores more generally, were criticized because of the lack of controls for prior achievement (Goldberger & Cain, 1982). A number of critics also made the point that Catholic school students looked better on the discipline and academic variables because they were primarily academic-track, college-bound students. If Catholic school students were compared with academic-track public school students, the differences would disappear.

Coleman and Hoffer responded to the first of these criticisms by incorporating controls for sophomore achievement differences in their regressions for estimating Catholic school effects on the schooling variables. The argument about Catholic school students being best compared with academic-track public school students is based on a faulty premise, however. The argument assumes that all of the Catholic students would be placed in an academic track if they were in the public sector. But that is not supported by the data. Catholic school students are indeed much more likely to report being in an academic or college-preparatory program of studies than public school students with comparable social backgrounds. Overall, about 70% of Catholic school seniors reported being enrolled in an academic program, versus about 40% of public school students. But when the effects of sophomore achievement scores, SES, parent expectations, and the other social background variables on program are controlled for, the 30% sector difference reduces to about 18%, which is far from having disappeared (Coleman & Hoffer, 1987). In other words, there is a substantial independent effect of Catholic school attendance on the likelihood of academic program enrollment.

Coleman and Hoffer (1987) present an analysis that parallels Coleman and colleagues' base-year explanatory effort, but extends the original analysis to include the track variable and better measures of coursework. Coleman and Hoffer also carried out the analysis separately for minority (Black and Hispanic students combined) and non-Hispanic White students. The discipline variables were essentially the same as in the 1980 analysis and included indices of both individuals' own behavior and reports of school-wide disciplinary problems. The results showed that Catholic students completed more math, science, and foreign language courses; completed more homework; had better attendance; and saw fewer school-wide discipline problems than public school students with similar sophomore achievement and social backgrounds (Coleman & Hoffer, 1987).

When these schooling variables were entered into the achievement regressions, Coleman and Hoffer (1987) found that the academic variables (track placement, homework, and coursework) explained most of the Catholic school effect on verbal skills and all of the effects on mathematics scores. These findings have been largely corroborated by other researchers using the HS&B data (Lee & Bryk, 1988) and, to a limited extent, the NELS:88 data (Gamoran, 1996).

CONCLUSIONS: WHY ARE CATHOLIC SCHOOLS MORE EFFECTIVE?

The main points from the review and extension of empirical research are as follows:

- Catholic high schools have positive effects on verbal and mathematics achievement, but no discernible effects on science. The main evidence here is still from HS&B, but preliminary analyses of the NELS:88 data confirm the pattern at least for the last 2 years of high school.
- Catholic school effects are greater for students from disadvantaged backgrounds, especially with respect to family structure and functioning. The evidence for "common-school effects" is consistent but statistically weak for low-SES students.
- The main "schooling" mechanism accounting for the Catholic school effects is the greater concentration of academic course taking among Catholic school students. Discipline climate variables explain a small amount the Catholic school effects on achievement gains. The evidence is still largely from HS&B, and NELS:88 replications and extensions are needed.
- The main "macro" theories of the Catholic sector effects are (1) aggregate-student composition, (2) market competition, (3) institutional charter, and (4) functional community. Counter evidence from HS&B weakens the case for (1), but the other hypotheses have not been rigorously addressed with available survey or archival data.

One important shortcoming in the research to date is the lack of specificity about the presence and size of Catholic school effects at different grade levels. The most glaring gap in the research record is the lack of data to assess effects of Catholic elementary school attendance. The

NAEP fourth-grade aggregated data can be used in a very limited way to compare sector differences at grades 4, 8, and 12, controlling for parent education only. But new studies are needed to collect data that would allow the kinds of comparisons that have been done with the High School and Beyond and NELS:88 data. This need will be met with the Early Childhood Longitudinal Study (like HS&B and NELS:88, directed by the U.S. Department of Education's National Center for Education Statistics) started in fall 1998 with a national sample of 23,000 kindergartners in more than 1,000 schools. These children will be surveyed and assessed through the fifth grade.

The problem of when Catholic schools have their effects is also present in the high school years. The NELS:88 data suggest that the Catholic school effects are small, if present at all, in ninth and tenth grades, but resemble the effects estimated with the HS&B data in eleventh and twelfth grades. Why this inconsistency should occur is not anticipated in any theories encountered in this review and should be investigated more carefully.

Several other limitations of research on high school achievement also can be noted. One concerns the achievement criteria upon which public and Catholic schools are compared. While the tests administered by NAEP, HS&B, and NELS:88 are valid indicators of achievement, the achievement they measure is mainly recall of facts and concepts, and literal reading comprehension, rather than problem solving and ability to "go beyond the text." These tests may measure necessary but not sufficient conditions for applications of intelligence, and further research might examine whether public and Catholic school students differ in the higher-order thinking skills too.

A second limitation of the research to date is that it has not shed much light on the inconsistency of Catholic school effects across subject areas. In particular, it is not clear why Catholic schools do not have positive effects on science achievement. Detailed comparisons of coursework should be done, using the NELS:88 transcript data.

Third, the "internal" explanatory efforts are most successful for math and less successful for reading. This may reflect the quality of coursework measures in verbal skill areas. Future data-collection projects should look hard to develop stronger "opportunity to learn" indicators for language arts (and social studies).

Where does the research stand with respect to the "big theory" explanations that have been advanced? As we have seen, individual selection accounts for at least half of the overall public–Catholic differences in verbal skills and mathematics in high school, and all of the sector difference in science. But neither the individual-selection nor the aggregate-student composition explanation holds up for the positive effects of Catholic schooling on growth in verbal skills and mathematics over the last 2 years of high school.

What about the competing explanations of the positive effects of Catholic schools? The inconsistency of the Catholic advantages across subjects and grade levels is difficult to reconcile with the competitive market model, which predicts that Catholic schools should be more effective for all of their students than the public alternative. The institutional charter and functional community hypotheses, in contrast, are not as exacting in their predictions about achievement effects. Catholic schools may have strong charters with respect to academic emphasis and internal community, but those structures may not carry over to consistently higher performances at all grades and in all subjects. The strongest test of the charter hypothesis would be to assess the extent to which the structures and beliefs that Bryk, Lee, and Holland (1993) posit are in fact present and operative in Catholic schools. The specific conditions under which those structures and beliefs translate into academic excellence, however, remain to be identified.

Similarly, the functional community hypothesis is most directly tested not by achievement comparisons, but by assessing the extent to which the social networks that Coleman and Hoffer (1987) predict are in fact found. Data are available in the NELS:88 survey for assessing the hypothesis with respect to parent contacts with other parents, and parent involvement in the schools, but the analyses remain to be done. Again, the specific conditions under which these community relations translate into higher achievement need to be identified and assessed.

In conclusion, the issue of the relative effectiveness of public and Catholic schools in promoting academic achievement remains unresolved in several respects. One aspect on which there is no debate is whether the Catholic schools do worse than their public counterparts in any area, after taking into account student background. No study has produced evidence of lower effectiveness. Further, where positive effects of Catholic schooling have been found, researchers also have been largely successful in linking the advantages to specific mechanisms, particularly greater academic demands. While the larger theoretical issues of markets, charters, and communities need further development and testing, the model of higher academic standards that Catholic schools have come to at least symbolize, if not always embody, has likely had a positive effect on contemporary American education, public and private.

Acknowledgments. The author would like to thank David Baker and James Youniss for their encouragement and support of the study, Patrick Bova for a comprehensive computer-based bibliographic search on the topic, and Polly Hoover for helpful comments on an earlier draft.

REFERENCES

Alexander, K. A., & Pallas, A. M. (1985). School sector and cognitive performance: When is a little a little? *Sociology of Education, 58,* 115–128.

Barr, R., & Dreeben, R. (1983). *How schools work.* Chicago: University of Chicago Press.

Bidwell, C. E., & Kasarda, J. D. (1980). Conceptualizing and measuring the effects of school and schooling. *American Journal of Education, 88,* 401–430.

Bryk, A. S., Lee, V. E., & Holland, P. B. (1993). *Catholic schools and the common good.* Cambridge, MA: Harvard University Press.

Campbell, J. R., Reese, C. M., O'Sullivan, C., & Dossey, J. A. (1996). *Trends in academic achievement, 1994.* Washington, DC: National Center for Education Statistics.

Chubb, J., & Moe, T. (1989). *Politics, markets, and America's schools.* Washington, DC: Brookings Institution.

Coleman, J. S., & Hoffer, T. (1987). *Public and private high schools: The impact of communities.* New York: Basic Books.

Coleman, J. S., Hoffer, T., & Kilgore, S. B. (1982). *High school achievement: Public, Catholic, and private schools compared.* New York: Basic Books.

Gamoran, A. (1996). Student achievement in public magnet, public comprehensive, and private city high schools. *Educational Evaluation and Policy Analysis, 18* (1), 1–18.

Glass, G. V., McGaw, B., & Smith, M. L. (1981). *Meta-analysis in social research.* Beverly Hills, CA: Sage.

Goldberger, A. S., & Cain, G. G. (1982). The causal analysis of cognitive outcomes in the Coleman, Hoffer, and Kilgore report. *Sociology of Education, 55,* 103–122.

Greeley, A. M. (1982). *Catholic high schools and minority students.* New Brunswick, NJ: Transaction Books.

Hoffer, T. B. (1998). Social background and achievement in public and Catholic high schools. *Social Psychology of Education, 2,* 7–23.

Hoffer, T. B., Greeley, A. M., & Coleman, J. S. (1985). Achievement growth in public and Catholic schools. *Sociology of Education, 58,* 74–97.

Ingels, S. J., Dowd, K. L., Baldridge, J. D., Stipe, J. L., Bartot, V. H., Frankel, M. R., & Quinn, P. (1994). *NELS:88 second follow-up: Student component data file user's manual.* Washington, DC: U.S. Department of Education.

Jencks, C. (1985). How much do high school students learn? *Sociology of Education, 58,* 128–135.

Lee, V. E., & Bryk, A. S. (1988). Curriculum tracking as mediating the social distribution of high school achievement. *Sociology of Education, 61,* 78–94.

McPartland, J. M., & McDill, E. L. (1982). Control and differentiation in the structure of American education. *Sociology of Education, 55,* 77–88.

National Center for Education Statistics. (1994). *NAEP data on disk: 1992 almanac viewer.* Washington, DC: U.S. Department of Education.

National Commission on Excellence in Education. (1983). *A nation at risk: The imperative of educational reform.* Washington, DC: U.S. Government Printing Office.

Schiller, K. (1994, August). *When do Catholic schools have effects?* Paper presented at the annual meeting of the American Sociological Association, Los Angeles.

Shah, B. V., Barnwell, B. G., Hunt, P. N., & La Vange, L. M. (1992). SUDAAN user's manual. Research Triangle Park, NC: Research Triangle Institute.

Willms, D. J. (1985). Catholic-school effects on academic achievement: New evidence from the High School and Beyond follow-up study. *Sociology of Education, 58,* 98–114.

PART II

Minority Students in Catholic Schools

THE SECOND PART OF THIS BOOK is focused on minority students in Catholic schools. This topic has been grounds for much controversy that recently has put Catholic schools in the public spotlight (see Chapters 2 and 5). As was stated in the Introduction, the Catholic schools that serve urban minority students are at risk financially and need to be supported in new ways, if they are to be maintained. The chapters in Part II are designed to provide basic information about Catholic schools that serve these students, the very information that is missing from public discussion but necessarily must be considered for the making of intelligent policy.

In Chapter 6, Joseph O'Keefe and Jessica Murphy report on a national census of 311 Catholic schools that enroll more than 50% minority students. The authors note how useful this census might be in light of the abstract discussion that has been focused on the education of minority populations. In the study reported here, the authors give details about the students' family structure and income, about the schools' teachers and staff, about costs and tuition, and about the students' religious backgrounds.

These data are embedded in a brief review of the literature on Catholic schools and minority students, on the one hand, and well-crafted implications regarding the future of this kind of education. The authors are especially clear about the potential tension between Church leaders' interest in maintaining these schools and practical considerations, such as costs, which threaten to undermine the bishops' theological and civic-minded purpose.

In Chapter 7, Vernon Polite presents a unique portrait of select Catholic schools that originally were established for the education of African American students. These schools have a rich history that has been overlooked by scholars and unknown to laypeople. Polite remedies these

omissions in a straightforward narrative style that also uncovers historical relations between the Catholic Church and the general African American population.

Polite's further contribution is in reporting structural and administrative details on these schools. Catholic schools in general have been
discussed recently because of their role in educating minorities. These
schools stand out from secondary schools as a whole because they were
designed to educate a Black Catholic elite. There is a plaintive tone in
Polite's analysis as he observes the now familiar coupling of rising costs
with rising tuition. These schools are at risk, and were they to close, an
asset to the African American community would have been lost.

In Chapter 8, Sheila Nelson reports on a longitudinal study of 33
inner-city elementary schools in Chicago. More than a decade ago, she
visited the schools to collect basic data on their structure, finances, and
perceptions of their administrators. In 1996, she revisited these schools
in order to assess the degree to which they had changed.

Her major findings are that these schools did indeed change. Several
closed, others had to be consolidated in order to remain open, and still
others survived by raising tuition and starting to serve a wealthier student body. It is reasonable to read into these data a potential future trend
of instability for inner-city schools. The presumed factors that provoked
change are still at work and unless concerted interventions are instituted,
more closings, consolidations, and rising costs can be anticipated.

In Chapter 9, Stewart Lawrence presents previously unpublished
data on the degree to which post-1970 Catholic immigrants to the United
States utilize Catholic schools for the education of their children. From
1870 to World War II, Catholic schools served a dual function of helping
new immigrants maintain their ethnic identities and facilitating their ac-
climation to American culture. Indeed, the term *Catholic Church* often
was associated with the concept of immigrant Church.

Lawrence then asks whether recent immigrants, notably Mexicans,
Haitians, Koreans, Filipinos, and Vietnamese, among others, are being
educated and enculturated through Catholic schools. The answer is that
they are not, at least to the degree that occurred with prior immigrants.
Lawrence explores some of the factors that might account for this fact,
for example, whether rising tuition has preempted enrollment. He finds,
by the way, that this hypothesis is only partially correct and that other
factors must be at work. He also finds wide variations among these immigrant groups on measures of income, location, proclivity for English,
and history of Catholic education in their countries of origin.

This comprehensive look at the status of the Catholic schools that serve minority populations is sobering. It shows how fragile these schools are and presents a challenge for those who want to see these schools continue this educational and social mission. This is especially poignant regarding recent immigrants, given the historical role that Catholic schools played in the education and civic socialization of many immigrant groups from the late 1800s through the 1920s.

CHAPTER 6

Ethnically Diverse Catholic Schools: School Structure, Students, Staffing, and Finance

JOSEPH M. O'KEEFE, S.J., & JESSICA MURPHY

THE CLAIM THAT CATHOLIC SCHOOLS are particularly effective for children of color has been made by many researchers conducting secondary analyses of national data sets and qualitative case studies. This finding is important enough to warrant a comprehensive look at these schools. The present chapter reports results of our national survey of 311 ethnically diverse Catholic elementary and secondary schools. We will report on their administrative structure, the students, the staff, and their financial condition. We found that these institutions differ from traditional parochial schools in being less dependent on particular parishes, in serving children from a wide variety of religious backgrounds, in the disparity between the ethnicity of the staff and of the students, and in the complexity of demands on administrative leadership. We will first review the salient literature, describe our methodology and findings, and conclude with reflections about the current status and future direction of these schools.

REVIEW OF THE LITERATURE

The literature related to ethnically diverse Catholic schools can be divided into five areas: secondary analyses of national data sets, primary data collection about particular schools, qualitative studies, historical studies, and theological scholarship.

Secondary Analyses of National Data Sets

Convey (1992) provided a comprehensive review of studies that used national data sets. He concluded that ethnically diverse Catholic schools differed from public schools on achievement and other important measures. York (1996) extended this review by focusing on 14 studies, from 1973 to 1993, that assessed African American students in Catholic schools. Results also pointed to differences from public schools. Other major studies (Bryk, Lee, & Holland, 1993; Coleman & Hoffer, 1987; Coleman, Hoffer, & Kilgore, 1982; Greeley, 1982) found that Catholic schools were particularly effective in educating ethnic minority groups. More recently, Gamoran (1996) repeated the positive Catholic school effect on tests of academic achievement in the National Educational Longitudinal Study (NELS) data set. In their analysis of NELS, Teachman, Paasch, and Carver (1997) reported a lower dropout rate in Catholic than in public high schools. This result coincides with Sander and Krautmann's (1995) analysis of High School & Beyond (HS&B) data, in that sophomores in Catholic schools, compared with sophomores in public schools, were more likely to graduate with their class. Jones's (1997) analysis of the National Assessment of Educational Progress (NAEP) data on math achievement of fourth graders, found that students from less supportive family environments achieved higher scores when they attended Catholic rather than public schools. Neal (1997) used census data and the annual survey from the National Catholic Educational Association (NCEA) to show higher graduation rates for Catholic school students.

Primary Data Collection About Particular Schools

In Kealey's (1990) results of a 1989 survey of 907 Catholic elementary schools, 17% self-identified as inner-city schools. In 67 of these schools, more than 75% of the children came from communities of color. The average tuition was $804, the per-pupil cost was $1,476, and 20% of the schools had an endowment program. Forty-four percent of the schools reported having new extended-day programs, indicating a restructuring to meet new needs. In the 103 surveys he received in a follow-up study, Kealey (1995) found increases in average tuition to $1,433 and in per-pupil cost to $2,186. Also, 55% of the schools had a prekindergarten, 37% had an endowment, and 66% had extended-day programs.

Vitullo-Martin (1979) reported that Catholic schools were more effective than their public school counterparts in engaging parents in the educational process and in reinforcing family values. Cibulka, O'Brien, and Zewe (1982) surveyed private inner-city elementary schools in New York, Newark, Washington, Detroit, Chicago, Milwaukee, New Orleans, and Los Angeles, in 1979–1980. They surveyed 50 principals, 339 teachers, and 3,995 parents in 56 Catholic schools that were eligible for Title 1 funds and in which 70% or more of the students belonged to ethnic minority groups. Their most notable finding was the nonelitist character of the students, as measured by admission, retention, and the income level of families. They also found that the schools were characterized by local control and shared decision making among administrators and teachers. The teachers, representing a balance of age and experience across the professional life span, had credentials virtually identical to those in public schools. One-third of them were members of religious communities. While extolling the strengths of these institutions, Cibulka and colleagues identified several factors that put these schools at risk. They include the socioeconomic condition of parents who use the schools, the prospects of maintaining quality faculty and physical plant, and a tendency of school system administrators to use ad hoc planning methods when dealing with inner-city schools.

Benson, Yeager, Wood, Guerra, and Manno (1986) reported on 106 Catholic high schools nationwide in which more than 10% of the students were from families with incomes below $10,000. In the first phase of their work, conducted in 1983, principals were sampled in 14 areas that ranged from administrative handling of teachers to religious education, through development and finance. Benson and colleagues complemented these data with scores of students' academic achievement and surveys of teachers. In comparison with more affluent schools, low-income schools are more likely to be diocesan and parochial than private and to have a larger percentage of women religious and priests on staff. However, the two types of schools exhibit a similar level of religious vitality, morale, academic emphasis, and discipline.

More recently Harris (1996) provided information about the long-term viability of inner-city schools in an overarching study of the financial structure of Catholic institutions in the United States. He found that from 1983 to 1993, across all Catholic populations, school expenses grew at nearly triple the rate of parish revenue. Harris speculated that the continued accessibility of Catholic education to low-income children will require a dramatic increase in income, through either philanthropy or government assistance.

Qualitative Studies

Bryk, Lee, and Holland (1993) complemented their statistical analyses
with qualitative field studies at seven schools. They found that students
in these high schools outperformed peers of equivalent social and ethnic
backgrounds in public and other private schools. They attributed this
result to a strong emphasis on academic achievement without tracking,
high levels of student engagement and teacher commitment, decentral-
ized governance based on the principle of subsidiarity, explicit moral
norms based on the principle of personalism, and recognition of the
power of religious symbols as an integrative force.

Much of the qualitative research is autobiographical. Studies about
the Catholic school experience for African Americans (Foeman, Brown,
Pugh, & Pearson, 1996; Irvine & Foster, 1996) and Hispanics (Carger,
1996) are typical of the genre. Biography is another appropriate vehicle
for reflection. As a White middle-class man, the lead author studied successful graduates of two Catholic high schools (O'Keefe, 1994). Through
their experience, he began to understand the deep ambiguity they experienced in a White middle-class environment. A Jewish author recently
published an anecdotal account of his experience in an ethnically diverse
inner-city Catholic high school in Jersey City (Gerson, 1997); unfortunately, using solely his own experience, he generalized about the inferi-
ority of public education. On the other side of the political spectrum, a
recent ethnography of a Catholic high school (Oldenski, 1997) provided a
glimpse into the ethos of liberation theology in a low-income, ethnically
diverse Catholic high school.

Historical Studies

Recent historical studies also provide important factual information.
Along with a recent general history of parochial schools (Walch, 1996),
the most significant are Irvine and Foster's (1996) volume on the education of African Americans and McGreevy's study (1996) of the presence
of African Americans in northern parochial schools. Walch and Mc-
Greevy document the dramatic shift in demographics, from White to
Black and Hispanic, that has occurred in many urban elementary schools
in the north. Irvine and Foster provide information about Black schools
in the south as well as urban schools in the north.

Theological Scholarship

In *The Church and Racism: Towards a More Fraternal Society*, Church officials
eschewed a model of assimilation to European cultural patterns and adopt-

ed a philosophy of cultural pluralism. They proposed that solidarity and communion do not demand uniformity, but require a positive appreciation of the complementary diversity of peoples. Catholic institutions must enhance a "well-understood pluralism" that can resolve "the problem of closed racism" (Pontifical Commission for Peace and Justice, 1988, p. 45).

In their major document on the issue, *Brothers and Sisters to Us*, the Catholic bishops of the United States explored the subtle and covert racism that permeates capitalist culture, which is as salient today as it was when it was written. The bishops called for a new look at the past, one freed from the cultural lens that "obscures the evil of the past and denies the burdens that history has placed on the shoulders of our Black, Hispanic, Native American and Asian brothers and sisters" (National Conference of Catholic Bishops, 1979, p. 5). The bishops saw clearly that racism is a fundamental sin, a primary pathology in human society, "a radical evil dividing the human family and denying the new creation of a redeemed world. To struggle against it demands an equally radical transformation in our own minds and hearts as well as the structure of society" (p. 10).

The pastoral letter called for the conversion of Catholics from this social sin, recruitment of people of color to ministry within the Church, social programs for migrant workers and undocumented aliens, fair employment practices in Catholic institutions, responsible investment of the assets of those institutions, financial support of groups advancing the cause of racial minorities, and the continuation and expansion of Catholic schools in the inner cities and other disadvantaged areas. The bishops argue that "no sacrifice can be so great, no price can be so high, no short-range goals can be so important as to warrant the lessening of our commitment to Catholic education in minority neighborhoods" (p. 13). The role and future of Black Catholics were further articulated in a collection of essays published in 1996 (Committee on African-American Catholics of the National Conference of Catholic Bishops).

In *The Hispanic Presence: Challenge and Commitment* (National Conference of Catholic Bishops, 1983), the bishops argued from history in advocating positive steps to enhance the welfare the burgeoning Latino population:

> Historically, the Church in the United States has been an "immigrant Church" whose outstanding record of care for countless European immigrants remains unmatched. Today that same tradition must inspire in the Church's approach to recent Hispanic immigrants a similar authority, compassion and decisiveness. (p. 4)

Likewise, the National Catholic Educational Association (1987) called for redoubled efforts among Catholic educators in favor of Spanish-speaking peoples in the document *Integral Education: A Response to the Hispanic Presence*. In the NCEA's *A Catholic Response to the Asian Presence* (1990), the authors found that immigrant parents look to Catholic schools for education in faith, discipline, moral training, a countercultural value system, and security. Many Asian Americans indicated that they would like to send their children to Catholic schools but that high tuition costs are beyond their ability to pay. *The People: Reflections of Native Peoples on the Catholic Experience in North America* (National Catholic Educational Association, 1992) not only assists teachers of all children in the development of an honest and faithful curriculum about the experience of Native Americans, but supports the Church's educational efforts on behalf of indigenous populations.

Chineworth's (1995) edited volume provides Catholic educators with insights into the reality of racism and the Black experience; it upholds the rationale for maintaining inner-city schools, even when the percentage of Catholics in those schools is very low. Martin (1996) offers a rationale for multicultural education based on the Church's self-understanding. Outside of the U.S. context, a recent pastoral letter (Committee for Community Relations of the Bishops' Conference of England and Wales, 1997) articulates a rationale for maintaining schools that serve children from a variety of religious communities.

METHODOLOGY

The 1995–96 census of Catholic elementary and secondary schools, conducted jointly by the National Catholic Educational Association and the market research firm Market Data Retrieval, served as the springboard for our study. Whereas each Catholic secondary school in the nation was invited to participate in the study, only elementary schools deemed urban or inner city were drawn from the overall population of Catholic elementary schools. Census data were then used to identify urban elementary schools that served low-income students through Title I funding, which eventually numbered just over 1,000 schools. Introductory letters describing the focus of the study were sent to diocesan superintendents and then surveys were distributed to identified school principals.

The secondary and elementary school versions of the survey are composed largely of parallel items to allow for comparative analysis. These items are focused on school characteristics, student body demographics, teacher and principal characteristics, family information, schools' community involvement, curriculum and instruction, school finances and development, school religious identity, and 5-year trends.

Data were collected primarily during the 1996–97 academic year, yielding a final sample size of 510 Catholic secondary schools and 398 Catholic elementary schools. The subsample of focus for the present report consists of schools in which minority student enrollment was equal to or greater than 50% of the total student body. The result is a subsample of 100 Catholic secondary schools and 211 Catholic elementary schools.

SCHOOL STRUCTURE

The survey examined administrative structure and the location of schools.

Administrative Structure

Table 6.1 illustrates the considerable differences in administrative structure at the secondary and elementary levels. The majority of the elementary schools are parish-related schools (63% of elementary schools vs. 14% of secondary schools), whereas secondary schools are much more likely to be private (43% of secondary schools vs. 4% of elementary schools). In relation to all Catholic schools, the ethnically diverse schools are more reliant on the diocese than are their counterparts (Milks, 1997).

Location of Schools

The ethnically diverse schools in the study are found in all sections of the nation (see Table 6.2). However, 86% of the target elementary schools and 87% of the target secondary schools are located in the mideast, Great Lakes, and west regions. Using demographic data from updates of the 1990 U.S. census (CACI, 1997), we explored the racial and socioeconomic characteristics of each zip code in which each of the schools in the sample is located. Compared with the national averages, both elementary

Table 6.1. Administrative Structure of 311 Schools (percent)

	Elementary		*Secondary*	
Type of school	*Sample*	*All*	*Sample*	*All*
Parish	63	82	14	11
Interparish	12	12	—	13
Diocesan	19	3	41	35
Private	4	4	43	42
Other	2	—	1	—

Table 6.2. Location of 311 Schools (percent)

	Elementary		Secondary	
	Sample	*All*	*Sample*	*All*
New England (CT, ME, MA, NH, RI, VT)	3	7	3	8
Mideast (DE, DC, NM, NJ, NY, PA)	30	27	28	28
Great Lakes (IL, IN, MI, OH, WI)	24	26	15	21
Great Plains (MO, KS, MN, IO, NE, ND, SD)	3	12	3	12
Southeast (Al, AK, FL, GA, KY, LA, MI, NC, SC, TN, VA, WV)	8	12	7	14
West (AL, AZ, CA, CO, HI, ID, MN, NM, OK, OR, TX, UT, WA, WY)	32	17	44	18

and secondary schools are in racially diverse areas. For example, while, on average, 82% of the nation's zip code tracts are White, only 42% of the population surrounding the minority elementary schools and 55% of the population surrounding the minority secondary schools are White. Moreover, both have a higher than average percentage of individuals living below the poverty line. Whereas the national average is 16% of the population, 28% of the individuals inhabiting the elementary school areas and 21% of the individuals living in the areas of the minority secondary schools live below the poverty line. The per capita income in the elementary schools areas is $14,337 versus the national per capita income level of $15,597. The result differs for the areas in which the secondary schools are located. The per capita income of the areas in which the minority secondary schools are located is $20,192 versus the previously cited national average of $15,597.

STUDENTS

The survey examined a number of characteristics of the students in these schools, including socioeconomic status, race, ethnicity, family structure, religion, educational aspirations, gender, enrollment, and retention.

Socioeconomic Status

Information on the socioeconomic status of students is difficult to obtain because of principals' concerns for confidentiality. In light of that limitation, we attempted to estimate socioeconomic status through students' place of residence, principals' perceptions, and the financial aid students receive.

As indicated in Table 6.3, over half of the students attending these elementary schools enjoy proximity between school and residence, suggesting that these schools are largely neighborhood institutions. In contrast, the majority of students attending secondary schools tend not to live near their school.

These data plus those discussed above for schools' zip codes allow the conclusion that elementary school students tend to have a lower per capita income and are more likely to live below the poverty line than the general population. Elementary principals claim that 46% of the students are eligible for free lunch, arguably a reliable indicator of a student's poverty status. Principals estimate that 33% of their students live below the poverty line, defined in the survey as a gross income of $9,655 for a two-person family and $15,141 for a four-person family. They also estimate that 17% of the students live in low-income, government-subsidized housing and that 1% have been homeless at some point. The total percentage of students receiving financial aid in these elementary schools is 18%. However, it must be noted that nearly 90% of the principals reported some type of variable scale based on the factors of family income, siblings in the school, membership in the local parish, or religious affiliation more broadly.

The secondary principals were asked a variety of items, appropriate to their setting, that tapped into student and community economic prosperity. They reported that 17% of their students are without health care coverage. In addition, 14% of the principals reported that their students reside in low-income, government-subsidized housing. When asked to estimate the percentage of students in their school living at or below the poverty threshold, 56% reported that more than 10% of their students lived at or below the poverty line. It is important to note that schools were putting forth effort to make education available to these students. Of the minority secondary school students, 62% receive some form of financial aid, with 4% of them receiving full tuition remission.

Table 6.3. Distance Between Student Residence and School (percent of students)

	Elementary	*Secondary*
0.5 mile or less	33	6
0.5 to 1 mile	21	8
1 to 3 miles	21	23
3 to 5 miles	16	21
5 miles or greater	10	50

Table 6.4. Racial/Ethnic Identity of Students (percent)

	Elementary	*Secondary*
White, non-Hispanic	13	23
Hispanic	37	35
Black, non-Hispanic	39	25
Asian	8	10
Native American	1	3
Other	2	3

Note: "Secondary" percentages total less than 100 due to rounding.

Race

The elementary schools are more racially diverse than the secondary schools (see Table 6.4). Of the elementary schools with 50% or more students of color, 17% were completely non-White, while 6% were completely non-Black, 12% were without an Hispanic presence, and over 23% of the schools enrolled no Asian American students. Five-year trend data for these schools indicated that only 3% of the elementary school principals said that their minority enrollment had decreased over the previous 5 years; 58% of the principals said that their enrollment of minority students had remained stable, and 35% stated that their minority enrollment had increased.

Of the predominantly minority high schools, about 11% enroll no White students. Nine schools have no Black students, about half of the minority schools report fewer than 15% Black students, and three-quarters of the schools have fewer than 38% Black student enrollment. Eighteen schools are at least 50% Black, and two schools are 100% Black (see Polite, Chapter 7, this volume). There are no Hispanic students in six schools and half of the schools have 31% or fewer Hispanic students. Twenty-six schools are at least 50% Hispanic, and two schools are 100% Hispanic. Principals in 16 schools report a total absence of Asian Americans, and two-thirds of the schools have fewer than 10% Asian American students. Only four schools are over 50% Asian American. Although present in 29 of the minority schools, the percentage of Native American students is minuscule. Only two schools report more than 3% enrollment of Native Americans; not surprisingly, these schools are located on reservations. Regarding the presence of students of color during the past 5 years, 3% of the minority school principals report a decrease, 56% report no change, and 41% report an increase in minority student enrollment.

Ethnicity

Principals also commented on the presence of foreign-born students within their schools. On average, 8% of the students in the minority elementary school sample are foreign born versus 9% of the students in the secondary school sample. While only 7% of the elementary school students have limited English proficiency, over 15% of the students in the secondary school sample fall into that category.

Family Characteristics

Principals' reports about family characteristics are shown in Table 6.5. Eight percent of the elementary school parents and double that percentage of the secondary school parents are foreign-born. Ten percent of the elementary school parents and approximately one-sixth of the secondary school parents have limited English proficiency. Forty-four percent of the elementary school students and 53% of the secondary school students come from families that are not constituted by a biological father and mother. Many principals neglected to estimate the educational attainment level of parents, and several wrote that such information was unobtainable. From those reporting, however, we speculate that the parents of these students, especially at the elementary level, have lower levels of educational attainment than the general population.

Religion

The religious identity of non-Catholics has remained unexamined in NCEA reports and elsewhere. Our data on religious affiliation reveal the

Table 6.5. Characteristics of Students' Caregivers (percent)

Caregivers	Elementary	Secondary
Single parents	35	38
Guardians	3	7
Grandparents	6	8
Foreign-born	8	16
Limited English proficiency	10	15
High school graduate or GED only	30	38
College graduate	12	35

truly ecumenical nature of the schools, especially in regard to mainstream Protestants. In elementary schools with 50% or more students of color, 69% are Catholics, 15% are Baptists, and 8% are from other Christian faiths. In secondary schools, 73% of the students are Catholics, and 10% each are Baptists or other Christians.

Only 13% of the principals of the minority elementary schools said that enrollment of non-Catholics had decreased over the past 5 years. About half (49%) said that non-Catholic student enrollment had remained the same, while 37% of the elementary school principals stated that their non-Catholic student enrollment had increased over the past 5 years. Similar trends were reported by secondary school principals; 8% reported a decrease in the number of non-Catholics, 62% reported no change, and 30% reported an increase in the number of non-Catholic students within their school.

Educational Aspirations

Elementary school principals, reporting that all of their students continue on to high school, also specified the kind of secondary school their graduates attended: Catholic 64%, public 30%, public with special focus 4%, and private non-Catholic 2%. The 5-year trends for the number of graduates going on to Catholic high schools were: decreasing, 20%; the same, 53%; and increasing, 27%.

Principals of secondary schools report that most of their students (70%) attended a Catholic elementary or middle school. The next largest group of students (24%) came from public elementary or middle schools. Only 7% of the students attending the minority Catholic secondary schools previously attended private, non-Catholic schools. Secondary school principals' estimates of what their graduates did after high school indicated that 72% of the students went on to 4-year colleges and 21% enrolled in 2-year colleges. These estimates agree with the fact that 92% of the students were enrolled in a college preparatory curriculum. Over the past 5 years, 7% of the minority secondary school principals report a decrease, 72% report no change, and 21% report an increase in the number of their students who enroll in a Catholic college or university.

Enrollment and Retention

During the 1995–96 academic year, the average total enrollment for the 211 Catholic elementary schools under study was 269 students; the average daily attendance rate was 93%. When asked to assess trends in enrollment over the past 5 years, 14% of the minority school principals reported a decrease, 44% reported no change, and 39% reported an increase in enrollment. Average total enrollment for the 100 high schools was 499 students; the average attendance rate was 96% of the total daily enrollment. When asked to estimate trends in enrollment over the past 5 years, 30% of the principals reported a decrease, 25% reported no change, and 45% reported an increase.

STAFF

The survey examined characteristics of principals, other administrators, teachers, and nonteaching professionals.

Principals

Eighty-one percent of the elementary schools principals are female, and 53% are members of religious communities. Unlike the diverse population of students they serve, 84% of the principals are White; of the rest, 6% are Black, 7% are Hispanic, 3% are Asian American, and less than 1% are Native American. Not surprisingly, 98% of the principals are Catholic. The mean annual salary is $28,768.

In secondary schools, 49% of the principals are males and 52% are females; 56% are members of religious communities. Ninety percent of the principals are White, with Hispanics (7%) the next highest represented ethnicity. Only two principals are Black, and no principals are Asian American or Native American in our secondary school sample. Ninety-seven percent of the secondary school principals identify themselves as Catholic; those principals who are not Catholic are either Baptist or describe themselves as "other Christian." The mean annual salary for these principals is $35,000. With regard to the educational attainment of the minority secondary school principals, 58% have at least one master's degree, 21% have a master's plus further study, and 15% have doctorates.

Other Administrators

Seventy-seven percent of the secondary school principals and 45% of the elementary school principals report that they have an assistant principal to help with administrative duties, and 76% of the secondary school principals report having at least one full-time chaplain on staff. Also, 89% of the secondary school principals report the presence of a paid development officer, whereas only 14% of the elementary schools report this position.

Teachers

Characteristic of today's Catholic schools, few priests (1% elementary level, 3% secondary level) and relatively few members of religious communities (11% elementary level, 14% secondary level) belong to the teaching staff of these predominantly minority student schools. Seventy-three percent of the secondary school teachers and 44% of the elementary school teachers are certified by the state. The teachers within these minority schools are mostly White (65% elementary level and 77% secondary level), with smaller numbers of Blacks (18% elementary level, 6% secondary level), Hispanics (13% elementary level, 12% secondary level), and Asian Americans (3% elementary level, 3% secondary level). The teachers are mostly Catholic (about 85%); there are small numbers of Baptists (7% elementary level, 2% secondary level) and other Protestants (6% elementary level, 9% secondary level). Only 10% of the elementary school principals and 13% of the secondary school principals report an increase in the number of non-Catholic teachers on their staffs.

When schools were heavily staffed by religious communities, teachers had an extensive spiritual formation and grounding in the theology of the Church. It is hoped that the ethos of the Catholic school will be carried on by alumni/ae of Catholic educational institutions from prekindergarten through university (Jacobs, 1997). It is interesting, therefore, that principals estimate that less than one-third of the teachers attended Catholic elementary or secondary schools and less than one-quarter attended Catholic colleges or universities.

In these ethnically diverse institutions, both elementary and secondary school teachers reflect similar levels of commitment, as evidenced by their length of stay in their particular school. Seventy-seven percent of the elementary school teachers and 84% of the secondary school teachers had taught at the same school for more than 3 years.

Nonteaching Professionals

When asked which professionals are paid for at least 5 hours of work per week, principals indicated the following:

> Nurse (26% elementary level, 33% secondary level)
> Speech therapist (14% elementary level, 2% secondary level)
> Psychologist (14% elementary level, 18% secondary level)
> Police officer (3% elementary level, 7% secondary level)
> Social worker (11% elementary level, 18% secondary level)

The vast majority of the high schools (83%) have a paid guidance counselor on staff.

FINANCES

The survey examined a number of financial features that merit reporting.

Physical Plant

While most of the secondary schools have enjoyed a long history, they are not, on average, as old as the elementary schools. The oldest of the predominantly minority elementary schools was founded in 1825 in the building that it still occupies; the newest was founded in 1994. In contrast, the oldest of the minority secondary schools was founded in 1860 and occupies a building that dates back to 1881. Of the elementary schools, 18% have merged with another institution; only 12% of the minority high schools have merged with another Catholic secondary school. Both the minority elementary and secondary schools were operating at approximately 81% of capacity.

Eighty-five percent of the minority secondary school principals submitted information about annual income from tuition, diocesan subsidy, parish subsidy, grants, alumni/ae gifts, nonalumni/ae gifts, nonalumni/ae bequests, fund-raising events, rental of physical plant, and other sources (see Table 6.6). Principals report that during the 1990s they have

Table 6.6. Source of School Income (percent)

	Elementary	*Secondary*
Tuition	63	69
Diocesan subsidy	8	4
Parish subsidy	7	0
Grants	4	4
Individual gifts	4	0
Alumni/ae gifts	—	4
Nonalumni/ae gifts	—	4
Nonalumni/ae bequests	—	1
Fund-raising events	6	5
Other	9	9

Notes: Average total income was $537,440 for elementary schools and $42,630,511 for secondary schools. "Elementary" percentages total more than 100 due to rounding.

become less tuition-dependent, with small increases in grants and bequests in schools that have such activities. While the data reveal positive trends in increases from nontuition sources, tuition is the primary source of income, as 69% of secondary and 63% of elementary school income is derived from tuition. The implications are rather clear that tuition-dependence puts these schools at risk, thereby thwarting the theological call to justice reviewed in the previous section. The per-pupil cost for elementary schools (total operating budget divided by the number of students in the school), as reported by principals, is $2,096. For the high schools, the figure is double that amount at $5,298.

DISTINCTIVE ASPECTS OF ETHNICALLY DIVERSE URBAN SCHOOLS

This study was designed to complement previous reports about Catholic schools that serve children of color. The goal was to provide details that are not available in multipurpose surveys, but that would provide substantive information about the structure of these schools, their student populations, staffs, and finances. We will discuss our findings in terms of six aspects of structure: dependence on diocese, ethnicity of students and staff, socioeconomic status of students, fiscal viability, staffing patterns, and religious issues.

Compared with all Catholic schools nationwide, these schools are less dependent on a local parish; they tend to have diocesan, interparish, or private-school structures. In that sense, they should not be classified as "parochial," where the principal is responsible to the local pastor, with little control coming from the central diocesan office. Rather, they are institutions sponsored by the larger Catholic community that often serve children with no church affiliation. These changing circumstances require new models of management and leadership.

Most of the students in these schools are Black or Hispanic. The student body is far more ethnically diverse than the adults who staff the institution. This has serious implications for instruction, curriculum, and school culture. How do Catholic schools confront the reality of racism? Where do they find ethnically similar adult role models for students? How does the curriculum in social studies, literature, and religion, designed and taught by White people, reflect the experience of people of color? Catholic schools also tend to be monocultural. Analysis of the data reveals that ethnically diverse schools have very large percentages of students of color, and White schools are very heavily White.

Although there is not one precise measure of the socioeconomic status of students in these schools, several indicators challenge the notion that these institutions, as private schools, are elitist. A very high percentage of those who apply for admission are accepted and very few drop out. Nearly one-half of the elementary students are eligible for free lunch, they live in zip-code areas with significantly higher levels of poverty than the national norm, half of them come from families without two biological parents, and principals estimate that one-third of them live below the poverty level. Even with a sliding scale of tuition, a higher percentage should be receiving financial aid. In the high schools, two-thirds of the students receive some form of financial aid, but only 4% receive full tuition remission. Given the nonelitist nature of the student body, it is remarkable that so many elementary students go on to private Catholic secondary schools and that so many high school students go to college.

If these schools are to survive and thrive, breaking the pattern of the past 20 years (O'Keefe, 1996), they must reduce their dependency on tuition, which now accounts for about two-thirds of their income. Expenditures undoubtedly will increase; aged facilities require significant capital expenditure, and staffing patterns that have relied heavily on members of religious communities and a veteran corps of teachers, will need to be replaced. Efforts at institutional advancement are firmly in place at the secondary level; similar efforts must be increased in the elementary schools.

Several staffing issues warrant attention. First, these schools have a higher percentage of religious than their counterparts among teachers and especially among principals, half of whom fit that category. Given the decline in vocations to religious life, a daunting question looms: How can their replacements have their level of educational attainment, knowledge of Catholicism, and ability to work for a very low salary? Moreover, since so few of the teachers are alumni/ae of Catholic institutions, who will carry on the charisms and cultures that provide religious distinctiveness? Well over half of the elementary teachers and one-quarter of the secondary teachers do not have state certification. This not only raises questions about professional competency, but, given the impending teacher shortage nationally, one must wonder about the ability to attract professionally trained teachers at lower salaries in the years to come. Second, there is a stunning lack of nonteaching professionals, especially at the elementary level. How can these schools provide adequate social and medical services to students from low-income urban settings? It is unlikely that they will find the means to hire such expertise, and, with the decline in vocations to religious life, it is unlikely that schools can develop a cadre of volunteer professionals (nurses, social workers, psychologists, speech therapists). Schools without nonteaching professionals will need to form alliances with other agencies to provide for the diverse needs of youth and their families (O'Keefe, 1998).

The overwhelming number of students and adults in these schools are Christian. A significant and increasing number belong to non-Catholic denominations, especially African American Baptist churches. Until now, surveys have sought information simply on the number of non-Catholics, ignoring the ecumenical dimension of these institutions. It is also important to note that a significant number of those who identify themselves as Catholics do not belong to the local parish or to any parish at all. The Catholic character of these schools cannot be taken for granted. Since many of the schools are not self-supporting, the question arises: Why should a diocese or religious community devote scarce resources to provide educational opportunities to non-Catholics or marginal Catholics? Depending on one's theological perspective, denominationally diverse Catholic schools may present a wonderful opportunity for Christian dialogue or be a serious dilution of religious character. The future of these schools ultimately depends on the Church's self-understanding.

REFERENCES

Benson, P. L., Yeager, R. J., Wood, P. K., Guerra, M. J., & Manno, B. V. (1986). *Catholic high schools: Their impact on low-income students.* Washington, DC: National Catholic Educational Association.

Bryk, A. S., Lee, V. E., & Holland, P. B. (1993). *Catholic schools and the common good.* Cambridge, MA: Harvard University Press.

CACI. (1997). *Sourcebook of zipcode demographic* (7th ed.). Fairfax, VA: Author.

Carger, C. L. (1996). *Of borders and dreams: A Mexican-American experience of urban education.* New York: Teachers College Press.

Chineworth, M. A. (Ed.). (1995). *Rise 'n' shine: Catholic education and the African-American community.* Washington, DC: National Catholic Educational Association.

Cibulka, J. G., O'Brien, T. J., & Zewe, D. (1982). *Inner-city private elementary schools: A study.* Milwaukee: Marquette University Press.

Coleman, J. S., & Hoffer, T. (1987). *Public and private high schools: The impact of communities.* New York: Basic Books.

Coleman, J. S., Hoffer, T., & Kilgore, S. B. (1982). *High school achievement: Public, Catholic, and private schools compared.* New York: Basic Books.

Committee for Community Relations of the Bishops' Conference of England and Wales. (1997). *A struggle for excellence: Catholic secondary schools in urban poverty areas.* London: Catholic Education Service.

Committee on African-American Catholics of the National Conference of Catholic Bishops. (1996). *Keep your hand on the plow*. Washington, DC: United States Catholic Conference.

Convey, J. J. (1992). *Catholic schools make a difference: Twenty-five years of research*. Washington, DC: National Catholic Educational Association.

Foeman, A. K., Brown, T., Pugh, D., & Pearson, M. (1996). In our own words: Academically successful and unsuccessful low-income African-American young men talk about academic life. *Howard Journal of Communications, 7*(3), 257–269.

Gamoran, A. (1996). Student achievement in public magnet, public comprehensive, and private city high schools. *Educational Evaluation and Policy Analysis, 18*(1), 1–18.

Gerson, M. (1997). *In the classroom: Dispatches from an inner-city school that works*. New York: Free Press.

Greeley, A. M. (1982). *Catholic high schools and minority students*. New Brunswick, NJ: Transaction Books.

Harris, J. H. (1996). *The cost of Catholic parishes and schools*. Kansas City: Sheed & Ward.

Irvine, J. J., & Foster, M. (Eds.). (1996). *Growing up African American in Catholic schools*. New York: Teachers College Press.

Jacobs, R. (1997). *The grammar of Catholic schooling*. Washington, DC: National Catholic Educational Association.

Jones, A. M. (1997). *Differential effectiveness: Catholic and public school fourth graders on the 1992 NAEP mathematics assessment*. Unpublished doctoral dissertation, Boston College.

Kealey, R. J. (1990). *United States Catholic elementary schools and their finances*. Washington, DC: National Catholic Educational Association.

Kealey, R. J. (1995). *Balance sheet for Catholic elementary schools: 1995 income and expenses*. Washington, DC: National Catholic Educational Association.

Martin, S. P. (1996). *Cultural diversity in Catholic schools*. Washington, DC: National Catholic Educational Association.

McGreevy, J. T. (1996). *Parish boundaries: The Catholic encounter with race in the twentieth-century urban north*. Chicago: University of Chicago Press.

Milks, M. J. (1997). *United States Catholic elementary and secondary schools 1996–1997*. Washington, DC: National Catholic Educational Association.

National Conference of Catholic Bishops. (1979). *Brothers and sisters to us*. Washington, DC: United States Catholic Conference.

National Catholic Conference of Bishops. (1983). *The Hispanic presence: Challenge and commitment*. Washington, DC: United States Catholic Conference.

National Catholic Educational Association. (1987). *Integral education: A response to the Hispanic presence*. Washington, DC: Author.

National Catholic Educational Association. (1990). *A Catholic response to the Asian presence*. Washington, DC: Author.

National Catholic Educational Association. (1992). *The people: Reflections of native peoples on the Catholic experience in North America*. Washington, DC: Author.

Neal, D. (1997). The effects of Catholic secondary schooling on educational achievement. *Journal of Labor Economics, 15*(1), 1, 98–123.

O'Keefe, J. M. (1994, April). *No strangers here? A study of the experiences of low-income students of color in high school.* Paper presented at the annual meeting of the American Educational Research Association, New Orleans.

O'Keefe, J. M. (1996). No margin, no mission. In T. H. McLaughlin, J. O'Keefe, & B. O'Keeffe (Eds.), *The contemporary Catholic school: Context, identity and diversity* (pp. 177–197). London: Falmer.

O'Keefe, J. M. (1998). Leadership for solidarity: How Catholic human service providers can work together. In R. Haney & J. M. O'Keefe (Eds.), *Conversations in excellence: Providing for the diverse needs of youth and their families* (pp. 149–160).

Oldenski, T. (1997). *Liberation theology and critical pedagogy in today's Catholic schools: Social justice in action.* New York: Garland Press.

Pontifical Commission for Peace and Justice. (1988). *The church and racism: Towards a more fraternal society.* Rome: Author.

Sander, W., & Krautmann, A. C. (1995). Catholic schools, dropout rates and educational attainment. *Economic Inquiry, 33*(2), 217–233.

Teachman, J. D., Paasch, K., & Carver, K. (1997). Social capital and the generation of human capital. *Social Forces, 75*(4), 1343–1359.

Vitullo-Martin, T. (1979). *Catholic inner-city schools: The future.* Washington, DC: United States Catholic Conference.

Walch, T. (1996). *Parish school: American Catholic parochial education from colonial times to the present.* New York: Crossroad.

York, D. E. (1996). The academic achievement of African Americans in Catholic schools: A review of the literature. In J. J. Irvine & M. Foster (Eds.), *Growing up African American in Catholic schools* (pp. 11–46). New York: Teachers College Press.

CHAPTER 7

Cornerstones: Catholic High Schools That Serve Predominantly African American Student Populations

VERNON C. POLITE

> The stone that the builders rejected has become the Cornerstone. By the Lord
> has this been done; it is wonderful in our eyes.
>
> —*Psalm* 118:22–23

AN EXCERPT FROM *When Work Disappears: The World of the New Urban Poor*,
the 1996 treatise on life in contemporary urban America by sociologist
William Julius Wilson, illustrates the stereotypical reactions of urban employers to urban job applicants:

> The employers who volunteered information on the schools they recruited
> from usually mentioned Catholic schools or those public schools from Chi-
> cago's largely White Northwest Side communities. Although employees re-
> cruited from the Catholic schools were more likely white, black students
> from Catholic schools were also viewed more favorably than those from
> public schools. For example, one employer at a suburban department store
> pointed out that although minority students fail the skills test more fre-
> quently than white students, the minorities [Blacks] that go to parochial
> schools test as well as the whites. They come here dressed as well, and this
> is a totally different act. Now this is the difference that I can spot, is be-
> tween your parochial school and your public school. (p. 134)

What factors, present among inner-city Catholic schools, seem to
minimize the significance of race among African American[1] students,
making them desirable to employers and institutions of higher educa-

tion? An answer to this question is important for policy makers who grapple with issues of equity and economic opportunity in inner cities and for religious communities that financially support these schools.

A High School Consortium was established in 1995 under the direction of the National Black Catholic Congress as a result of earnest concerns for the future of Catholic high school education in predominantly African American communities. The Congress, housed in Baltimore, Maryland, has identified some 31 schools in urban and otherwise marginalized communities of the country where the student populations of African Americans exceed 75%. The overarching goal of the Consortium is to put in place national strategies and support systems that will ensure the survival of these schools and their service to the African American community for decades to come (African American Bishops of the United States, 1984).

The 31 predominantly African American Catholic high schools, or the "Cornerstones," as I affectionately refer to them in this chapter, are located in Baltimore, Birmingham, Brooklyn, Detroit, Chicago, Kansas City, Los Angeles and its nearby urban communities, Montgomery, Newark and its nearby urban communities, New Orleans, St. Louis, and Washington, D.C. and nearby urban communities. The histories of these schools are particularly interesting in that 10 of the 31 schools are historically Black in that they were founded for the express purpose of educating African American high school students. The remaining 21 schools evolved as predominantly African American as a result of shifting racial demographic patterns that occurred over the past 20 years in urban America.

The purpose of this chapter is to describe the social contexts of these schools. The overarching question that guided my research is: What are the commonplace characteristics and practices of Catholic high schools that serve predominantly African American student populations?

In an effort to understand the commonplace characteristics and practices of the African American Catholic high schools, I asked the 31 principals for the 1996–97 academic year to complete the African American Catholic High School Survey,[2] a 75-item instrument made up of both multiple-choice and descriptive items designed to provide focused school-specific information on a wide range of topic areas, including the school building; students; the principal; curriculum and instruction; finances and development; Catholic identity; and African American cultural identity. Additionally, I conducted site visits to 22 of the identified schools to collect additional qualitative data, utilizing procedures that I have developed and implemented nationally with urban principals and that involve reflective conversations (in-depth interviews) and document analysis (Polite, McClure, & Rollie, 1997).

I collected and analyzed qualitative data using a variety of means: One in-depth reflective 60-minute conversation with the principals; school building tours; examination of official and informal documents; and school and classroom observations. Each in-depth conversation provided both factual information regarding the principal's perceptions, beliefs, and values, and the school's historical and present operations; and also valuable perception-based data needed to develop realistic frames of the schooling context.

THE CORNERSTONE SCHOOLS

The Cornerstones are found mainly (26 of the 31 schools) in communities described as inner city/urban. An additional four schools are best described as near-central-city schools because they are located either within the first or second geographical ring surrounding an urban metropolis (Polite, 1993). Although the majority of the Cornerstones are located in so-called "economically challenged" communities, several others are found in rather established and stable urban environments.

The Cornerstones have organized largely following the traditional U.S. patterns of grade grouping for secondary school-aged students, with 25 of the 31 schools offering grades 9–12. The remaining six schools are structured more within the fashion of the private academy, with grades 7–12. The schools collectively enroll approximately 12,000 students, with an average enrollment of 390 students per school. The largest school, Bishop Loughlin in Brooklyn, enrolled 913 students during the 1996–97 school year, while the smallest school, the newly formed Loyola High School in Detroit, served 115 students during that same period. When compared with the previous academic year, 20 of the principals reported that their student enrollment remained stable, while another six reported slight increases in enrollment over the previous year. Nine of the 31 schools have enrollments of 300 or fewer students. For purposes of this chapter, the Cornerstones are divided into three categories: privately owned, diocesan, and historically African American.

Fifteen of the Cornerstones are diocesan schools, while the remaining 16 are privately owned. The 16 privately owned schools enroll 6,011 students collectively, with an average student population of 375 and an average tuition rate of $3,188. By close contrast, the diocesan-owned schools enroll 5,806 students, with an average school enrollment of 405 and an average tuition rate of $3,108. The privately owned schools, supported primarily by Catholic religious communities of nuns, priests, or brothers, were established in late 1800s and early 1900s. The diocesan-owned schools were formed in the second half of the twentieth century, mainly in the 1950s and 1960s.

From the personal accounts of the principals, the continuing existence of each of the Cornerstones represents a true mission to the African American community; however, the privately owned schools, without exception, reflect special commitments to the African American community on the part of Catholic religious communities, many of which are grappling with a multiplicity of concurrent issues, including aging membership, declining vocations, and diminished resources (Diamond, 1997; Galetto, in press). For example, St. Mary's Academy in New Orleans was established in 1867 by the Sisters of the Holy Family, a vowed group of African American nuns.

After completing site visits to 22 of the 31 schools and analyzing the survey data received from the principals, I believe it is accurate to assess the physical condition of the schools, collectively, as good, with 23 needing minor repairs to the physical plant. Given, however, that the majority of the Cornerstones are operating under extremely austere budgets, the additional financial resources needed to redress minor repairs often are not available, resulting in the subsequent need for major repairs at substantially greater cost.

Finally, special notice should be given to the third category of Cornerstones, the historical Cornerstones (see Table 7.1). The 10 historical Cornerstones include both privately owned and diocesan-controlled schools. These schools, from their origin, were designed and structured with the specific mission of evangelization and academic preparation of the African American community where they are housed. The oldest of these schools, St. Frances Academy of Baltimore, has been in existence for 167 years. St. Frances Academy [for Colored Girls] opened in Baltimore 19 years before Elizabeth Cady Stanton would organize the first American women's rights convention (Sellers, 1976) and more than 30 years prior to the signing of the Emancipation Proclamation. At the time this chapter was written, the newest of these schools Loyola High School, formed in 1993, had not experienced its first graduating class. Each of these historical Cornerstones has a special history and contribution, often in an economically challenged community. The Cornerstones are historical artifacts of the African American Catholic experience in the United States. The principals provided numerous examples of the historical significance of their schools. As a representative example of the impact that these historical schools have on the lives of their students and the com-

Table 7.1. Historically African American Cornerstones

	City	Founded	Owner-ship	Enroll-ment	Tuition ($)	Grad-uates (%)	College attend. (%)
St. Frances Academy	Baltimore	1828	Private	240	3,500	96–100	96–100
St. Mary's Academy	New Orleans	1867	Private	627	1,400	96–100	96–100
Xavier Prep.	New Orleans	1915	Private	515	2,600	96–100	96–100
St. Jude	Mont-gomery	1934	Other	156	1,800	96–100	96–100
Holy Family	Birming-ham	1943	Private	190	1,725	96–100	91–95
St. Augustine	New Orleans	1951	Private	680	2,700	95–100	96–100
Hales Franciscan	Chicago	1963	Private	334	3,100	96–100	96–100
St. Martin de Porres	Detroit	1967	Diocesan	700	3,100	96–100	91–95
Cardinal Ritter	St. Louis	1979	Diocesan	257	2,800	96–100	96–100
Loyola	Detroit	1993	Other	115	2,500	—	—

Note: St. Mary's Academy enrollment figure represents grades 7–12.

munity at large, the comments of Geraldine Perry, principal of St. Jude High School in Montgomery, are particularly insightful:

> St. Jude High School, established in 1946 has the distinction of being situated in the birthplace of the civil rights movement, is recognized by the African American community for its role in the civil rights marches of the 1960s, and sits along an historical civil rights route. We have the unique opportunity to host and be a part of newsworthy African American events in our city because of the rich heritage of the school and our student body. We proudly utilize our school facility as a showcase of African American art, poetry, the most prominent of which is a 7 foot bronze sculpture of Jesus that graces our foyer [sculpted by Richard Barthe, an African American].

Table 7.2. Graduation and College Plans, as Reported by Schools for 1996–97

Percentage of seniors	Number of schools
Graduated	
91–95	5
96–100	26
To attend college	
81–90	4
91–95	14
96–100	13

THE CORNERSTONE STUDENTS

In this section, I discuss those characteristics that define the 12,000 students who presently attend the 31 Cornerstone schools. The majority (54%) of the students attending these schools describe themselves as non-Catholic Christians, with approximately 46% identifying themselves as Roman Catholic.

The good news regarding the Cornerstone schools remains the academic success that each continues to enjoy as measured by the number of students that go on to attend 4-year colleges upon graduation, at least 91% across the schools. Table 7.2 shows the percentages of Cornerstone students who graduated and planned to attend college during the 1996–97 academic year. My efforts did not explore students' performance on standardized examinations; however, several principals remarked during their personal interviews that standardized testing is an area of concern. In fact, when I questioned several groups of students (15 focus groups, representing the students from half of the schools) across the country, the concern that surfaced was centered around college-entrance scores (ACT and SAT) that were not as high as the students had expected, resulting in their having to make choices among second-tier colleges as opposed to first-tier colleges and Ivy League schools. Given the educational outcomes of their counterparts in local public schools, the concern becomes rather amusing. Bryk, Lee, and Holland (1993) found that Catholic schools appear to have an independent effect on achievement, especially in reducing disparities between disadvantaged and advantaged students. Bryk and colleagues argue, and I concur based on my work with the Cornerstones, that success experienced by African American students in Catholic schools is realized as a result of deemphasizing tracking and creating small, caring learning communities. The following are commonplace educational practices among the Cornerstones:

1. Most have an open tracking system, meaning that students commonly are grouped by ability, but there is open flexibility and movement in and out of tracks. In most cases, the number of students dictates the diversity of academic options. When limited, the Cornerstone curriculum tends to focus on the more academic course. The Cornerstones tend to track their students "high."
2. The majority of the Cornerstone high schools require that incoming ninth graders who are deficient in major academic areas participate in a summer remedial program prior to entering the school. These programs are sponsored by the individual Cornerstones and are central to establishing an environment conducive to learning.
3. Each student is valued as an individual and as a contributing member of the learning community. Each school offers a full course of co-curricular activities, meaning that, given the average size of the schools (390), most students are involved in nonacademic endeavors that provide additional opportunities to interact with caring adults.
4. Students who are unsuccessful in specific course areas during the academic year generally are required to make up the deficiency during the summer.
5. Each Cornerstone community places strong emphasis on guidance and counseling, preparing students for college or entry-level jobs in the workplace.
6. The climate at each school is centered on academics.
7. Students who are unwilling or unable to comply with school guidelines are not allowed to continue. This does not mean that all disruptive students are removed. The principals report that on average five students (or 1%) are dismissed annually due to severe disciplinary infractions. The result is a safe and orderly environment that is conducive to learning.

Principals reported that much of the success experienced at the Cornerstone schools is attributed to the personal support that each student receives, the caring teachers and staff, and explicit Christian values that influence many aspects of the schooling process.

Predominantly African American Catholic schools are not utopian learning communities. The principals' surveys reveal emerging trends that implore further research and attention. These trends are related to racial composition, levels of student poverty, special needs, abusive parents and households, and disciplinary problems.

The percentage of African American students attending the Cornerstone schools is increasing and the students represent lower-income families. As previously discussed, a special category of schools exists among the Cornerstones, the historically African American Cornerstones. Each of the 10 schools (refer to Table 7.1) reports enrollments of African American students between 96 and 100%. In fact, in interviews with the principals of these schools, I was able to identify only five non-African American students out of the 3,814 students enrolled in schools classified as historically African American. The remaining 21 schools, those that evolved as African American due to shifting demographic trends in urban and suburban communities, report on average 85% African American student enrollments. Two factors emerge as important. The first is that these nonhistorical schools, that are already beyond 75% African American, are reporting increasing overall numbers and percentages of African American students, meaning that non-African American parents rarely shy away from predominantly African American Catholic schools despite their proven ability to graduate extremely high percentages (96–100%) of students and send more than 91% of their graduates on to 4-year colleges.

The second factor is equally interesting from a sociological perspective. Nearly half of the schools report that they are serving increasing numbers of students who are living in poverty, indicating that upper-middle-income African American parents are not likely to select predominantly African American Catholic schools for their children.

It appears that, with respect to the schools showcased in this chapter, once a Cornerstone is identified as serving the marginalized and the lower middle income, few upper-middle-income parents chose that school. The result is limited financial resources.

Increasing numbers of African American students matriculating in Cornerstone schools are perceived by their principals as having special needs. Sr. John Francis, principal of St. Frances Academy in Baltimore, reported that "whenever middle-income parents come with their children, I know immediately that the child has either a discipline problem or special needs." More than half of the Cornerstone principals indicated that they have received increasing numbers of students who are eligible for special education programs under federal guidelines. It remains no secret that the public sector has been overwhelmed by the numbers of students requiring special educational assistance. This problem has been magnified in recent years with the passage of the Americans with Disabilities Act. In fact, research reports that African Americans, particularly African American males, have been ill served by special education programs in public schools (Harry & Anderson, 1994). It seems entirely logical, as Sr. John Francis indicated, that frustrated parents of children requiring special education services might opt for a Catholic school where there are smaller classrooms and ostensibly more one-on-one interaction. One of the obvious concerns is the fact that teachers and administrators in pre-dominantly African American schools most often have not been trained in the skills and techniques of special education.

An increasing number of students are "affected" by human immunodeficiency virus or HIV (the virus that causes acquired immunodeficiency syndrome or AIDS). The fact that eight principals reported that they had experienced increasing numbers of students "affected" by the AIDS virus is an indication of a potential, emerging problem, a problem that perhaps Catholic principals are ill prepared to address. Given the social stigma attached to the HIV/AIDS problem, it is possible that many other principals may not be aware of this serious problem affecting their students. The term *affected*, of course, could mean a number of things: personally infected or affected by infected family members or by friends (National Catholic Educational Association, 1992).

The Cornerstone principals report two less significant trends among their students that also merit some attention: *Nine schools reported increasing numbers of students who are habitual behavior problems; and the principals of 10 schools indicated that they are receiving increasing numbers of students who are living in abusive households.* These two issues pose a potential negative impact on the overall stability of the student population.

CORNERSTONE PRINCIPALS

The individuals presently serving as principals at the 31 Cornerstone schools, collectively, represent a well-educated group. Table 7.3 shows the principals' highest level of education obtained. Thirty of the principals have earned at least one master's degree. It is significant that 1 out 5 holds a master's degree in religious studies or divinity.

I also examined additional demographic descriptors of race, gender, and status in life. There are 15 men and 16 women principals. Obviously,

Table 7.3. Highest Academic Degrees Earned by Principals

	Number
Bachelor's	1
Master's	22
Two master's	6
Doctorate	2
Total	31

the overwhelming majority are Roman Catholics; however, two principals identified themselves as "non-Catholic." There are presently nine
professed religious administering individual Cornerstone schools. The
remaining 22 are laypersons.

Finally, the data regarding the salaries were less well defined due
to the fact that 10 of the principals failed to provide salary information.
However, it is clear from the information gleaned from those 21 principals who did provide personal income information that there are great
disparities from school to school as well among religious and laypersons.
The salary range for religious was between $18,000 and $60,000. By contrast, the salary range for the lay principals was between $35,000 and
$80,000. Obviously, many factors contribute to the disparities, including
geographical location, cost of living, religious stipends, and so forth.

CORNERSTONE CULTURE/IDENTITY

One question often raised regarding the Cornerstone schools is, "Are
they truly Catholic?" The question is particularly interesting given that,
from my best estimates, the majority (at least 56%) of the students who
attend predominantly African American Catholic schools are not professed Roman Catholics. Two factors skewed my understanding of the
exact number of African American Catholic students who attend predominantly African American Catholic high schools: (1) several Cornerstone schools no longer record or collect information on the religious
affiliation of their students; and (2) there is no uniform manner of categorizing students by religious affiliation across the schools (i.e., schools
have adopted very different ways of categorizing their students—some
schools record the specific religious denomination for each student, other
schools merely distinguish Catholics from non-Catholics, others specify
Christian and non-Christian, etc.). It is, however, clear that the majority
of students are not Roman Catholics.

As I moved from one school to the next, city to city, I clearly noticed
the presence of a commonplaceness of culture and/or identity. This Cornerstone culture/identity includes the following core components:

1. A code of behavior, dress, values, discipline, and language that
   is grounded within the Christian traditions of love of God and
   love of one's neighbor
2. Catholic religious rituals practiced as an affirmation of the African American culture of the students

3. A focus on ministry and evangelization (not conversion to Catholicism)
4. A strong commitment to a set of beliefs that evolved from the American Catholic traditions and the traditions and histories of Africans and African Americans, especially the teachings of prominent African and African American Catholics

Catholic culture/identity, however, is best demonstrated in predominantly African American Catholic schools by their emphasis on ministry, with preference for the poor and marginalized of the African American community. The Cornerstone school spreads the Word to those young persons who have not yet developed mature notions about the purpose of life. Education empowers them with Catholic morals and values needed to enhance the quality of their everyday lives. Catholic identity, then, is best measured by the extent to which the school prepares young men and women to live moral and decent lives and participate in the evangelizing mission of the Church. This ministry to the African American community was mentioned repeatedly by principals of the various Cornerstones. For example, one principal of a midwestern high school spoke typically about the ministry of Catholic schooling:

> Catholic schools are an extension of the larger Roman Catholic Church. They are an important organ of the ministry of the Church, specifically to the African American community. . . . *There is no separation!* . . . We share in the overall ministry of the Church. Our position(s) are not just simply jobs. We attempt to hire people who have a *deeper sense of commitment* specifically to minister to the African American community. *Hear what I am saying!* . . . I have worked with wonderful, committed teachers in public schools, but I am talking about Catholic school teachers who have a clear commitment to Catholic *ministry* to African American youth. . . . Our parents sense the difference [between Catholic schooling and public schooling]. (emphasis added)

The African American Catholic community historically has played an influential role in the Catholic education of African Americans also. In fact, the First Colored Catholic Congress elucidated the purpose and distinction of Catholic schools for African American youths in its 1889 general statement to its assembly:

> The education of a people being the great and fundamental means of elevating it to the higher planes to which all Christian civilization tends, we

pledge ourselves to aid in establishing, wherever we are to be found, Catholic Schools, embracing the primary and higher branches of knowledge, as in them and through them alone can we expect to reach the large masses of colored children now growing up in this country without a semblance of Christian education. (cited in Three Catholic Afro-American Congresses, 1893/1978, p. 68)

The late Archbishop James Lyke (1991), the first African American archbishop, addressed the National Congress on Catholic Education and included this comment regarding Catholic schools for African American students:

The Catholic school in the African American community enhances the vitality of the [Catholic] Church, for the Church is not a closed social system, but rather an open global Church that is more "colorful" with each passing year. The school continues to reach out into the environment and draws in all people without respect to race, culture, or financial status. This is the will of God and the mission of God's people. The Second Vatican Council, the popes of the second half of the 20th century, and the National Conference of Catholic Bishops have consistently reminded the Church of its true mission in their pastoral letters: *The Church in the Modern World, The Declaration on Christian Education, A Call to Action* of Pope Paul VI, *To Teach as Jesus Did*, and Pope John Paul II's *Address to Catholic School Leaders and to the Black Catholic Leadership*, in May of 1987.

In my observations at the various schools, I paid special attention to evidence of Catholic culture and found that there were numerous examples of the Catholic tradition among these schools. I observed a lesson on the sacrament of baptism at Loyola High School in Detroit, and a Holy Week Prayer Service at Hales Franciscan High School (Chicago); there were gospel choirs in rehearsal at Archbishop Carroll (Washington, D.C.) and Verbum Dei (Los Angeles). I even noticed a religion class in prayer before the altar of the Holy Martyrs of Uganda at St. Augustine's High School (New Orleans). I witnessed a lesson on Black saints and the popes of African heritage. The principals report the average number of school-wide masses celebrated per year is seven, with an average of five non-Eucharistic lituguries per academic year. All 31 schools offer a retreat program for students, and 26 offer a retreat program for teachers and staff.

AFRICAN AMERICAN CULTURAL IDENTITY

Theorists define an affective curriculum as one that provides learning opportunities that have positive influences on students' appreciation, at-

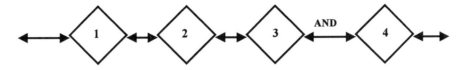

Figure 7.1. African American cultural continuum. Category 1: education to teach basic knowledge and appreciation of African American culture and history, particularly as it pertains to the Catholic Church; category 2: education to teach competence in and mastery of African American culture and history, particularly as it pertains to the Catholic Church; category 3: education to place African American culture and history, particularly as it pertains to the Catholic Church, at the center of the cognitive and affective development of all students; category 4: education to prepare agents of social change for the betterment of the African American people, particularly Catholics of African descent in the United States. Nine Cornerstones fell into category 1, seventeen into category 2, and five into category 3 (there were none in category 4).

titudes, beliefs, and values. In this regard, I found an appreciation of African American students' race, ethnicity, and culture to be particularly important for the Cornerstone learning communities. I discovered in my reflective conversations with the Cornerstone principals that each of them expressed a genuine concern for a cultural-learning agenda geared specifically toward African American students.

The Cornerstone schools can be grouped into four categories with respect to their expression of African American culture and history (for an example of a multicultural curriculum reform that stresses four specific levels of multiculturalism, see Banks, 1988). Figure 7.1 depicts a continuum of African American culture that reflects a combination of how the principals described the cultural experiences of their schools, as well as the information that I gleaned personally from analysis of documents collected from the various Cornerstones and school observations. The continuum is a useful model for illustrating African American cultural expressions as currently practiced at the Cornerstones nationally. In reality, however, the schools do not fall so nicely into one of four categories, but rather appear at various points along the continuum with fluid movement, both to the right and to the left (demonstrated by the arrows) depending on the quality and quantity of resources and personnel available to them. The special care that the principals afford to cultural identity is probably best expressed in the detailed written comments of concerns provided by the principals, which serve as an indication of how serious the question of cultural identity was considered.

Category 1 schools are those schools that teach basic knowledge and appreciation of African American culture and history. Only 29% of the

Cornerstones fall into this category. Cultural experience is seen as a separate entity, distinct from the academic domain and experienced most commonly as add-on celebrations, special events (i.e., Black History Month, Rev. Dr. Martin Luther King, Jr., celebrations, and so forth). As an example of a category 1 school, one principal wrote:

> We have several yearly programs—religious and historical—we call it "Celebrate Us." On career day, we attempt to invite mostly African Americans. We will add an African American studies course to the curriculum for 1997–1998. We urge all teachers to add African American emphasis to all courses, but it is not a definite plan in place.

By contrast, category 2 schools have moved to ensure competency in and mastery of African American culture and history. The majority (17) of the 31 Cornerstones are in this category, demonstrating efforts to incorporate African American culture into more than merely extracurricular activities, but through some specific curriculum modification. One of the principals in New York described his school as category 2 and added this statement as evidence of his school's cultural experience:

> It is very difficult for us to determine where we are with African American cultural experience. Our students are 85% African American, but that cultural expression is further subdivided into many cultural experiences (American-born, southern-born, native-born Africans, Haitians, all Caribbean islands, Guyana and Belize, the eastern coast of Central America and Panama). The emphasis on African American culture is most seen in the academic areas of history, English, and religion . . . in the extracurricular activities, in our assemblies, in our art. We must follow closely the guidelines set up by New York State. Nevertheless, within those strict guidelines, the contributions of African Americans are well-reflected in our textbooks. I have discussed this matter with key staff who concur with this statement [and we are confident] the African American presence, identity, and pride are not tacked on to a static program and we are moving closer to centering our academic program around the African American culture.

Category 3 schools represent those schools that have undergone extensive curriculum modifications designed to place the African American culture and history at the very center of the academic curriculum. This Afrocentric curriculum is rare among the Cornerstone schools, with only five of the schools falling into category 3. One principal described her category 3 school as follows:

> Within the last 5 years, our school has completely restructured the academic program. Instead of the previous modular schedule, we now use an integrated curriculum with teams of teachers working in block schedules. . . . We feel that our curriculum now is centered on the needs, interests, and history of our African American students.

Finally, Figure 7.1 indicates a fourth category that appears somewhat distanced from categories 1, 2, and 3. While there are no schools that currently fall in this category, for Catholic schools serving predominantly African American students, the category represents an ideal of education to promote social change or relief to social problems affecting the African American community. Archbishop Lyke (1991) expressed his vision of urban Catholic schools as agents of change:

> Inferior educational opportunity is one of the most deplorable outcomes of historical racism and discrimination in this country. This systemic injustice must be firmly addressed—not with platitudes, but with a commitment to search and find practical programs of action. A Catholic school in [a] blight-stricken community is more than a mere "bright spot." It prepares its students by providing the tools needed to attack social injustice intellectually, economically, and spiritually.
>
> As Catholics, we are not to be afraid to be out of step with the rest of the world. It is not our calling to conform to those trends in society that bolster social injustice. We must collaborate in revamping the social order that allows our people to be caught in webs of poverty, inadequate educational programs, slum housing and unemployment.

Education for social change within the inner-city Catholic high school might include the use of the dialogue method of teaching (for examples of this approach, see Shor & Freire, 1987; Ternasky, 1995). The late Paulo Freire popularized this approach to teaching, which posits that schooling, especially for the marginalized, must focus on social, political, and economic inequalities in the larger society through dialogues within the context of the classroom. The goal is to prepare students to become productive adults with the knowledge of true social justice and the skills needed to transform the African American community economically, politically, socially, and spiritually.

The idea of teaching African American culture is indeed an important one for Catholic schools that serve largely African American students. There are no guidebooks that provide step-by-step procedures, but clearly the matter has been addressed in these Cornerstone schools and is seen as an essential part of the holistic education of African American students.

FINANCES AND DEVELOPMENT

It is rather difficult to make general statements regarding the finances and approaches to development associated with the Cornerstone schools. Each school is unique. Although each school is different with varying resources, one way to think of finances is to look at two model budgets, one for a private school and the second for a diocesan school. I considered these two schools to be typical of the Cornerstone schools in enrollment, tuition, and student–teacher ratio.

Hales Franciscan High School was chosen to represent the private school (see Table 7.4). Hales Franciscan was founded in 1963 by the Franciscans of the Sacred Heart Province and the Archdiocese of Chicago. It is the only historically Black, Catholic, all-male, college-preparatory high school in the state of Illinois. The school is accredited by the North Central Association and the Illinois State Board of Education. Hales is owned and operated by a lay board of trustees. The school's motto is In Virum Perfectum (Unto Perfect Manhood). Hales enrolled 334 students during the 1996–97 year, with a student–teacher ratio of 16 to 1. Tuition revenues represent less than half of total income. Interestingly, Hales raises more revenue through special fund raising than through tuition. Each student at Hales is eligible for a $3,250 grant per year.

By contrast, Junipero Serra High School is a diocesan high school. The school was founded in 1950 by James Francis Cardinal McIntyre and the Marianist Order. The school is a coeducational, 4-year, Catholic, college-preparatory school in the Los Angeles Catholic Archdiocese. Serra is accredited by the Western Association of Schools and Colleges, Western Catholic Educational Association, College Board, and California

Table 7.4. Operating Budget for Hales Franciscan High School, 1995–96

Income	Percent	Amount ($)
Tuition	44	968,000
Special fund-raising	46	1,012,000
Individual gifts	10	220,000
Total operating budget		2,200,000

Table 7.5. Operating Budget for Junipero Serra High School, 1996–97

Income	Percent	Amount ($)
Tuition	77	1,357,539
Diocesan subsidy	6	105,782
Private grants	6	105,782
Special fund raising	11	35,261
Total operating budget		1,604,364

Scholastic Federation. Serra depends largely on the revenue raised from tuition (77%), as indicated by Table 7.5.

Cornerstone principals are delighted by the academic success of their students. There appears to be, however, a ceaseless concern for the financial stability of all the schools. In the case of some Cornerstone schools, an increase or decrease of 10 students could make the difference between remaining open or closing. The private schools rely on financial support from religious communities that are experiencing financial difficulties. The diocesan schools most often depend on tuition, special fund-raising efforts, and support from the diocese. In the case of Serra, the diocese provided $105,000 of support, but that diocesan support amounts to only 6% of the total budget.

CONCLUSION

The histories of African Americans and American Catholicism, particularly Catholic schooling, have been entangled from the earliest years of the colonial era. Beginning with the establishment of St. Francis Academy for Colored Girls in Baltimore in 1828, the long history of Catholic schooling, specifically for African Americans, has emerged as a prominent factor (Polite, 1996). History may never fully disclose the true effect of Catholic schooling on African Americans and the country at large. For those who might wish to explore comprehensive works on this topic, I would recommend Fr. Cyprian Davis's *The History of Black Catholics in the United States* (1990) and Jacqueline Irvine and Michele Foster's *Growing Up African American in Catholic Schools* (1996) as two excellent resources.

The opportunities for the nation's inner-city children to acquire a quality education seems to become more disputable with each passing academic year. A Catholic school, such as the Cornerstone schools showcased in this chapter, in a plight-stricken community, is more than a mere bright spot; it prepares its students by providing them with the tools needed to attack social injustices intellectually, economically, and spiritually. Value education, social action programs, local school-based management, community building among staff and students, parental involvement, and volunteer support—these aspects are commonplace realities in most predominantly African American Catholic schools. Given their safe and orderly environments, their focus on basic academics and high expectations for all students to achieve, and their success in moving their graduates into 4-year colleges, the Cornerstones are national examples of what the late Ronald Edmonds (1979) referred to as "effective schools":

> While recognizing the importance of family background in developing a child's character, personality, and intelligence, I cannot overemphasize my rejection of the notion that a school is relieved of its instructional obligations when teaching the children of the poor. I reject such a notion partly because I recognize the existence of schools that successfully teach basic skills to all children. Such success occurs partly because these schools are determined to serve all of their pupils without regard to family background. At the same time these schools recognize the necessity of modifying curricular design, text selection, teaching strategy, and so on, in response to differences in family background among pupils in the school. (p. 21)

African American students and parents must realize that Catholic schools are more than havens for students who otherwise would attend less desirable neighborhood schools. They are institutions in which well-defined values and morals are taught explicitly through the curriculum and implicitly through the daily routines and co-curricular activities. An essential part of the mission of the Cornerstones is evangelization and the teaching of Christian traditions and values. Such a mission compels the leadership of urban Catholic schools, where the majority of the students are African Americans, to consider the history and traditions of this people when planning religious instruction and services. It is crucial that African American students be afforded the opportunity to practice the traditions of the Catholic Church without compromising their cultural and historical heritages.

As the United States becomes more ethnically and racially diversified, urban Catholic schools increasingly are reflecting the multifaceted dimensions of our nation. The onus, however, is on all Americans to contribute in whatever manner possible to improve the education of this population. Catholic schools contribute significantly by providing both Christian values and a quality education for many African American students. African American Catholics and others who benefit from Catholic schooling in urban communities must plan *now* if these schools are to be preserved. For example, the principal and leadership of St. Martin de Porres in Chicago announced that the school would be closed at the close of 1999 due to many problems, including low enrollment and financial issues. The answers seem to lie in heightened political organization, new and creative strategies for raising funds, the development of specialty schools, and regional consolidation. It is in the best interest of concerned African American parents whose children attend Catholic schools to actively participate at the local level in strategic-planning meetings and to become actively involved in efforts to generate funds to maintain their children's schools.

NOTES

1. In acknowledgment of past and present usage, the terms *Colored, Negro(es), Black(s),* and *African American(s)* are used interchangeably throughout the chapter to refer to individuals of African descent who reside within the United States and its territories and former colonies of European nations.

2. Sections of the survey were adopted, with permission, from the *Catholic Elementary School Survey* developed by J. M. O'Keefe, Boston College.

REFERENCES

African American Bishops of the United States. (1984). *What we have seen and heard: A pastoral letter on evangelization from the African American bishops of the United States.* Cincinnati, OH: St. Anthony Messenger Press.

Banks, J. A. (1988). Approaches to multicultural curriculum reform. *Multicultural Leader, 1*(2), 1–3.

Bryk, A. S., Lee. V. E., & Holland, P. B. (1993). *Catholic schools and the common good.* Cambridge, MA: Harvard University Press.

Davis, C. (1990). *The history of Black Catholics in the United States.* New York: Crossroad.

Diamond, D. (1997). Leadership behavior and self efficacy of Catholic secondary school administrators. Unpublished Ph.D. dissertation, Catholic University of America, Washington, D.C.

Edmonds, R. (1979). Effective schools for urban poor. *Educational Leadership, 37*(1), 15–18, 20–24.

Galetto, P. (in press). Religious knowledge and belief of lay religious teachers in Catholic elementary schools. In J. A. McLellan, J. Youniss, & J. Convey (Eds.), *The Catholic characters of Catholic schools.* Notre Dame, IN: University of Notre Dame Press.

Harry, B., & Anderson, M. G. (1994). The disproportionate placement of African

American males in special education programs: A critique of the process. *Journal of Negro Education, 63*(4), 602–619.

Irvine, J. J., & Foster, M. (Eds.). (1996). *Growing up African American in Catholic schools.* New York: Teachers College Press.

Lyke, J. P. (1991, November). *Catholic schools: The lifeblood of evangelization.* Paper presented at the special meeting of the National Congress on Catholic Schools, Washington, DC.

National Catholic Educational Association. (1992). *AIDS, A Catholic educational approach to HIV: Teacher's manual.* Washington, DC: Author.

Polite, V. C. (1993). If only we knew then what we know now: Foiled opportunities to learn in suburbia. *Journal of Negro Education, 63*(3), 337–354.

Polite, V. C. (1996). Making a way out of no way: The Oblate Sisters of Providence, St. Frances Academy, and the African American community. In J. J. Irvine & M. Foster (Eds.), *Growing up African American in Catholic schools* (pp. 62–75). New York: Teachers College Press.

Polite, V. C., McClure, R., & Rollie, D. (1997). Emerging reflective urban principals: The role of the shadowing encounter. *Urban Education, 31*(5), 466–489.

Sellers, T. E. (1976). *Twentieth-century missionaries or teachers.* Unpublished Ed.D. dissertation. Stanford University, Stanford, CA.

Shor, I., & Freire, P. (1987). What is the "dialogical method" of teaching? *Journal of Education, 169*(3), 11–31.

Ternasky, P. L. (1995). Why should we talk to them? The ethics of disagreement. *Educational Horizons, 74*(1), 13–20.

Three Catholic Afro-American Congresses. (1978). *Proceedings of the First Colored Catholic Congress* (1889 January). New York: Arno Press. (Original work published 1893)

Wilson, W. J. (1996). *When work disappears: The world of the new urban poor.* New York: Knopf.

CHAPTER 8

Black Catholic Schools in Inner-City Chicago: Forging a Path to the Future

M. SHEILA NELSON

THE INITIAL RESEARCH FOR THIS CHAPTER was done in 1987–88 when I interviewed pastors and principals of 33 Black inner-city Catholic elementary schools in Chicago in an attempt to understand the relationship between a Catholic school's mission and its organizational effectiveness, and between these schools' adaptation strategies and their organizational survival. I then divided the schools into four categories based on how the schools procured resources, defined themselves and their mission, and focused administrative energies. After conducting a case study of a school in each category, I made some predictions about the schools most at risk, the strengths and limitations of each category, and the most significant challenges each category had to meet in order for the schools to succeed. My research revealed an interesting interplay between proactive change (careful planning and deliberative decision making) and environmentally induced adaptation and/or death. (For a more complete discussion of these research findings and the organizational theory underlying them, see Nelson, 1994.)

In 1996–97 I returned to these same schools to examine the accuracy of my predictions, to look for patterns in school closures and in school survival, and to identify new trends and directions. While most of my original expectations were met, several things surprised me. One category, the externally linked schools, had stabilized and appeared stronger than I had predicted. Even more important, I found a growing convergence of the other three categories toward external linkage.

OVERVIEW OF THE FOUR CATEGORIES

Before discussing my most recent findings, I will describe briefly the four categories of schools, their strengths, and their limitations as I had identified them. Then, having presented my expectations for each category, I will discuss what has been happening to the surviving schools and how well their particular strategies have enabled them to cope with the challenges they have encountered.

The Parish-Centered Schools: The Most Traditional Form

Thirteen schools fit the category I called parish-centered and were parochial schools in the traditional sense. The local parish gave the school legitimacy, a sense of identity, and its mission. As the largest schools in my 1988 sample (a mean enrollment of 326 compared with a sample mean of 271), they had been better able to withstand environmental change without major organizational changes (Hannan & Freeman, 1988).

The parish-centered schools were specialist organizations (Hannan & Freeman, 1988), structured to meet the needs of a culturally distinct population; African American heritage, values, and symbols provided the context in which the Catholic faith was celebrated, taught, and ritualized. This emphasis helped bridge the religious and socioeconomic diversity common to these schools and similarly helped integrate parish and school communities.

I had concluded in 1988 that parish-centered schools, more easily than most of the other schools I studied, were able to create an atmosphere and community conducive to learning. The vibrant school community, with its rich value climate, enhanced academic effectiveness (Purkey & Smith, 1988). Similarly, a clearer sense of mission and identity strengthened the schools' legitimacy to organizational participants (Meyer & Scott, 1983); this attracted new families into the school and activated parish resources on behalf of the school. The strong sense of ownership made the parish-centered school more resistant to outside or environmental challenges that threatened its survival (Meyer & Zucker, 1989). Thus, while principals in these schools found the environment challenging, they tended to view the future positively and were less likely to feel overwhelmed or powerless.

I was concerned, however, that their almost exclusive reliance on the parish put these schools organizationally at risk. Despite the emphasis on a common culture and a significant overlap between the church and school populations, competing interests and goals at times erupted in conflict. Unless the parish/school community was well established with a strongly united leadership, in times of financial crisis the relationship between the school and the parish worship community became tenuous at best, and the interdependence of church and school seemed likely to dissolve.

A second concern focused on loss of enrollment. Because of their large size, these schools had been able to lose a significant number of students without it threatening their existence. But if enrollment continued to drop, at some point the parish-centered approach would no longer be feasible.

The Isolated School: Going It Alone

I classified eight schools as isolated schools because they were geographically isolated in some of the most badly deteriorated neighborhoods of Chicago. They lacked not only the financial support traditionally provided by the parish, but the legitimacy and the political support as well. While the parish-centered school was recognized as a vital and essential component of the parish, the isolated school was considered too heavy a burden. To quote one pastor: "There was no money left to be church; other parish staff had been discontinued. The parish had to get the school off our back so that the church could be church." Radical racial or socioeconomic change, diverse church and school populations, and a lack of access to alternative resource providers contributed to the isolation of a school.

Despite the death of resources, two strengths were evident in these schools. The first was administrative autonomy for the principal. Without the conflicts of interest between parish and school, a charismatic leader was able to shape the school's mission and philosophy in a more generalist way in order to attract a wider group of people from the local community (Hannan & Freeman, 1977). The second was that these schools were more likely than schools in the other categories to be neighborhood schools (with an average of 80% of their students living within a mile-and-a-half radius of school), thus making it easier to build community, involve families and build a sense of ownership for the school, and establish a strong reputation in the neighborhood, factors that Comer (1988) identifies as critical in inner-city schools. Unfortunately, the vibrant community that I found in a few of the isolated schools was very dependent on a charismatic principal—and easily could be lost if the principal moved on. The isolated school lacked the parish supports that facilitated the process of institutionalizing school spirit and a sense of ownership.

Because these schools were so isolated, without outside groups to provide resources or to fight for the school's survival, I expected this group to be the most vulnerable to school closings; survival depended on the isolation being temporary and leadership moving the school to another form of adaptation. The one exception I foresaw was that when a school was *the only* source of Catholic education in an area, the archdiocese might continue to subsidize the school in order to make Catholic education available in all parts of Chicago.

The Cooperatively Linked School: Regional Catholic Schools

Six schools had responded to organizational challenges by restructuring from a parochial to a regional Catholic school system. Demographic shifts had led to relatively rapid decline in some of these schools; while they still had resources available to them, losses were inevitable. Thus they were looking proactively for ways to stabilize their future by joining forces with nearby schools that faced similar challenges. Others in this group looked very much like the isolated schools; they had made structural changes out of absolute necessity. The case study school of the cooperatively linked group, for example, declined from 700 to 186 students in a 20-year period, while the parish decreased by 1,400 families.

As in the isolated schools, interaction between the local parish and the school was limited. But pastors in this category were much more committed to their schools, viewing them as a way to legitimize the parish's presence in the neighborhood. Pastors were relieved of the financial burden of the school because the parish and school finances usually were separated in the process of restructuring; the cooperating schools began functioning under a joint budget with archdiocesan subsidy. This change freed the principals to focus on operational and educational matters rather than on finances.

This regional approach to Catholic education provided support for the team of principals and increased autonomy within the parish setting; the school became less vulnerable to pastoral whims and political struggles characteristic of isolated and parish-centered schools. This approach was therefore beneficial to both parish and school. In addition, because they now depended directly on the archdiocese for subsidy, the restructured schools were more likely to know and to take appropriate action to meet the criteria by which the archdiocese evaluated schools, thus securing the assistance of the diocese. I therefore predicted that the cooperatively linked schools would be the most likely to survive.

On the other hand, while restructuring stabilized resources, the newness of the structures made the school much more vulnerable organizationally (Hannan & Freeman, 1977; Meyer & Zucker, 1989; Singh,

House, & Tucker, 1986). Schools suffer a loss of identity, a loss of legitimacy, and a loss of community as leadership focus shifts from intra-school relations to creating new structures and building bridges between schools. As a result, I expected to see continued declines in student enrollment until a new school identity had been established. Additionally, because of the schools' increased dependence on the archdiocese—no longer mediated by a parish—I also expected these schools to be vulnerable to repeated restructuring attempts.

In some ways these schools are caught in a vicious cycle: Change leads to loss of legitimacy and declining enrollment and the intended economy of scale is not realized. This stimulates the need for further restructuring, which the school cannot resist because it lacks the political clout of older, more established institutions (Hannan & Freeman, 1988; Meyer & Zucker, 1989).

The Externally Linked School: Marketing an Education

Six schools were externally linked; while they had lost the traditional connections with their respective parishes, they had found ways to market themselves as credible *academic* institutions to a broader audience and had established alternative sources of financing, political support, and legitimacy. The administrators of these schools were more entrepreneurial than others. While pastors were extremely supportive and most were actively involved in fund raising for the school, I found in this group no concerted effort to forge a unified church/school community.

Although these principals experienced more autonomy than in the parish setting, they were vulnerable to political interference and competing demands from various groups of supporters. The school's mission and identity were often ambiguous, allowing for adaptation to the expectations of varied supporters (Wagner, 1977), but in the long run this tends to affect school climate negatively. Similar to the cooperatively linked school, administrators tended to be more attentive to outside resource providers than to the educational climate and faculty expertise within the school. As a result, community was weakened, teachers were alienated, and the school's effectiveness was compromised (Purkey & Smith, 1988). This seemed more likely to occur when a school had not yet established a strong academic reputation (Meyer, Scott, & Deal, 1983). I therefore suspected that until the school's academic reputation was firmly established—as was the case in some but not all of these schools—the externally linked schools would continue to face major turbulence: teacher, student, and possibly administrative turnover, and sizable fluctuations in enrollment.

Once the school's reputation *was* strongly established, however, I expected these schools to do quite well and to experience more stability than most. Increased flexibility in funding and less reliance on parish and archdiocesan subsidy would increase their autonomy. Additionally, because of the entrepreneurial atmosphere of the schools, they were better able to respond to fluctuating enrollment than either the isolated or the cooperatively linked schools, where students tended to be drawn from a limited geographic area.

NINE YEARS LATER: CHICAGO'S BLACK INNER-CITY SCHOOLS REVISITED

Three types of data provided me with new information on these schools: personal interviews with the principals of my four case study schools, surveys of administrators of the remaining schools in my study, and the Office of Catholic Education's (OCE) "School Profile" on each of my surviving schools. These data sheets present official summary characteristics such as enrollment from 1991 through 1995, ethnic information, "yellow flag criteria" that indicate the viability of the school from the archdiocesan perspective, whether and when the school completed each of eight planning processes recommended by the archdiocese, rates of transfer in and out of the school, and tuition information. In addition, I interviewed the OCE director of research and the planning consultant most involved with the inner-city schools in which I was interested.

Administrators in all but four of the surviving schools provided me with input on their schools. I began with a mail survey, which, due at least in part to timing, yielded a poor response rate (43%). I then followed up with telephone interviews and one on-site interview. Two principals declined phone interviews because they were new to the job (one having only been in the school 1 month). Additionally, three surveys were returned blank—two new principals did not feel able to answer the questions, and the third did not have time to respond. I obtained some information from the assistant principal of one of the schools that had returned a blank survey.

Of the 33 schools studied in 1988, five had closed completely by 1996. Seven others were involved in consolidations in which three buildings closed (see Table 8.1). While there were major changes in enrollment in some of the schools, enrollment averages in the surviving schools remained amazingly similar—271 per building in 1988, and 279 in 1995. An average of one-third of the students in these schools live in poverty (see Table 8.2), but the poverty rate climbs as high as 59% in individual

Table 8.1. Changes in School Structure

Category in 1988	Structure of school in 1996				
	Closed	New collaboration	External links	Further reorganization	No change
Parish-centered (n = 13)	1	2	1		9
Isolated (n = 8)	3	3	1		1
Cooperatively linked (n = 6)	0	1		4	1
Externally linked (n = 6)	1	1			4
Total (n = 33)	5	7	2	4	15

schools. Some schools are no longer receiving any parish subsidy, while others still receive over half of their budget from such subsidy (the archdiocesan recommended limit is 35%); the schools in my sample had an average parish subsidy of 24% (see Table 8.3).

Having presented this brief overview of the surviving schools, I will examine patterns of variation by category.

The Parish-Centered Schools: Continuing the Tradition

At first glance, it appears that 10 of the 13 parish-centered schools were continuing to operate in 1996 without any major restructuring. Closer

Table 8.2. School Characteristics by Category, 1995

Category in 1988	Mean enrollment	Students living 1.5 miles or more from school (%)	Students in poverty (%)	Subsidy as share of budget (%)
Parish-centered (n = 12)	289	41	26	16
Isolated (n = 5)	244	39	45	30
Cooperatively linked (n = 11)	241	40	36	38
Externally linked (n = 5)	320	53	39	19
Total (n = 33)	279	44	33	25

Note: In the cooperatively linked schools category, I counted each of the buildings of consolidated schools separately to provide a more accurate enrollment picture. For example, one "school" had an enrollment of 893 in 1995, but those students were located on three separate campuses. So for this table, the *n* counts the three separately. There were only six cooperatively linked schools in my study—but they encompassed 11 separate buildings.

Table 8.3. Average Revenues and Costs, 1995 (dollars)

	All schools (n = 28)	Parish-centered (n = 12)	Isolated (n = 4)	Externally linked (n = 6)	Cooperatively linked (n = 6)
Tuition for first child	1,630	1,577	1,364	1,961	1,581
Fees	147	170	142	90	165
Fund raising	170	150	150	154	250
Total	1,947	1,897	1,656	2,205	1,996
Cost per student	2,284	2,113	2,404	2,465	2,336
Revenues per student	1,744	1,713	1,674	2,081	1,448
Parish subsidy as share of budget	24.2%	18.4%	30%	19.3%	38%
School-generated revenues as share of budget	75.8%	81.6%	70%	80.7%	62%

examination, however, revealed that one of these actually had developed important external links, which I will explain below. Of the other three, one had closed in 1994, and two had consolidated. The two schools involved in consolidations had had strong histories and reputations but, while both now served a Black student body, one of the parishes remained almost entirely elderly Polish, while the other served a racially mixed population. Thus, it was hard to build the kind of parish/school community necessary for this model. Not surprisingly, both of the consolidating schools had had low enrollments for this category in 1988, between 200 and 235 students.

Of the two remaining low-enrollment, parish-centered schools, one recently had redefined the parish/school identity at the time of my 1988 research and by 1996 had gained 130 students—a growth of 65%. The final school remained fairly stable, but is unique in its racial diversity: 57% Black, 20% Hispanic, with White, biracial, Asian American, and Native American students.

The mean enrollment for the self-contained schools in this category was down slightly, from 326 to 305. Three schools showed significant declines in enrollment of between 23 and 51%, with most of the loss taking place between 1988 and 1991. Since then, enrollment remained quite stable in the three schools.

A return to the case study school revealed how well the parish-centered approach can and does work in a strong parish. The school went through a very smooth transition to a new principal, hiring (as was this school's pattern) a parishioner who had held leadership roles in both school and parish. Enrollment is strong. Connections between the parish Church and the school have continued to grow; parish volunteers work in the classrooms, provide a six-session parish orientation to new school families, sponsor a youth group, and provide a male mentoring ministry program for students. As was the case in 1988, various teachers are actively involved in the Church, and administrators and teachers very deliberately organize opportunities to involve parents in the school. The integration of gospel and African values creates a strong school culture and a positively charged educational climate. The principal pointed out that while 7 of 19 Catholic elementary schools in this particular council have closed in the past 4 years, her enrollment has held steady at over 500 and the school is financially strong. When all the pieces come together for this model, the strength of the parish-centered school is undeniable.

Adaptations to the Weaknesses of the Parish-Centered Model. While the vast majority of the parish-centered schools seemed to be operating with no major structural changes, some of the weaknesses of this pattern were becoming more apparent. Finances were a major concern for these schools, as they were for most of the schools in my study. Nine of 12 principals in this group specifically named finances as one of the greatest challenges the school will have to meet in order to survive the next 10 years. Even schools that were basically self-sufficient reported financial concerns about maintaining enrollment and about technological upgrading of the school.

Parish-centered schools in poorer parishes were leading the movement of these schools toward finding new sources of financial support. They reported that even with archdiocesan subsidy, there was never enough money. Annual reductions in subsidy required them to seek new sources of support. One former principal, for example, had earned a master's degree in philanthropy and returned as the school's director of development. In a style characteristic of a strong parish-centered school, the parish had helped one of its teachers earn a master's in administration so that she could take over as principal. This development office planned to raise $250,000 in funds through direct solicitation, and with this more diverse donor base to secure the school's operating budget. The school is attempting, in the words of the development director, to "take control of our own destiny," securing the kind of autonomy that traditionally has been missing from parish-centered schools. This was the only school in this category, aside from the case study school, that described its funding base as "stable"; two of the others described it as "extremely insecure," and the others as "somewhat insecure."

While this school was the most dramatic example of the switch toward developing an outside funding base, a number of principals in this category spoke of the growing need to rely on fund raising and gifts. What keeps these schools distinct from the externally linked, however, was that they maintained a parish identity in the midst of this transition. School leadership reported, as they had in parish-centered schools 9 years earlier, a strong focus on the internal school community; this focus is very different from that of the typical externally linked or even cooperatively linked school where outside funders invariably hold center stage.

Trouble with pastors was another major concern raised by principals in parish-centered schools, a concern that goes beyond my focus on competing *financial* interests to competing philosophies. Two principals specifically mentioned this as a problem, while several others expressed concern about what will happen when the current pastor's tenure is up. The best example is one of the schools involved in a consolidation; the pastors disputed among themselves during and after the planning process. Amid much political intrigue, ownership of the school was transferred from one parish to another. While the previous parish had been vitally involved in the school, the new parish sponsor is indifferent and difficult to work with. Relationships with both parishes are strained, and disputes over usage of the original parish property add to the tension. The frustrated principal complained that the school had had eight different pastors in 9 years. Pastoral problems, from her perspective, contributed to a high staff turnover—six out of ten teachers are new this year. She explained that Catholic teachers wanting to work in *Catholic* schools were frustrated with how complicated the relationship with the Church had become. She and her teachers had functioned well in the parish-centered school and apparently were grieving its loss. The principal expressed hope that the consolidated school soon would become an archdiocesan school, freed from the parochial disputes in which it was currently embroiled.

Several other principals commented on the major changes that faced their schools after a change in pastor. They are convinced that a pastor can make or break a school—and a few even hinged their predictions of the school's survival on pastoral leadership and the direction that would take.

Can the Parish-Centered School Survive? When asked candidly whether they thought their schools would survive the next 10 years as currently structured, many responded less optimistically than 9 years earlier. Some of these schools are reaching a point where they have to do things differently or they will not survive. Six in this category responded that their school would survive. Two did not answer; two made survival contingent on additional funding, and one contingent on finding "a dynamic and *very* effective administrator who will remain over a long period of time." The final respondent did not expect the school to survive as currently structured, but she was hopeful that with a combination of creative financing and new and dynamic administration, survival would be possible.

The Isolated Schools: Rapidly Disappearing Form

As expected, this category of schools had the highest organizational mortality rate. Three of the eight schools closed completely, including one whose principal had told me the archdiocese would never allow them to close because they were the only school in the area. Three others were involved in consolidations that resulted in two more buildings closing. Only two remained as self-contained schools, and only one of them could still be considered an isolated school. It is located in a very poor inner-city neighborhood near several strong parish-centered schools and one externally linked school—none of which at this time is experiencing enrollment difficulties or other challenges that would push it in the direction of consolidation. The principal stated that the schools "can't survive with each trying to exist in its own world," but complained that collaboration was impossible because the schools in the area functioned as "every family on its own," a description very appropriate for the parish-centered model.

The poverty rate for the surviving schools in this category was higher than for any other category, 45% compared with an overall mean of 33%. As predicted, finances were a major concern. Principals in all but one of these schools identified finances as one of the greatest challenges and threats to their future. The final principal rated the school's funding base as "somewhat insecure," adding that they live from paycheck to paycheck. Even the principal who described the school's funding base as "very strong" quickly added, "but vulnerable to the stroke of a pen."

Consolidating changed the neighborhood character of the isolated schools. An average of 39% of these schools' students now came from outside the neighborhood, while the rate for the two remaining self-contained schools in the category was 18.5%, less than half that of the newly consolidated schools.

Attempts at Overcoming Isolation. It is becoming increasingly obvious that isolated schools cannot survive as isolated schools, and their principals therefore are attempting to establish new relationships capable of providing resources and increased stability. When possible, these schools seemed to be choosing to consolidate; when that was impossible, leadership tended to look for outside supporters. This was the case in the final self-contained school in this group.

This school is geographically isolated on the outskirts of Chicago. When it became clear that the local parish would close, a task force studying ways for the Church to remain connected to the neighborhood, identified the school as the best way for the Church to continue to serve the area. One of the task force members assumed responsibility for fund raising for the school and secured operational funding for the school for a 5-year period. He has promised to continue raising money to subsidize the school as long as he is able. So while the future is far from secure, the principal reported that at present they have everything that they need. This outside support makes it possible to keep tuition minimal at $750—less than half of what it is in most of the other schools (see Table 8.4). But even at that, because of the extreme poverty of the area, 40% of families receive a reduced tuition rate. Funds raised by the school's new sponsor also pay full tuition for any eighth-grade graduate of the school who attends a Catholic high school. After a period of extreme turmoil, the principal rates her financial situation as "stable but dependent." Additional assistance comes from the Inner City Teaching Core, which provides three or four volunteer teachers each year. The now externally sponsored school grew by 87% between 1988 and 1995 (from 125 to 234).

Table 8.4. Range of Revenues and Costs, 1995 (dollars)

	Low	*High*
Tuition	750	3,725
Fees	0	300
Fund raising	0	425
Cost per student	1,401	4,324
Revenues per student	1,013	4,104
Parish subsidy as share of budget	0%	51%
School-generated revenues as share of budget	49%	102%[a]

Note: It is significant to note that in the school with a tuition of $750 for the first child, the tuition is $820 for two children, and $835 for three or more. Yet 40% of their families request and receive a further reduction in their tuition.

[a] School-generated revenues exceeded yearly budget.

Dangerously low enrollments pushed two schools in this group to consolidate, with both consolidations involving a building closing; enrollment has since stabilized at around 275. The three schools in this category that closed all had enrollments of around 200 in 1988. The two schools that consolidated have had very different experiences from each other. The first school has gone from an isolated school to an isolated consolidation. Pastoral attitudes and behaviors that previously isolated the school from the local parish continue to cause conflict and financial problems in the consolidation. In the second, the consolidation has helped to move the school to stronger links with external supporters.

The case study school for this category illustrates the plight of the isolated consolidation. While the previous principal had built a strong school community, enrollment had declined by 29% to a dangerously low 175 students, while a neighboring school had declined to 100. By consolidating and closing the neighboring building, enrollment initially rose to 300, and then settled at approximately 275. But cultural differences between the two adjacent neighborhoods presented the new school with major problems. The newcomers were "a tougher, less protected, more streetwise population." Staff was not prepared for the attitudes and behaviors of the incoming children and their parents. In addition, the newly formed school inherited the financial problems of the dissolved school—uncollected tuition and unpaid bills. While ideally the two pastors should have equal power in the school, only the on-site pastor is actually involved; the other has even withheld archdiocesan subsidy intended for the school. In addition, at present only one member representing the closed building serves on the school board for the consolidated school.

The consolidation was clearly a crisis point for this school, but with strong leadership from the principal, the school seems to have recovered much of its family spirit and the positive energy that characterized the school in 1988. To all appearances, the original culture of the school was strong enough to overcome the onslaught of opposing attitudes. The future, however, remains uncertain. Finances are a major obstacle to which there is no apparent solution. A dynamic principal is currently carrying the school, but it appears that over the long run an isolated consolidation will be no stronger than a solitary isolated school. The consolidation at least temporarily stabilizes the school's situation by increasing enrollment, but, once again, what is needed is a more permanent solution.

A more promising approach is being taken by two other schools in this category. In addition to consolidating, they are establishing additional external links. One principal is utilizing strong connections with a sharing parish to sponsor 35 students. These schools also are networking with other Catholic institutions to provide needed medical and social services to students. Principals spoke of the need for financial officers who will secure grants for the school, thus freeing the principal to be an instructional leader. These are the kinds of efforts that will move the school—whether consolidated or not—beyond the isolation that threatens the survival of inner-city schools.

The Cooperatively Linked Schools: Creating New Alternatives

As expected, all of these schools lost enrollment, averaging a 27% decline. The greatest loss of enrollment occurred in two schools that consolidated with each other in 1994 and lost 64% of their enrollment by 1996. While enrollment had been dropping quite steadily in these two schools since 1988 (from approximately 900 students in 1988 to 700 in 1994), it dropped dramatically to 450 in 1995, the year after the consolidation, and then down another 125 students the second year. Half of the schools in this category lost between 40% and 50% of their enrollment. Only one school in this category had fewer than 200 students in 1988, and that school had the lowest loss of enrollment in the intervening years—only 5%.

The case study school in this category did surprisingly well with enrollment. Having gone through repeated rounds of restructuring, the buildings that remained a part of the consolidation showed an enrollment loss of 20%. Besides enrollment loss, the cooperatively linked schools also experienced high rates of student mobility; most schools regularly experienced shifts of between 25% and 50% of their student bodies. The only school where this was not the case was located in a fairly stable neighborhood described by the principal as "the last stop before the suburbs."

In addition to fluctuating enrollment, a loss of autonomy and vulnerability to further restructuring also threaten the survival of the newly consolidated school, as can be seen in the case study school. Despite the consistent leadership of a dedicated and talented principal throughout the past 10 years, the school—which originally restructured in 1984—has gone through three more major restructurings since 1988. The original restructuring consolidated *nine parish* schools into a *regional* Catholic school with *six* campuses, then a regional school with *four* campuses, then a single *parish* school with *three* sites, and finally an *archdiocesan* school with three sites. Restructuring efforts were complicated by conflict between pastors, and the school repeatedly was caught in the middle. Finally, in order to get out of an impossible situation, the Cardinal unilaterally decided to make the school Chicago's first archdiocesan elementary school.

The principal expressed frustration at having to go through organizational changes every couple of years; she complained that it is exhausting, and a waste of time and energy, to be constantly setting up new models—or to spend time planning changes that are never implemented. Outside facilitation resulted in decisions beyond the control of those most closely affected by them (Meyer & Zucker, 1989). While the principal has managed to protect her school community from much of the disruption, it has been a real drain on leadership: "This is *not* normal. No other schools have to deal with this every other year."

While the separation of parish and school contributes to the vulnerability of the school to repeated restructuring, that same separation provides the school community some measure of protection from the turmoil the restructuring otherwise might cause. The impact of such changes could be far more devastating on a parish-centered school where the relationship between school and parish is a vital resource to both communities.

Other than complaints about restructuring, the case study school was doing very well. Enrollment and finances were stable despite yearly reductions in diocesan subsidy. Principals in this category were, however, concerned that they could no longer afford to hire specialists—music and art teachers, counselors, directors of religious education, and special education people—that had been on staff in 1988, specialists that most schools in other categories had not been able to afford. Some of the financial advantages of the cooperatively linked school were disappearing as archdiocesan funding levels dropped.

Collaboration Without Loss of Control. Two principals in this category were new to their schools and returned their surveys blank, but the others all expressed a belief that their schools could survive with the restructuring that currently was occurring. While recognizing that individual buildings may have to close, they expect the school itself to continue. The new forms of restructuring being explored by four of these schools retain more local control than in previous consolidations; principals will have more autonomy and fewer archdiocesan regulations to meet.

New cooperative ventures also differ in the way in which they are financed. Development work is a central part of the efforts of these schools to secure their financial future. The archdiocese is viewed as the most important of *many* donors, rather than as the *sole* source of support. In addition, these schools are linking into health and social services that can be provided by other Catholic institutions in the school setting, thus creating a "full-service school," which is vitally important to inner-city families.

Several of these principals admitted that their school would not be able to survive if left "out here by ourselves," but if the planning group makes the needed contacts, "if we're in the right place at the right time, we'll survive; otherwise we won't." Another common concern was the reliability of archdiocesan subsidy; this concern intensified as Chicago waited to hear who Cardinal Bernardin's successor would be. Just as the pastor is crucial to the fate of the Catholic school, the Cardinal is crucial to the fate of the system. Principals recognized that the archdiocese would not be able to subsidize the schools forever, but expressed concern that "if all subsidy is withdrawn sooner than we plan, we won't survive." This group of principals clearly was working toward self-sufficiency, but admitted that it would take time.

The Externally Linked Schools: Growing Stronger

The six externally linked schools were doing surprisingly well. Only one had closed, but that building now houses the older students of a recently established Catholic "free school" sponsored by a religious congregation. The other five schools showed an average increase in enrollment of 13%, with average enrollment now higher than in any other category. Only one of these was a neighborhood school; an average of 53% of the students in these schools came from outside the immediate vicinity of the school. Parish subsidy varied greatly, ranging from 2% to 39%, and the poverty rate in these schools was quite high—ranging from a low of 30% to a high of 60%.

My case study school, while the most innovative of the group, also had been the most at risk in 1988 because of goal displacement, an unclear mission, an alienated faculty, disenchanted parents, and ineffective academic programs. Administrative turnover has been great in this school—there have been five principals in the past 6 years. Key to the school's survival is a pastor whose 36-year tenure has provided it with a strong network of supporters. In most externally linked schools, the long tenure and consistent leadership of principal and/or pastor clearly has facilitated the process of securing outside funding.

The principal who took over in 1988 discussed with me the problems she had inherited. She succeeded in putting the school on sound financial footing—paying back bills and fines, maintaining a budget, reestablishing the school's credit, and securing $80,000 in grants for the school. She cleaned up the school, created a climate for learning, built up the school's audiovisuals, educated the school board as to their role, and improved public relations, teacher morale, and parent involvement. She spoke, for example, of walking children home after school to discuss their tardiness with a parent, and of visiting homes to bring truants to school. She described herself as working "7 days a week and half the night."

Unfortunately, when she left 3 years later, things began to deteriorate again. Last year's principal said that her predecessor (one of two who served between the two I interviewed for this chapter) had created a "financial disaster," which ultimately resulted in the establishment of a strong finance committee and the hiring of a business manager to be shared by school and parish. Since diocesan cuts, the school needs to earn $200,000 a year through fund raising in order to stay afloat—and the current goal is to be financially independent of the archdiocese by the year 2000. A variety of programs help to raise the needed money, but also build bridges between the school and the surrounding community, which holds some of Chicago's wealthiest as well as some of its most impoverished people.

When principals focus on strengthening the school community, contributions made by external supporters are utilized more effectively. The stronger the school, the stronger the appeal that can be made to outside funders. And the stronger those networks with outside funding sources, the more resources are available to the school to strengthen its programs and personnel. This case highlighted, however, the vital role a principal plays; no matter how large an external network a school has, if the principal is not providing strong and effective leadership, it is likely to veer off course very quickly.

The principals in this category talked more frequently and enthusiastically than others about outside resources available to schools. While a few principals in the other categories expressed the hope that such resources existed, they had just begun to explore the possibilities. In contrast, these principals *knew* what was there and had begun to activate their support networks, to pursue new sources of financial assistance, and to reap the benefits of their endeavors.

One other externally linked school, which also serves a very poor part of Chicago, was maintaining its external links but adding some cooperative links with neighboring schools as well. When asked about this shift in direction, the principal replied that she was moving in this direction not because her school needed this change, but because the survival of the neighboring schools depended on this collaboration.

The three externally linked schools with locational advantages that market strong academic programs, had a much more stable environment. This was reflected in more stable enrollments, although two of these schools showed higher percentages of students transferring in and out than the actual enrollment numbers would have led one to expect.

All the principals in this category expect their schools to continue through the next 10 years; they continue to look for creative ways to finance the school—and they express a stronger sense of autonomy and control over their situation than most principals in other categories.

A VIEW OF INNER-CITY SCHOOLS FROM THE CENTER: THE OFFICE OF CATHOLIC EDUCATION

Because the archdiocese has been and remains the most important source of support for inner-city Catholic schools, no study of these schools would be complete without considering the perspective of archdiocesan leadership. In light of my discussions with principals, the issues of most concern to me were the ongoing restructuring, which was apparently beyond the control of local administrators, and the future of archdiocesan school subsidy.

A planning consultant from the Office of Catholic Education admitted that multiple restructurings have been a serious problem for consolidated schools in the inner city. She attributed this in part to the lack of central planning for these schools; most decisions had been made in a chaotic manner in response to crisis or political maneuvering in the parish. The planning process was initiated by the parish, and, if the parish chose to utilize the services of the OCE, a planning consultant directed the process. With each parish pursuing its own interests, planning was often shortsighted, and the core problems confronting these schools were not addressed.

At the time of this research, however, a task force first commissioned by Cardinal Bernardin was studying the long-term educational needs of the entire archdiocese of Chicago. For the first time a master plan was being drafted that considered the need for new schools as well as for school consolidations and closings. Two work groups were involved: the first to study school availability and viability, and the second to find ways to fund the schools that the first group would identify as viable and necessary.

This innovative approach reverses the usual process of finance-driven decision making. Here the educational needs of the parish or local Church community determine the amount of financial support needed, and then professional financiers find ways to meet those needs. The goal of this planning process is to ensure that a Catholic school is available to every Catholic family that chooses it. Schools that remain after this plan is implemented should survive and meet the educational needs of the Chicago archdiocese for the long term.

The master plan also will change the way subsidy is distributed. Currently it is very uneven and often built on historical dependencies; certain parishes have always been subsidized and have come to expect that support. Little or no attention has been paid to new needs and new populations of poor people in noncentral city parishes. Similarly there is the problem of the poor paying much higher tuition because the wealthy parishes can afford to give more support to their schools. The OCE reported that archdiocesan school solvency averaged 81%, but in many of the African American parish schools on Chicago's south side, tuition provided 100% of the school costs—these schools receive no parish or archdiocesan subsidy. I found this to be the case especially in my parish-centered schools. The new process will address these inequities and should result in increased stability for the schools that survive the screening.

Much hard work has already gone into the process, and the consultant is confident that good will come of it. One limitation, however, is that the plan looks only at Catholic education—it does not attempt to assess availability and viability of Churches. As a result, pastoral autonomy will remain an issue, with pastors able to subvert or squelch the plan if they feel it threatens their parish. While a public relations group is attempting to keep people informed and involved, the consultant stated that in order for the plan to move forward, a way to protect parish interests must be developed.

Once the plan has identified the schools that will be a part of the Chicago Catholic School System, the OCE will oversee the development of a master technology plan to address the computer and technology needs of these schools. The OCE recognizes what so many principals said to me, that today's educational technology is simply beyond the schools' financial means.

The OCE's perspective on subsidy is extremely important since funding was a major concern for all four categories of schools. While archdiocesan schools need to diversify their funding base, the planning consultant acknowledged that poor parishes will continue to need subsidy from the archdiocese. At present, archdiocesan subsidy comes from two sources. First, parishes pay a 10% tax overall to the Pastoral Center, and the majority of the grants given to poor parishes come from these funds. That pool of money must increase. Second, the Cardinal's Big Shoulders Fund solicits money from corporate donors specifically for Catholic schools; this fund grew to $63 million in 10 years, and another $50 million is expected to be raised by 2002. In addition, the finance task force mentioned earlier is working hard to procure future funding. So while the schools are experiencing continuing cuts in subsidy, the OCE is committed to providing some level of ongoing support—although there was concern here, too, that Cardinal Bernardin's successor might be less supportive of Catholic schools. (This interview took place before Cardinal George, Bernardin's successor, had been appointed.) In terms of state or federal aid to Catholic education, neither the planning consultant nor the principals who spoke of vouchers, saw them as the solution to school financing problems. Funding for textbooks, school transportation, and title funds were, however, welcome sources of assistance.

A FEW PARTING IMPRESSIONS:
COMMON CRIES FROM THE INNER CITY

One of the most important things I discovered in talking to these principals was that no matter what their school's primary strategy of adaptation previously, there has been a convergence of strategies that I had not expected to see. Two things seem to be pushing the schools toward this common ground: financial necessity, and an awareness that Catholic schools in the inner city are becoming increasingly elitist, that unless we find ways other than tuition to support the schools, the poor will not be able to afford them. Over and over I heard principals agonizing that those who need the schools most, those whom they most want to serve, are being priced out. The result was that principals were moving toward development directors or financial directors, toward grants and creative ways to raise money for their schools.

Their organizational shift, however, combined the best of several strategies. The most promising seemed to be retaining the culture and strong community identification of the parish-centered school with the fund-raising methods of the externally linked. The major difference I saw between these new attempts and the 1988 externally linked schools was that schools were now using their own strengths to build bridges to outside funders, rather than shaping the school to be what funders wanted.

A second powerful cry I heard from principals was a cry for ministry, for teachers who view teaching as a ministry rather than a job. It was interesting to me how frequently the language of "ministry" was used and the great significance placed on that interpretation of teachers' work. I heard this both in schools that were very stable and in those that were struggling. Principals reported that the sense of ministry makes a difference, and they were looking to hire teachers who had that sense—or trying to pass that sense on to their current teachers. While probably used as a legitimizing myth (Meyer, Scott, & Deal, 1983), it also appeared to be a necessary component for building a Catholic school community, for creating the "difference" that justified the school's existence.

The commitment and dedication of these inner-city principals is inspiring; they are accomplishing so much with so little in situations where the need is so great. The problems their schools face are not unique; while they vary in intensity and degree, the same challenges threaten the survival of Catholic schools throughout our nation. There is much we can learn from the experience of these inner-city schools, but I suspect that solutions available to them will not be as readily available to Catholic schools in middle America. The very desperation of the situation in our central cities calls forth a response that is not likely to be found elsewhere.

REFERENCES

Comer, J. P. (1988). Educating poor minority children. *Scientific American, 259*(5), 42–48.

Hannan, M. T., & Freeman, J. (1977). The population ecology of organizations. *American Journal of Sociology, 82*, 929–964.

Hannan, M. T., & Freeman, J. (1988). The ecology of organizational mortality: American labor unions, 1836–1985. *American Journal of Sociology, 94*, 25–52.

Meyer, J. W., & Scott, W. R. (Eds.). (1983). *Organizational environments: Ritual and rationality.* Newbury Park, CA: Sage.

Meyer, J. W., Scott, W. R., & Deal, T. E. (1983). Institutional and technical sources of organizational structure: Explaining the structure of educational organizations. In J. W. Meyer & W. R. Scott (Eds.), *Organizational environments: Ritual and rationality* (pp. 45–67). Newbury Park, CA: Sage.

Meyer, M. W., & Zucker, L. G. (1989). *Permanently failing organizations.* Newbury Park, CA: Sage.

Nelson, S. (1994). Catholic elementary schools in Chicago's Black inner city: Four modes of adaptation to environmental change. *Nonprofit and Voluntary Sector Quarterly, 23*(3), 209–225.

Purkey, S. C., & Smith, M. S. (1988). Effective schools: A review. *The Elementary School Journal, 83*, 427–452.

Singh, J. V., House, R. J., & Tucker, D. J. (1986). Organizational change and organizational mortality. *Administrative Science Quarterly, 31*, 587–611.

Wagner, J. (1977). *Misfits and missionaries: A school for Black dropouts.* Newbury Park, CA: Sage.

CHAPTER 9

"New" Immigrants in the Catholic Schools: A Preliminary Assessment

STEWART LAWRENCE

SCHOLARS HAVE LONG RECOGNIZED the important, if at times paradoxical, role of Catholic school education in the adaptation of Catholic immigrants to American society in the late nineteenth and early twentieth centuries (see Walch, 1994). However, little if any attention has been focused on the role of Catholic school education in the lives of American immigrants who arrived since 1965. These immigrants arrived with many of the same ethno-religious aspirations as their predecessors, but they encounter a Catholic Church that has already assimilated the previous generations and is loathe to acknowledge, let alone accommodate, the need for "national" parishes and schools. At the same time, these "new" immigrants (many of them at least nominal Catholics) are arriving in major metropolitan areas where Church attendance among Euro-Americans has declined precipitously and where large numbers of Catholic schools are in danger of being closed. Thus, how the American Church responds to this latest wave of immigration surely will be fundamental not only to the capacity of successive immigrant generations to adapt successfully to American life but also to the ability of the institutional Church to survive in its current form.

This chapter takes a preliminary look at the question of immigrant participation in the Catholic schools. It seeks to address, through available statistics as well as ethnographic research, the extent to which selected immigrant groups are enrolling their children in Catholic schools and the reasons why some groups appear to be using the schools more than others. Most of the data collection and the analysis are geared toward producing for each group a reliable estimate of its "rate of participation"—a ratio defined by the percentage of its total school-aged population that is enrolled in Catholic schools. The study takes as a given that Catholic school is costly for immigrants, perhaps more so than for the population at large. However, it seeks to challenge the widespread and largely untested assumption that immigrants are simply "too poor" to attend the Catholic schools. This assumption seems to reflect a pervasive ignorance of the extraordinary diversity of the current U.S. immigrant population, much of which is well educated, has a high earning potential, and is strongly committed to Catholic education. Some immigrant groups do indeed have extremely low rates of participation—rates far below those of the native-born. However, other groups have surprisingly high rates—in some instances, rates that are far *above* those of the native-born. Some of the causes of these variations are beyond the scope of policy intervention but others clearly are not. Even those causes not immediately susceptible to policy intervention should be better appreciated because they tell us a great deal about the nature of Catholic school choice among an increasingly significant segment of the U.S. population.

HOW THE STUDY WAS CONDUCTED

This study was conducted over a period of 3 months in the spring of 1997. Because the time frame was narrow, the study's scope is limited. The sections below describe the research design and the methods used to gather and analyze the data.

The Sample

The immigrant groups selected for this study were Mexicans, Cubans, Central Americans, Haitians, Vietnamese, Koreans, and Filipinos. These groups were chosen because they are the largest of the post-1965 Catholic immigrant groups for which at least some data are available. Also chosen were Puerto Ricans, who by law are U.S. citizens, but whose pattern of migration between Puerto Rico and the U.S. mainland is similar to the migratory patterns of other groups.

The 18 dioceses selected for special study were chosen for both their size and diversity. Fifteen of these dioceses are ranked among the largest 20 dioceses (out of 175) nationwide, including major dioceses in the eastern, central, and western parts of the country. Since the vast majority of U.S. immigrants congregate in a relatively small number of established metropolitan areas, it made sense to focus on the dioceses in these areas. At the same time, some of the dioceses selected are either new or tiny by comparison. These dioceses were chosen for other reasons. Orange, California, has the largest number of Vietnamese refugees and immigrants of any U.S. diocese. El Paso, Texas, has the most Hispanic-dominated (overwhelmingly Mexican) population of any U.S. diocese. The Washington metropolitan area (which encompasses the Arlington diocese and the Archdiocese of Washington) is one of the major receiving areas for Central Americans. In short, the sample, although small, is highly representative of the contemporary Catholic experience with immigrants.

Data-Collection Methods

Only a few Catholic dioceses collect and gather statistics on school enrollment that specify the *nationality* of the student. Miami, for example, has collected data on Haitians since 1985 and on Nicaraguans since 1991. Boston has collected data on Haitians since 1991. San Jose has collected data on specific Asian nationalities, including Filipinos, Koreans, and Vietnamese, since 1985. Los Angeles has collected data on Filipinos since 1991. However, most dioceses collect data only in the five ethnic categories specified in the Basic Educational Demographic Survey (BEDS) form used by federal and state education authorities to allocate funds to public and private schools. These categories are White, Native American, Black, Asian, and Hispanic—none of which are immigrant categories per se.

In some dioceses, however, the school-aged population in a particular ethnic category is overwhelmingly represented by a particular immigrant group, and thus the ethnic figure can be used as a *proxy* for nationality. For example, Mexicans are the *overwhelming* majority (75–95%) of the Hispanic school-aged population in the following seven dioceses: Los Angeles, San Jose, Orange, Oakland, El Paso, Houston, and Omaha. Puerto Ricans are the *overwhelming* majority (i.e., more than two-thirds) of the school-aged population in only two dioceses: Philadelphia and Cleveland. However, Brooklyn, Boston, and Newark have school-aged populations that are *majority* Puerto Rican, and Orlando and Rockville Centre have *near-majority* Puerto Rican school-aged populations that are more than double the size of the next closest group. Finally, Cubans constitute over 40% of the Hispanic school-aged population in Miami and almost four times the size of the next largest group. Therefore, for the purposes of analysis, the Hispanic rates in these 15 dioceses will be used as proxies for either the Mexican, Puerto Rican, or Cuban rate.

Additional Collection

Enrollment data on Haitian immigrants in Brooklyn, Newark, and Boston were gathered firsthand through telephone interviews with Catholic school principals in all schools that reported having students with Haitian ancestry. Principals who did not have figures on national origin readily available were asked to analyze their enrollment lists and, in some cases, to conduct a fresh "head count" of students who are Haitian. Of the more than 25 Catholic school principals interviewed, only one refused to comply. A small portion of students were identified as of "mixed" ancestry because their parents did not share the same national heritage. For statistical purposes, students were considered "Haitian" if one or both of their birth parents were Haitian.

Interviews also were conducted with local informants in eight dioceses to obtain ethnographic data on the Catholic faith and educational practices of specific immigrant groups. The most important dioceses covered were Brooklyn, Chicago, Miami, San Jose, Boston, and New Orleans. Some of these local informants were first interviewed in 1996 as part of a separate study of Catholic pastoral practices toward "newcomer" immigrant groups in nine Catholic dioceses (see Foley, 1997). In both sets of interviews, these informants provided critical insights into the diverse motivations and incentives of immigrant families to participate in Catholic parishes and schools.

Limitations of Data

The data presented in this study have two main limitations. First, not all of the participation rates reported for Hispanics are, strictly speaking, *immigrant* rates of participation. In many U.S. dioceses, particularly those in the southwest, Catholic school students identified as "Hispanic" would almost surely include large numbers of native-born Hispanics whose parents also might be native-born. The ancestors of a family may have arrived decades earlier, but the family would continue to identify itself by its original nationality (for example, "Mexican"). In the data presented in this study, there is no obvious way to distinguish first-generation Mexican immigrants from Mexican Americans or "Chicanos" who have lived in the United States for decades. The same would be true for the general category "Asians," which in some dioceses would include large numbers of Japanese Americans and Chinese Americans whose families arrived at the turn of the century. Nevertheless, the specific Asian groups analyzed in this study (Koreans, Filipinos, and Vietnamese) comprise largely immigrants who arrived in recent decades.

Second, all of the rates of participation reported here are for 1990. The data are based on 1989–90 Catholic school enrollment statistics collected by diocesan education departments as well as demographic data contained in the 1990 U.S. Census, including the School District Data Book, which contains specially tabulated data on the school-aged population only. Because of time and funding constraints, as well as some inherent limitations in the 1980 census data, it was not possible to present rates of Catholic school participation for 1980 and to compare these with those for 1990. A more comprehensive trend assessment of immigrant school participation will be the subject of future research.

MAIN FINDINGS OF THE STUDY

The following sections describe the rates of participation for selected immigrant groups (and Puerto Ricans) and analyze some of the reasons these rates vary by group and by diocese. Income is obviously one factor that shapes these rates of participation, but there are other factors, too. While no formal test for the influence of these factors is possible on the basis of the available data, how they might interact to shape immigrant school choice is illustrated below.

Rates of Participation

Table 9.1 summarizes the rates of Catholic school participation that were calculated for the seven immigrant groups in those dioceses for which data could be found. In addition, a preliminary test of income as a cause of variation in these rates was conducted for Hispanic and Asian groups, using per capita or median income data available through the U.S. Census. Tables 9.2 and 9.3 compare the income levels for Hispanics and Asians, with their respective rates of participation in 17 of the 18 dioceses. Asians, who have consistently higher participation rates than Hispanics, also have higher per capita incomes. However, as discussed below, the *intra-ethnic* comparisons of income and rates of participation do not appear to support a causal relationship. Income is undoubtedly an important influence on immigrant rates of participation, but when considered alone, it does not consistently predict why some national groups utilize the Catholic schools more than others. Other factors affecting their Catholic school participation include prior exposure to Catholic schools, fluency in English, legal status, degree of integration into local parishes, and the "carrying capacity" of the Catholic schools, their tuition rates,

Table 9.1. Rates of Participation for Selected Immigrant Groups, Selected Dioceses, 1990

Group	Participation (%)	Diocese
Filipino	16.2	Los Angeles
	15.7	San Jose
Haitian	13.1	Brooklyn
	12.2	Boston
	4.0	Miami
Puerto Rican	12.9	Newark
	10.5	Philadelphia
	10.0	Chicago
	8.8	Brooklyn
	7.8	Cleveland
	3.7	Boston
	2.3	Orlando
Korean	5.0	San Jose
Vietnamese	4.5	San Jose
Mexican	6.8	Omaha
	4.0	Los Angeles
	3.8	Oakland
	3.2	San Jose
	2.6	Orange
	2.0	El Paso
	1.4	Houston
Nicaraguan	0.8	Miami

Sources: 1990 U.S. Census data (school-aged population by nationality); enrollment data from diocesan education departments or from local Catholic schools (Haitians in Brooklyn).

and the availability of financial aid. These factors are discussed at greater length in a later section.

Mexicans and Puerto Ricans

The seven Mexican-dominant dioceses have rates of participation ranging from 1.4 to 6.8, with the two lowest rates accounted for by dioceses in Texas (El Paso and Houston). The four California dioceses have rates ranging from 2.6 to 4.0. The highest rate is for Omaha. As indicated in Table 9.2, most of these rates of participation are far below the rates

Table 9.2. Hispanic Participation in Catholic Elementary and Secondary
Schools, per Capita Income, and Poverty Rate by Diocese, 1989–1990

Diocese	Participation (%)	Income ($)[a]		Share in poverty (%)[a]	
Puerto Rican dominant					
Newark	12.9	11,012	(6)	17.4	(10)
Philadelphia	10.5	7,575	(17)	35.5	(18)
Chicago	10.0	8,505	(13)	19.1	(11)
Brooklyn	8.8	9,014	(10)	25.9	(14)
Cleveland	7.8	8,791	(11)	26.3	(15)
Boston	3.7	8,555	(12)	31.3	(17)
Mexican dominant					
Omaha	6.8	8,048	(15)	13.9	(8)
Los Angeles	4.0	8,130	(14)	19.4	(12)
Oakland	3.8	11,791	(4)	10.5	(2)
San Jose	3.2	10,917	(8)	13.1	(6)
Orange	2.6	9,258	(9)	13.6	(7)
El Paso	2.0	6,251	(18)	30.7	(16)
Houston	1.4	7,578	(16)	22.8	(13)
Cuban dominant					
Miami	7.1[b]	10,989	(7)	15.6	(9)
Other					
Rockville Centre	6.5	12,754	(3)	7.9	(1)
Washington, D.C.	6.3	12,812	(2)	10.5	(2)
Arlington	5.1	13,208	(1)	10.7	(4)

Sources: The Hispanic participation rate is the ratio of the Hispanic enrolled population
(elementary and secondary) to the total Hispanic school-aged population (ages 5–17). Enrollment
figures were provided by the education department of each diocese or by the NCEA. The school-
aged population was calculated from school-district-level data in the 1990 Census School District
Special Tabulation. Income and poverty rate data are from the 1990 Census.

[a] Numbers in parentheses are rankings.

[b] Minimum estimate.

reported for dioceses in the northeast and southeast, where Puerto Ricans, not Mexicans, are the dominant school-aged nationality among
Hispanics. In fact, three of the five dioceses with the highest participation rates among Hispanics are dioceses with Puerto Rican-dominant,
school-aged populations. Newark (12.9) and Philadelphia (10.5), the dioceses with the two highest Hispanic rates, both have Puerto Rican-dominant, school-aged populations. The rates for Brooklyn (8.8) and Rockville
Centre (6.5) also place them among the top 8 dioceses on our list.

Income. How do income and nonincome variables influence the variation in these rates? Table 9.2 compares Hispanic rates of participation
with the Hispanic poverty rate and Hispanic per capita income in 17
dioceses. Four of the seven Mexican-dominant dioceses (Los Angeles, El

Table 9.3. Asian Participation in Catholic Elementary and Secondary Schools and per Capita Income by Diocese, 1989–1990

Diocese	Participation (%)	Income ($)[a]	
Chicago	14.4	14,140	(11)
San Francisco	13.6	14,286	(10)
Newark	13.0	18,013	(2)
Philadelphia	10.8	12,118	(15)
Houston	9.8	12,902	(14)
Cleveland	9.0	17,330	(3)
Rockville Centre	6.8	20,241	(1)
Omaha	5.8	10,367	(17)
San Jose	5.7	16,179	(5)
Los Angeles	5.5	14,635	(9)
Boston	5.2	13,041	(13)
Washington, D.C.	5.1	16,203	(4)
Oakland	4.8	14,834	(8)
Miami	4.4	13,531	(12)
Orange	3.6	14,849	(7)
Arlington	3.5	15,789	(6)
Brooklyn	3.0	11,851	(16)
El Paso	2.5	9,258	(18)

Sources: The Asian participation rate is the ratio of the Asian enrolled population (elementary and secondary) to the total Asian school-aged population (ages 5–17). Asian enrollment figures were provided by the education department of each diocese or by the NCEA. The Asian school-aged population was calculated from school-district-level data in the 1990 Census School District Special Tabulation. Income rates are from the 1990 Census.

[a]Numbers in parentheses are rankings.

Paso, Houston, and Omaha) rank at the bottom of the Hispanic income spectrum, and two others (San Jose and Orange) rank in the middle. At first glance, this lends some validity to the proposition that the lower the income, the lower the participation of Hispanic children in Catholic schools.

However, other evidence suggests that there is little correlation between income and school participation. Within the seven Mexican-dominant dioceses, El Paso and Houston have lower per capita incomes and lower participation rates than Los Angeles, but both San Jose and Orange have higher income levels and *lower* participation rates than Los Angeles. Omaha, which has the highest participation rate among the seven Mexican-dominant dioceses, has one of the *lowest* Hispanic income levels. Oakland, with a participation rate roughly equivalent to that of Los

Angeles, has an income level that is 45% higher. Income also does not appear to explain the variation in Puerto Rican rates of participation. Hispanics in Boston have one of the lowest per capita incomes and one of the highest poverty rates; however, Hispanics in Brooklyn and Philadelphia are as poor or poorer and yet in both cases the participation rate for Puerto Ricans is *more than twice as high.*

Supply and Demand Factors. Another important influence on Hispanic participation rates is the total number of Catholic schools available (the supply) relative to the total Hispanic school-aged population (the potential demand). Comparisons of Hispanic participation rates across different dioceses can be standardized using this ratio, which can be defined as the diocese's "burden" ratio. In addition, dioceses can be compared by dividing the number of Catholic schools by the total number of Hispanics who are enrolled. This second ratio (the "absorption" ratio) allows us to compare how many Hispanics, on average, are being incorporated into each diocese's schools.

Table 9.4 compares participation rates for Mexican-dominant and Puerto Rican-dominant, school-aged populations, with the number of Catholic schools, the number of Hispanics enrolled, and the total Hispanic school-aged population in 14 of our 18 dioceses. Omaha, with by far the highest participation rate (6.8), has a comparatively minuscule Mexican school-aged population (5,123) to incorporate within its 77 schools, and the diocese is absorbing, on average, just 4.5 Mexicans per school. Most other dioceses are faced with Mexican school-aged populations that are enormous, yet all but Los Angeles have fewer schools than Omaha. El Paso, with the second lowest participation rate, is absorbing, on average, 201.3 students per school, more than any other diocese. Los Angeles has 4 to 20 times more schools than any of the other dioceses, but also has a Hispanic school-aged population (1,096,481) that is 15 times as large as the other dioceses' school-aged populations *combined.* The Los Angeles burden ratio is on par with Orange and Houston, but Los Angeles is absorbing more than double the number of Mexican students per school.

These same supply and demand factors are also evident in the variation in the Puerto Rican rates. Orlando's low participation rate (2.3) is offset by the fact that it has the highest burden ratio of the seven dioceses listed. Boston has a burden ratio one-fifth the size of Orlando's but is absorbing only one-third as many students per school. Brooklyn has a burden ratio four times as large as Boston's but is absorbing 10 times as many students per school.

These results suggest that supply and demand factors have to be

Table 9.4. Catholic School Participation Rates, Burden Ratios, and Absorption Ratios for Selected Dioceses with Mexican-Dominant and Puerto Rican–Dominant School-Aged Populations, 1989–1990

Diocese	Participa-tion (%)	School-aged population	Enrolled pop-ulation	No. schools	Burden ratio	Absorption ratio
Mexican dominant						
Omaha	6.8	5,123	348	77	66.5	4.5
Los Angeles	4.0	1,096,481	44,017	289	3,794.1	152.3
Oakland	3.8	79,474	3,009	64	1,241.7	47.0
San Jose	3.2	68,512	2,226	35	1,957.5	63.6
Orange	2.6	157,267	4,040	42	3,744.5	96.2
El Paso	2.0	186,258	3,019	15	12,417.2	201.3
Houston	1.4	248,150	3,516	55	4,511.8	63.9
Puerto Rican dominant						
Newark	12.9	8,705	11,202	222	392.1	50.5
Philadelphia	10.5	37,083	3,895	308	120.4	12.6
Brooklyn	8.8	197,997	17,380	186	1,064.5	93.4
Cleveland	7.8	17,087	1,331	169	101.1	7.9
Rockville Centre	6.5	37,383	2,415	102	366.5	23.7
Boston	3.7	50,161	1,838	186	269.7	9.9
Orlando	2.3	39,999	929	31	1,290.2	30.0

Sources: 1990 Census School District Special Tabulation, NCEA, Diocesan education departments.

taken more seriously in any analysis of the variation in participation rates across dioceses. Omaha's high Mexican participation rate relative to other dioceses is evidently not related to income; the most important factor appears to be its relatively small Mexican population and its relatively large number of schools. Likewise, Orlando's relatively low Puerto Rican participation rate may be chiefly a function of the fact that the diocese has only 31 schools. On the other hand, Boston has a relatively large number of schools and a moderately sized Puerto Rican school-aged population; however, the Puerto Rican Catholic school participation rate is still extremely low. If we compare Boston with Cleveland, we see that they have comparable numbers of Catholic schools, comparable absorption rates, and comparable per capita income levels; however, the Cleveland participation rate is more than twice the size of Boston's. In this case, the key factor could be simply school demand: Cleveland's Puerto Rican school-aged population is roughly one-third the size of Boston's.

Prior Exposure to Catholic Schools. Puerto Rican rates of participation may be higher than Mexican rates for a third reason: the two groups' contrasting exposure to Catholic education in their respective territories of origin. Most Catholic schools in Mexico have long been concentrated in a handful of states, only one of which, Michoacán, has been a major sending area for migrants to the United States. In Mexico, there are two applicants for every place in the parochial schools, but the rate of Catholic school participation is only 7% (Grayson, 1992). As a result, despite the longevity of their migration, Mexicans have tended to be written off by the North American Church as candidates for Catholic school education (see Dolan & Hinojosa, 1994). In the southwest, nearly all of the Church's emphasis in the 1920s was on providing Mexican immigrant families with access to parish-based religious education classes (the Confraternity of Christian Doctrine, or CCD), on the assumption that their children would be attending local public schools. This historical emphasis (or neglect), coupled with income barriers, may well have created a profound aversion to Catholic school education on the part of Mexican immigrants and their descendants.

Puerto Ricans, by contrast, are far more likely to have been exposed to Catholic schools in Puerto Rico, thanks to a major campaign by the U.S. bishops in the 1950s to expose migrating Puerto Ricans to American-style religious practices and institutions. One pillar of this campaign was the Bishops' drive to expand the reach of the Catholic schools in Puerto Rico to even the remotest corners of the island through roving teaching staffs and subsidized tuition for the poor (see Dolan & Vidal, 1994). Meanwhile, within in the United States, the Bishops of several major dioceses instituted special "social action" programs for newly arriving Puerto Ricans and began a campaign to establish "integrated" parishes and schools among Puerto Ricans and Euro-Americans living in the same inner-city Catholic neighborhoods (Fitzpatrick, 1971). These campaigns evidently fell short of achieving the sweeping results envisioned by their proponents, but they stood in stark contrast to the relative neglect accorded the earliest Mexican immigrants. Even their staunchest critics acknowledge that these programs helped reduce the "social distance" between Puerto Rican migrants and the "official" U.S. Church (see Diaz-Stevens, 1993).

Cubans

The Cuban case further illustrates the need to take into account both the specific characteristics of the immigrant group and the historical and institutional peculiarities of the diocese in which it is located.

Roughly half of the total Cuban population in the United States resides within the Miami archdiocese. No other large immigrant group, Hispanic or non-Hispanic, has its numbers so concentrated in a single location. Moreover, the Cubans first arrived in the early 1960s when the Miami diocese was struggling just to survive and desperately needed a new mission. The Cubans were middle class and Catholic, and as frontline warriors in the Kennedy administration's anticommunist foreign policy, they were recipients of generous U.S. funding and political support. Serving the Cubans thus became a major part of the new bishop's plans for rebuilding his troubled diocese (see McNally, 1984).

The first Cuban refugees to arrive in Miami were not just Catholic, they were *devoutly* Catholic; some 80% had attended Catholic schools prior to fleeing Cuba (see Boswell & Curtis, 1983). By the mid-1960s, the refugees already had filled the Archdiocese's Catholic schools to capacity and waiting lists swelled. In response, several Catholic religious orders banded together to establish new parochial schools, but the demand continued to outstrip supply. A top Catholic prelate in Miami, quoted in the early 1980s, noted: "We could double the [Catholic school] enrollment today if we could build the schools fast enough . . . the inability to meet the demands for additional schools is one of the major problems we face" (Boswell & Curtis, 1983, p. 127).

The unique historical and institutional circumstances of the Cubans in Miami help explain why their rate of Catholic school participation is one of the highest among Hispanics. The Cuban rate of 7.1% in Miami is higher than the proxy rate for Mexicans everywhere but is lower than the proxy rate for Puerto Ricans in Brooklyn (8.8), Philadelphia (10.4), and Newark (12.9). However, this comparison is misleading on two counts. First, Miami in 1990 had only 46 Catholic schools, compared with 186, 308, and 222 for Brooklyn, Philadelphia, and Newark, respectively. At the same time, its Hispanic school-aged population of 214,868 was the largest of the four dioceses, larger even than Brooklyn's (197,997). Thus, Miami's burden ratio was 3299.5, higher than the rate for all Puerto Rican-dominant dioceses, and higher than the rate for several Mexican-dominant dioceses. Furthermore, Miami's absorption rate of 335.5 tops the list of all 19 dioceses in this study, with El Paso (201.3) and Los Angeles (152.3) a distant second and third.

Another reason the 7.1% rate is misleading is that not all the Cubans in Catholic school attend the "official" schools. Large numbers of Cubans also can be found in the so-called "Hispanic Catholic Schools" that are run independently of the Archdiocese but receive support from local parishes. The Hispanic Catholic Schools were set up in the 1980s by recently arrived immigrants from Cuba and Central America who did not feel comfortable in the parishes and who could not afford Catholic school tuition. The Hispanic schools provide elementary school and religious instruction to an estimated 10,000 students annually. While respecting their autonomy, the Archdiocese has insisted that teachers in these schools participate in its teacher certification program; it also has encouraged students in the schools to receive their first communion in the parishes.

No reliable estimate of the Cuban population in the Hispanic Catholic Schools is available. However, their estimated total enrollment of 10,000 students is two-thirds the enrollment level in the "official" Catholic school system. If we combine the two enrollment figures, the Hispanic participation rate in Miami jumps to 11.9%, second only to Newark (12.9%). Thus, the Cuban participation rate in Miami is either high or very high despite the fact that its Hispanic per capita income ranks somewhere in the middle.

Haitians

The complex interplay of income and nonincome variables is also apparent in the case of Haitians, who, like Hispanics, are overwhelmingly identified with Catholicism. The three dioceses with the largest Haitian concentrations are Brooklyn, Miami, and Newark. However, only two U.S. dioceses—Miami and Boston—collect data on Haitian enrollment in their Catholic schools. Miami began in 1985–86, Boston in 1989–90. To supplement these statistics, school-by-school surveys were conducted in Newark and Brooklyn in the spring of 1997. The results for all four dioceses are presented in Table 9.5.

Table 9.5. Haitian Enrollment in Catholic Schools, Selected Dioceses, 1985–1996

Diocese	85–86	89–90	90–91	91–92	92–93	93–94	94–95	95–96	96–97
Miami	680	—	—	938	958	1,015	1,111	1,093	—
Boston									
City	—	730	1,096	980	1,013	1,065	—	1,014	990
GMA	—	—	—	—	—	1,892	2,053	2,432	2,338
Newark	—	—	—	408	—	—	—	—	1,457
Brooklyn	—	—	—	—	—	—	—	—	3,402

Sources: Education departments, Boston and Miami; interviews with Catholic school principals in Brooklyn and Newark.

Notes: Brooklyn and Newark figures are for elementary schools only. "GMA" is the Greater Metropolitan Area.

Because of data gaps, it is not possible to estimate Haitian rates of Catholic school participation for all four dioceses. Moreover, the rates that can be estimated may be somewhat inflated, due to the census undercount and other statistical difficulties.[1] For Miami, the Haitian enrollment for 1991–92 compares with a total Haitian school-aged population of 26,574.[2] The rate of participation is 4.0%.

For Boston, the most reliable method for deriving the 1990 participation rate is to retain the City of Boston enrollment figure for 1989–90 and to limit the Haitian school-aged population to Haitians living in the immediate metropolitan area, including those areas most heavily populated by Haitians (i.e., Dorchester, Mattapan, Brockton, Cambridge, Somerville, and Lynn). Using this method, we arrive at a school-aged population of 6,001 and a participation rate of 12.2%.

For Brooklyn, we can calculate the *current* participation rate for Haitians (at the elementary level) by retaining the 1996–97 enrollment figure (3,402) and estimating the annual increase in the school-aged population that has occurred since 1990.[3] Through this latter method, we arrive at a 1996 participation rate (elementary only) of 13.1%.

Comparison of Hispanic and Haitian Rates. The Haitian rates of participation in Brooklyn and Boston are either higher or much higher than the Hispanic participation rates in all 18 dioceses. This is true even though the median family income of Haitians in 1990 was only slightly higher than that of Puerto Ricans and Mexicans. Two hypotheses could be advanced to explain these relatively high Haitian rates.

First, like Cubans, Haitians had a strong prior exposure to Catholic schools in their homeland. Some 90% of the elementary and secondary schools in Haiti were once owned by the Catholic Church. In 1972, out of 72 schools in the area of the capital, Port-au-Prince, alone, 30 were Catholic, with a combined enrollment of more than 10,000 pupils (Des Mangles, 1992).

Second, while costly for Haitians, U.S. Catholic schools are also viewed as an important vehicle for social advancement. Even poor Haitian immigrants place a high value on education for their children, to the exclusion of other personal and family needs. One U.S. priest with experience in Haiti summarizes the issue as follows:

Almost every parish in Haiti, even those way out in the hills, has a Catholic school. So a lot of our Haitian immigrants—I would say the majority of our people here—have gone through the Catholic school system in Haiti. They know what it is and they want to get their children into the Catholic schools here. And the parents will sacrifice almost everything else just to pay for their kids to attend.

Comparison of Haitian Rates Between Dioceses. Several hypotheses also might be advanced to explain why Haitian participation rates are so much higher in Boston and Brooklyn than in Miami. First, Haitians began arriving in large numbers in Miami only in the 1980s; by contrast, Haitian immigration to the northeast, particularly New York, dates to the 1960s. This longer period of settlement in the northeast has given immigrants there more time to become established in local parishes and to position themselves in the schools. Second, Boston and Brooklyn each have five to six times as many Catholic schools as Miami, and their burden and absorption ratios for Hispanics are much lower. Haitians in Boston and Brooklyn tend to reside in inner-city areas where many Catholic schools are desperate for new students just to say open. By contrast, the Catholic schools in Miami are dominated by Cubans and most schools already had substantial waiting lists long before the first Haitians arrived. Thus, length of residency and sheer availability of schools clearly would favor Haitians in the northeast.

A third factor is that Haitians in Miami tend to be poorer and far less fluent in English than their counterparts up north (see Stafford, 1987; Stepick, 1992). In Miami, Haitians congregate around three Haitian Catholic "missions" and attend mass and receive social services in their native Creole tongue. None of these Haitian missions has its own Catholic school; most school-aged children attend nearby public schools and roughly 1,000 attend weekly CCD classes in Creole.

One of the apparent anomalies in the data is that Haitian Catholic school enrollment is markedly higher in Boston than in Newark and Miami, even though the Haitian population in the latter two dioceses is estimated by Catholic sources to be twice as large. Two factors might explain this result. First, tuition levels are evidently much lower at the Catholic schools in Boston where Haitians are in attendance. For example, elementary school tuition at St. Angela, one of the largest Haitian parishes in Boston, is only $1,300; by contrast, the average tuition in Miami elementary schools is $3,750. Second, according to Catholic sources in Boston, nearly all Haitian students receive financial support either from the diocese or from two private corporations with an interest in promoting Haitian education.

Asian Groups: Filipinos, Koreans, and Vietnamese

The participation rates for Filipinos in San Jose (15.7%) and Los Angeles (16.2%) are the highest among the immigrant groups included in our study. These rates are nearly the same despite the fact that the Filipino school-aged populations and enrollment levels in the two dioceses are vastly different. Los Angeles has a Filipino school-aged population of 55,168 (with 8,941 enrolled) compared with 8,013 for San Jose (with 1,257 enrolled). Los Angeles also has 289 schools compared with just 35 for San Jose. Thus, the Los Angeles absorption ratio is 30.9 compared with 35.9 for San Jose.

It is tempting to interpret these high Filipino participation rates as largely a function of income. According to 1990 census data, the median family income of Filipinos was $47,794. This compares with $32,007 for Cubans, $25,556 for Haitians, and $21,585 for Mexicans. However, as we have seen, Haitian, Puerto Rican, and Cuban participation rates are also quite high, much higher than we would expect on the basis of income data alone. Haitian participation rates in Brooklyn and Boston are about 75% as large as Filipino participation rates in Los Angeles and San Jose. However, Filipinos on average earn nearly twice as much as Haitians do.

Comparison of Filipinos with another Asian group—Koreans—also casts doubt on income as the primary cause of variation in the rates of participation. Korean median income in 1990 was $33,406, which is higher than the median income for both Cubans and Haitians. However, in San Jose, the one diocese that collects statistics on Korean enrollment in the Catholic schools, the Korean participation rate was only 5.0%. Thus, Koreans in San Jose have a much lower participation rate than Cubans in Miami or Haitians in the Northeast.

Again, an important source of the explanation is likely to be prior exposure to Catholic schools. In the Philippines (which, like Haiti, is more than 70% Catholic), Catholic schools "have the highest esteem among the Filipino people," says a diocesan ethnic ministry coordinator. "Immigrants from the Philippines bring that level of esteem—and maybe with it, a high level of expectation—about the Catholic schools when they come to the U.S."

Prominent among these Filipino expectations is that Catholic schools will protect the virtue and moral standing of their daughters, which many Filipinos fear the public schools will not do. In addition, because of the unique sense of extended kinship ties in the Philippines, Catholic school teachers often serve as the "third parent" for young Filipina women.

Another factor in the Philippines is the price of the schools: While some of the expensive private schools are affordable only by the wealthy, the Church in the Philippines runs an extensive system of parochial schools that are "fairly inexpensive" and accessible to large numbers of Filipinos.

Koreans, by contrast, have no prior experience with Catholic schools back home. Korea's religious culture is primarily Buddhist, not Christian, and the dominant Christian group is Protestant not Catholic. Moreover, whereas education is extremely important in the Korean value system, it has never been viewed, even by Korean Catholics, as something to be carried out in denominational institutions. According to a priest with experience with the Korean community:

> It's not the role of the church, of religion, to socialize the individual in Korea. It's the role of the government, or in the language of Confucianism, it's the role of the king. He must provide for his subjects this sense of moral "uprightness" through education. That's why Catholic schools never caught on in Korea. It would be too different. Why shouldn't your child be socialized with all the other children? The whole point is to become Korean, to become an "upright" person. To separate the kids and send them to religious schools, people wouldn't want to do that. Even if they were ardent Catholics.

Another factor in the case of the Koreans is their relationship to local parishes. Cubans, Haitians, and Filipinos tend to be highly integrated into the life of these parishes: The parents are usually bilingual, and they frequently serve in important positions on parish pastoral councils; moreover, they generally encourage their children to receive religious instruction in English. Koreans, by contrast, almost always seek to organize their faith activities separately from other groups. Since the late 1980s, Korean Catholics have fought for and won the right to build 30 new Korean-language churches in California, New Jersey, Illinois, Maryland, Missouri, Texas, Oregon, Alaska, and New York. In addition, in 60 or more other locations, they have established Korean Catholic communities in existing Churches that function as a "parish within the parish." All of these Churches and quasi-parishes offer masses in Korean and some sponsor Korean-language classes. As many as 90% of the Korean children in these parishes attend a Korean version of CCD. No other Catholic immigrant group has achieved this degree of ethnic "autonomy" since the abolition of the old Euro-American "national parishes" in the 1920s. (For complete list of Korean Catholic communities in the United States and abroad, see Diocese of Seoul, 1996.)

The experience of the Vietnamese lies somewhere between that of the Filipinos and the Koreans. On the one hand, the Vietnamese are disproportionately Catholic relative to their brothers and sisters back home, and many first-generation immigrants and refugees have significant prior experience with Catholic schools. Thus, like the Filipinos, the Vietnamese are generally anxious to utilize local Catholic schools. At the same time, those Vietnamese Catholic communities that organize their faith activities separately from local parishes generally find that they do not have equal access to the parish schools. In San Jose, for example, the Vietnamese community comprises a semi-autonomous "apostolate" that pays monthly rent to the parishes to use Church facilities at nonpeak times. A priest who works with the Vietnamese community notes that because of this arrangement, Vietnamese applicants to the Catholic schools are considered "out of parish" and are not given the same priority as native-born American applicants. "There are some Vietnamese in the Catholic schools but not as many as we would expect [given our numbers]. There could be many, many more."

The 1990 Catholic school enrollment figure for Vietnamese in San Jose was 261. Comparing this figure with an estimated Vietnamese school-aged population of 5,820, we obtain a Catholic school participation rate of 4.5%. There is strong evidence to suggest that the Vietnamese participation rate is much higher in dioceses where the Vietnamese are more highly integrated into local parishes (Orange) or where they maintain their own quasi-national parishes (New Orleans). For example, in New Orleans, where the total Vietnamese population is estimated by Catholic sources at only 18,000, 387 Vietnamese schoolchildren recently attended a single Catholic school. If the Vietnamese school-aged population in New Orleans was estimated at 4,167, the rate of Catholic school participation would be an astounding 9.3%. This is more than double the rate in San Jose, where the Vietnamese population is estimated to be seven times larger. (No comparable data are available for Orange, whose Vietnamese population is even larger than San Jose's.)

Comparison of Immigrant and Nonimmigrant Rates

The relative contribution of Hispanic and Asian immigrants to the Catholic schools can be further gauged by comparing immigrant groups' rates of participation with those of other ethnic groups. These comparisons can be made only in those dioceses for which comprehensive data are readily available. Table 9.6 compares rates of participation for various groups in Los Angeles, San Jose, Oakland, San Francisco, Miami, Chicago, Brooklyn, Boston, and Philadelphia.

In the midwest and the northeast, the traditional bastions of Catholic school education, the White participation rate is larger than the rates for all other groups. However, in the west and the southeast, immigrants and their descendants generally have higher rates of participation than both Whites and Blacks. The Filipino participation rates in Los Angeles

Table 9.6. Catholic School Enrollment Rates for Immigrant and Nonimmigrant Groups by Region and City, Selected Dioceses, 1990 (percent of group's school-aged population)

West		Midwest		Northeast		Southeast	
Group	*Enroll. rate*	*Group*	*Enroll. rate*	*Group*	*Enroll. rate*	*Group*	*Enroll. rate*
San Jose		**Chicago**		**Philadelphia**		**Miami**	
Filipino	15.4	White	15.8	White	19.9	Cuban	7.1
White	6.3	Asian	14.4	Asian	10.8	Asian	4.4
Total Asian	5.7	Mexican	10.0	Puerto Rican	10.5	Haitian	4.0
Black	5.7	Black	7.2	Black	5.9	White	2.8
Korean	5.0					Nicaraguan	0.8
Vietnamese	4.5			**Brooklyn**		Black	0.7
Mexican	3.2			White	18.2		
				Haitian	12.1		
Los Angeles				Black	11.3		
Filipino	16.2			Puerto Rican	8.8		
Mexican	4.0			Asian	3.0		
Black	3.7						
White	3.3			**Boston**			
				White	13.8		
Oakland				Haitian	12.2		
Black	11.4			Black	6.5		
Asian	4.8			Asian	5.2		
Mexican	3.8			Puerto Rican	3.7		
White	1.7						
San Francisco							
Asian	13.6						
White	11.3						
Hispanic	10.4						
Black	7.7						

Sources: Diocesan enrollment data; 1990 U.S. Census; interviews with school principals.

and San Jose, for example, dwarf those of every other group, including Whites. In San Jose, White participation is still proportionately higher than Korean and Vietnamese participation and double the rate of participation of Mexicans. In Miami, however, both Cubans and Haitians have higher participation rates than Whites.

In Boston, the Haitian participation rate is nearly as large as that for Whites and is almost double the rate for Blacks. In Brooklyn, the Haitian rate is roughly the same as the Black rate and two-thirds the size of the White rate.

CONCLUSION

Most of the post-1965 immigrant groups do not seek to establish their own national parishes or schools. Within the context of a more "integrated" parish setting, these groups generally seek to utilize the existing Catholic schools; however, they do so at widely varying rates that are impossible to predict on the basis of a single factor. Mexicans, far and away the largest U.S. immigrant group, also have the lowest rate of Catholic school utilization. To the extent that Mexicans continue to dominate the U.S. immigrant population, the aggregate contribution of immigrants to the Catholic school system is likely to remain minimal. However, some of the smaller immigrant groups have rates of participation that are very high—indeed, in some cases much higher than for Whites or Blacks. In some dioceses, these high rates of participation also translate into impressively high percentages of the total Catholic school enrollment. Cubans account for 50–60% of the annual Catholic school enrollment in Miami, and in dioceses in the northeast and southwest, Hispanic groups constitute between 20 and 40% of total enrollment. Equally impressive is the fact that Filipinos now account for more than 10% of the total Catholic school enrollment in Los Angeles and San Jose.

The rate of immigrant participation in Catholic schools varies widely from group to group, and within each group may vary widely from diocese to diocese. This study has identified endogenous and exogenous (i.e., environmental) variables that appear to explain some of this variation. The most striking general conclusion is that income alone is a poor predictor of the variation in the participation rates among Hispanic and Asian immigrants. Other factors, including the immigrants' prior exposure to Catholic schools in their country of origin as well as obstacles or opportunities afforded by local school and parish environments, seem just as important in shaping their school-choice preferences and decisions.

Future ethnographic research needs to zero in on the mixture of constraints and incentives that inform these school-choice preferences and decisions. One important question is the extent to which immigrant use of Catholic schools expresses a specific commitment to *Catholic* education as opposed to a more general desire for quality education that is coincidentally Catholic. Other studies have shown that inner-city Catholics and non-Catholics may turn to the Catholic schools primarily to escape the drugs and violence and perceived lack of discipline in inner-city public schools. Among immigrant Catholics with prior exposure to Catholic schools, we might expect a greater commitment to the "Catholicity" of the schools. Evidence from New Orleans on the Vietnamese and from Miami on the Cubans would appear to support this view. For example, in Miami, despite a large and growing influx of non-Catholic Cubans since 1980, over 98% of the Catholic school population remains Catholic. By contrast, some of the evidence for Haitians appears to point in the opposite direction: In Newark, the Catholic school with the largest Haitian enrollment is dominated completely by non-Catholics, and, overall, non-Catholics account for over one-quarter of the total Haitian enrollment in the diocese.

Second, more needs to be known about the specific income levels of the families attending the Catholic schools. Most of the income data presented in this study were for Hispanic and Asians in the *diocesan population at large*. Income was not found to be strongly correlated with rates of participation; however, it could be that only the wealthier segment of each immigrant group is sending its children to Catholic school. If so, we would still need to know why one group's wealthier population is utilizing the Catholic schools at a higher rate than this same segment in another group. In short, income alone still does not seem to provide all the answers.

Third, more needs to be known about the *exogenous* variables that affect immigrant participation. It is striking that three dioceses whose Catholic school systems are reputedly among the best organized in the country—Chicago, Philadelphia, and San Francisco—have the highest rates of participation for both Asians and Hispanics, despite their contrasting locations, degree of Mexican-dominance, and Hispanic and Asian income levels. Are there exogenous influences—not only the size of the school system but also its *administrative capacity*—that at least partially overdetermine the endogenous influences? In addition to contrasting the sheer number of Catholic schools in the different dioceses, we need to know more about the variation in the size of the schools as well as the length of waiting lists and the tuition rates. The average tuition in some dioceses is two to three times the level in other dioceses. In addition, the perceived quality of the public schools varies from diocese to diocese, and from metropolitan area to metropolitan area. Some groups, particularly Asians, are more likely to live in the suburbs and to have additional income to dedicate to Catholic schools, assuming such schools are available. On the other hand, their proximity to the suburbs generally would afford them access to higher-quality public schools.

A final area of research concerns the impact of bilingual education, English as a Second Language (ESL), and other financial support and subsidies. Only a few dioceses appear to utilize the available federal monies, and two of these dioceses (Chicago and Brooklyn) have two of the highest participation rates for Hispanics and Asians. Some groups (e.g., Haitians) appear to be relying heavily on financial aid, and this may be boosting their participation rates, relative to other groups. A more systematic analysis of the language spoken by and financial resources available to immigrants in different dioceses, and the effects these might have on immigrant participation rates, should be of significance to Catholic policy makers seeking to chart the future of Catholic schools.

Acknowledgments. I want to thank the numerous diocesan staff and Catholic school principals who graciously consented to be interviewed for this project. I also want to thank the following people who helped me organize and conduct the research: Dr. Jeffrey Passel, a highly renowned demographer and immigration specialist with the Urban Institute, who introduced me to on-line data sources from the U.S. Census Bureau; Mary Jo Milks of the National Catholic Educational Association, who shared additional enrollment data that were not available from local dioceses; Michael Mihalecz, a graduate student in the Catholic University Psychology Department, who conducted most of the interviews with Catholic school principals and staff in Brooklyn and Newark.

NOTES

1. The 1990 Census School District Special Tabulation does not include "Haitian" as a possible race or nationality. The only available category for measuring Haitian nationality is the school-aged population identified as speaking "French or French Creole" at home. Depending on the region, this group could include large numbers of immigrant children from France and Canada (i.e., French Canadians) as well as French-speaking "Cajuns" who live primarily in Louisiana.

2. The Haitian school-aged population was derived from the French- and French Creole-speaking population. A careful review of the data revealed that the number of French or Canadian persons living within the Archdiocese was negligible. In addition, because so many of the Haitians in Miami are post-1980 arrivals, there is an unusually high number who speak primarily French Creole.

3. The method for doing so is as follows: Haitian sources in Brooklyn estimate that the Haitian population has increased by 7,000 persons annually since the 1990 Census. The 1990 Census also estimated that 34% of the Haitians arriving between 1987 and 1990 were school-aged children. If we assume this ratio also holds for the post-1990 period, then 14,280 school-aged Haitians have arrived since 1990. The total school-aged population (combining the 1990 and post-1990 figures) would be 25,874. However, this figure would not include untold thousands that may be undercounted by the Census.

REFERENCES

Boswell, T. D., & Curtis, J. R. (1983). *The Cuban-American experience.* Totowa, NJ: Rowman & Allanheld.

Des Mangles, L. G. (1992). *The faces of gods: Voudou and Roman Catholicism in Haiti.* Chapel Hill: University of North Carolina Press.

Diaz-Stevens, A. M. (1993). *Oxcart Catholicism: The impact of Puerto Rican migration on the Archdiocese of New York.* Notre Dame: University of Notre Dame Press.

Diocese of Seoul. (1996). *Handbook of the Pastoral Commission for Overseas Koreans.* Seoul: Diocese of Seoul.

Dolan, J. P., & Hinojosa, G. (Eds.). (1994). *Mexican Americans and the Catholic Church, 1900–1965.* Notre Dame: University of Notre Dame Press.

Dolan, J. P., & Vidal, J. R. (Eds.). (1994). *Puerto Ricans and Cubans in the U.S., 1900–1965.* Notre Dame: University of Notre Dame Press.

Fitzpatrick, J. (1971). *Puerto Rican Americans: The meaning of migration to the mainland.* Englewood Cliffs, NJ: Prentice-Hall.

Foley, M. (1997). *Welcoming the stranger: The Catholic Church and the new immigrants* (Working Paper No. 1, Program on Religion and the New Immigrants). Washington, DC: Catholic University Life Cycle Institute.

Grayson, G. W. (1992). *The Catholic Church in Mexico.* Washington, DC: Center for Strategic and International Studies.

McNally, M. J. (1984). *Catholicism in South Florida, 1868–1968.* Gainesville: University of Florida Press.

Stafford, S. B. (1987). Language and identity: Haitians in New York City. In E. M. Chaney & C. R. Sutton (Eds.), *Caribbean life in New York City: Sociocultural dimensions* (pp. 202–217). New York: Center for Migration Studies.

Stepick, A. (1992). The refugees nobody wants: Haitians in Miami. In G. Grenier & A. Stepick (Eds.), *Miami now! Immigration, ethnicity, and social change* (pp. 57–82). Gainesville: University of Florida Press.

Walch, T. (1994). The ethnic dimension in American parochial education. In T. Walch (Ed.), *Immigrant America: European ethnicity in the United States* (pp. 141–159). New York: Garland.

Conclusion: Catholic Education at the Crossroads

MAUREEN T. HALLINAN

THE END OF THE TWENTIETH CENTURY finds Catholic education at a critical juncture in its history. The world today is dramatically different from the one in which the Catholic school system originally was created and later thrived. Consequently, fundamental questions arise about the future of Catholic education. Should the mission of Catholic education be the same in the coming decades as it was in the past, when the American citizenry was less educated, less affluent, less mobile, and more homogeneous? Has expanded access to education for all social classes lessened the need for a Catholic school system? Are there better ways to engage in the ministry of education than by staffing Catholic schools? And, even if there are compelling reasons to continue Catholic schooling as it presently exists or in some new form, are these schools at all financially viable? The chapters in this volume provide important data to help answer these questions and to provide guidance for making decisions about the future of Catholic education in America.

As a number of chapters demonstrate, Catholic education is in a state of dramatic change. In the past, the Catholic school system evolved gradually, adapting to its environment as the nation grew. The accelerated rate of change that characterizes today's society requires that Catholic schools accommodate quickly to a new and different environment and that they take on challenges not confronted earlier in their history. At this crossroads in the life of Catholic education, it is imperative to engage in a reflective evaluation of Catholic schools, to ask honest questions about their future, and to ascertain whether they can continue to be a vital force in American society.

In order to assess fairly the current state of Catholic education, it is necessary to examine Catholic schools in their social context. Two factors pertaining to this context are relevant. First, the Catholic school system is a very small part of the educational enterprise in this country. Only about 6% of American students attend Catholic schools, with a smaller proportion attending other religious or nonreligious private schools. The overwhelming majority of students are enrolled in the public school system. Thus, the status and condition of the public schools, given their central role in educating American youth, is the appropriate baseline against which to evaluate the Catholic school system.

The second relevant factor about the social context of Catholic schools is the close relationship that exists between the Catholic and public school systems and the influence they have on each other. Due to strict separation of Church and state in America, Catholic schools are legally independent of the public school system. Public schools are supported by taxes, while Catholic schools are financed by tuition and private support, usually from the parish and diocese in which a school is located. Public schools are governed by district school boards, while Catholic schools have their own governing structure, usually a parish school board or council. Public schools must abide by federal and state regulations governing curriculum, length of school day and year, staff credentials, graduation requirements, special education mandates, and a host of other rules and regulations. Catholic school officials have greater freedom to make decisions about governance, curriculum, staffing, and students. They can make decisions about educational practice and policy without being constrained by some of the bureaucratic apparatus that governs the public schools.

Although the Catholic and public school systems are structurally and functionally independent, they maintain a close relationship and exert considerable influence on each other. Both public and Catholic school systems are societal institutions that serve a similar clientele, operate in the same community, and have the same purpose. This shared institutional mission creates numerous informal interdependencies between the two school systems.

One way the Catholic and public schools influence each other is through finances. In one sense, Catholic schools subsidize the public school system. Catholic schools save taxpayers a considerable amount of money by removing their students from the public schools. If the 2.5 million students who attend 8,000 Catholic schools were to enroll in the public school system, the budget implications would be staggering. At the same time, public schools indirectly provide financial resources to the Catholic schools. Several services that are not available in most Catholic schools, such as special education programs or bilingual programs, are provided by the public schools for Catholic school students. In addition, Catholic school students may participate in summer school classes, recreational activities, after-school programs, and other activities that are sponsored by the public school district.

Interestingly, the financial impact of Catholic and public schools on each other is not the same. Catholic schools subsidize public schools by saving public schools the per-pupil costs of educating children enrolled in Catholic schools. But the services public schools provide to Catholic school students, while benefiting Catholic school children, do not save the Catholic schools any money, and represent no significant cost to the public schools. They already provide these services for public school students.

The public and Catholic schools also influence each other through competition for students. This competition has remained covert for the past 2 centuries. However, recent proposals for educational reform, and particularly school-choice proposals, have brought competition to the surface. Proposals to fund private education by providing vouchers for tuition or fees from public school funds have underscored the concept of market competition for students. If voucher plans receive public support, schools will be competing overtly for students.

In addition, the two school systems influence each other by representing different models of school design, organization, and governance. Catholic schools typically are smaller than public schools; have less teacher mobility, greater discipline, and stricter rules and regulations; and emphasize social values and community service. Public schools are more heterogeneous with respect to student and faculty demographic characteristics and religion, offer a more diverse curriculum, service a higher percentage of disabled students, and stress the avoidance of deviant behavior more than the development of community responsibility. By comparing the two models, teachers and administrators in both school systems learn a great deal about how best to produce academically successful and socially responsible students.

In short, the Catholic school system, while small in comparison to the public school system, remains an important component of the educational enterprise in this country. Catholic schools serve a significant number of students, at a considerable cost savings to the public schools. Catholic schools influence the policies and practices of the public schools. Finally, Catholic schools provide an alternative to the public schools for parents who prefer the Catholic schools' religious and philosophical orientation. Given the significant role the Catholic schools play in the current educational enterprise in America, the future of Catholic schools necessarily will have a profound effect on the public school system and on education in general in the United States.

COMPARISON OF CATHOLIC AND PUBLIC SCHOOLS

Whether Catholic schools continue to operate in the same way they have in the past depends to a large extent on characteristics not only of contemporary Catholic schools but also of the public school system. One rationale for Catholic schools must be that they play a role in society not played by the public schools. If Catholic schools fail to make a unique contribution to society, then the Catholic school system is redundant and no longer justified.

In evaluating Catholic schools, four areas need to be considered: student academic achievement, religious education, social development, and citizenship. Student academic achievement is a fundamental goal of all schools. Catholic schools must, therefore, be judged by this standard, no matter what else they might provide. If Catholic schools fail to foster student learning, they fail as schools. Moreover, if Catholic schools provide a poor education to students, they also fail in their religious mission of modeling service and dedication to youth.

The quality of the public schools is one standard against which to judge the success of Catholic schools in terms of student academic achievement. However, the public schools vary widely in terms of student performance. A reasonable comparison would be between Catholic and public schools that are similar in relevant characteristics. Another comparison would be between the average achievement of public and Catholic school students. If Catholic schools performed significantly worse than comparable public schools, then any justification for their existence would be questionable.

The second area to consider in evaluating Catholic schools is religious education. The Catholic school system was founded to provide a religious as well as an academic education for Catholic students. American society is arguably more secular today than a century ago, and religious education has changed accordingly. The success of the Catholic schools in influencing religious belief and practice must be examined.

The third area to examine is student social development. All schools aim to teach students social skills and foster positive social interactions in a multiracial and multicultural society. In evaluating Catholic schools, one must ask whether they are as effective or more effective than the public schools in nurturing positive and respectful social relations among students, including those who vary in ascribed and achieved characteristics.

Finally, schools aim to prepare students for good citizenship. The impact of Catholic schools on student democratic participation and community responsibility must be compared with the accomplishments of the public schools in this regard. Training for democratic participation and for public and social leadership is the basis for evaluation.

Academic Achievement in Public and Catholic Schools

The public school system in America is a vast institution containing over 47 million students in elementary, middle, and secondary schools across the country. Some of these schools, including many in middle- and upper-class communities, and a few in urban areas, can be singled out for their academic excellence and outstanding social programs. The students in these schools consistently obtain higher standardized test scores and grades and have higher graduation rates than their peers in other schools. The large majority of graduates of these high schools attend and complete college. Many of them go on to graduate study at the most prestigious universities in the country or to professional schools or challenging employment. Typically, these outstanding public schools receive greater financial support from property taxes than schools in less affluent areas, and are less troubled by disciplinary problems and unmotivated students. As a result, they have the resources to provide quality education for their students.

At the other end of the continuum, many public schools in rural, suburban, and especially urban areas provide a poor education for their pupils. Low achievement test scores, high illiteracy rates, high dropout rates, and frequent occurrences of crime and violence characterize a significant number of public schools. Reform efforts have been unsuccessful in most of these schools in significantly improving academic performance. Inner-city schools, in particular, are viewed by many as virtually beyond saving, due to the physical condition of the buildings, the social conditions in the environment, and the disaffection of school administrators, teachers, and pupils. The impact of poverty on the education of children in inner-city schools has been profound and devastating.

In between the least successful and most successful public schools are the majority of schools that provide a somewhat adequate education but leave considerable room for improvement. International studies show that test scores in these schools lag behind those in countries with fewer resources than America. While the problems that plague most inner-city schools are less severe in an average public school, they are pres-ent. School administrators are faced with absenteeism, failure on school exit exams, low standardized test scores, dropouts, teenage pregnancies, and delinquent behavior.

Moreover, in many of these schools, opportunities for learning are distributed inequitably across students. For example, ability grouping or tracking, which is practiced in most public middle and high schools, widens the gap between high-achieving and low-achieving students (Hallinan, 1994). Typically, bright students are exposed to an interesting curriculum and challenged to succeed, while slower learners are as-signed to boring classes and given little motivation to perform. In ad-dition, administrative and disciplinary problems in schools consume considerable instructional time and deprive students of learning oppor-tunities. Dropout rates are high and college enrollment low.

In general, the public schools are functioning below expectation and below capability. They show a dramatic need for improvement. Among the many reasons critics cite for the failures of the public schools are that the public school system is unwieldy and difficult to manage, bureau-cratic regulations curtail creative solutions and innovative programs, socioeconomic factors limit the influence teachers have on student learn-ing, teacher morale and teacher turnover have a negative effect on in-struction, and students are not held to high standards of academic per-formance and social behavior.

Comparisons of the academic achievement of students in Catholic and non-Catholic schools by Coleman, Hoffer, and Kilgore (1982), Gree-ley (1982), and Bryk, Lee, and Holland (1993) demonstrate a small ad-vantage of Catholic schools over public schools in terms of student scores on standardized mathematics and verbal achievement tests. This Catholic school advantage persists under a variety of statistical models, procedures, and controls for selectivity (see, for example, Jencks, 1985). These scholars attribute the Catholic school advantage to a more rigor-ous curriculum, to stricter discipline, and to a greater sense of commu-nity in the Catholic schools.

Hoffer (Chapter 5) extends this body of work with a rigorous analy-sis of the *High School and Beyond* (HS&B) survey. In his chapter, Hoffer reports that the Catholic school advantage holds for mathematics and verbal achievement but not for science. He also shows that the Catholic school effect is greater for students from disadvantaged backgrounds. In addition, he finds that Catholic school students take a greater number of academic courses than public school students, suggesting that this may be the basis for the Catholic school advantage. Discipline differences have only a weak effect on academic outcomes. Hoffer also points out that organizational and institutional explanations of Catholic school achievement, such as student demographic and socioeconomic composition, market competition, institutional charter, and functional community have not yet been adequately tested.

These findings are open to different interpretations. One conclusion quickly reached by a number of researchers and practitioners is that the data provide evidence that Catholic schools offer higher-quality academic training than public schools. This appears to be a valid conclusion, based on numerous analyses of the highest-quality, national longitudinal surveys available. At the same time, the differences between the mean achievement in Catholic and public schools are not great and have not been examined for most subjects other than mathematics and English. In addition, individual schools may differ widely from the mean, so many public schools might have higher achievement than a given Catholic school and vice versa.

Another interpretation of the Catholic school advantage is that Catholic schools are doing well only in comparison to the low standard set by the public schools. One can argue that the observed differences between Catholic and public school achievement do not indicate that Catholic school students are receiving a high-quality education. Rather, the differences suggest that children in public schools perform poorly and those in Catholic schools merely less poorly.

One also may argue that the observed differences in mathematics and English scores are of little substantive significance because they are based on standardized test scores. These tests are seen by many as culturally biased and consequently an inappropriate measure of academic performance. A related argument is that standardized tests are measures of ability rather than achievement, and thus are inappropriate instruments for comparing student performance. Measures of school effects should tap into differences in learning based on instructional exposure, such as examinations based on curriculum content.

Another interpretation of the Catholic school advantage is that the age of the data on which many of the analyses were performed make them a poor measure of the status of contemporary Catholic schools. The HSB data survey was initiated in 1980 and most of the analyses were conducted on waves of this survey gathered during the 1980s. Since a number of educational reforms have been implemented in the public schools since that time, the results may not show the same achievement differences between the two school systems today. However, the more recent NELS data demonstrate a similar Catholic school advantage (Schiller, in press). Moreover, recent SAT scores also show higher results for Catholic school students.

One may ask whether the Catholic school advantage extends to subjects other than mathematics and English. One area that demands close scrutiny is science. Catholic schools typically have not had the resources available to public schools to purchase laboratory equipment and supplies for science courses. Hoffer found no difference in the science achievement of students in Catholic and public high schools, possibly indicating that resource limitations in Catholic schools dampen the advantages provided by typical Catholic school characteristics. Vocational education is another area in which the Catholic schools may lag behind the public schools because Catholic schools generally do not have the machinery or equipment needed for viable programs. An accurate comparison of Catholic and public schools' educational outcomes should include not only academic achievement, but outcomes such as college aspirations, career aspirations, educational attainment, and employment outcomes.

The Catholic school advantage also must be evaluated on the basis of which students benefit most from attending a Catholic school. Hoffer's research shows that the difference between test scores in Catholic and public schools is greater for disadvantaged students than for their more advantaged peers. Coleman and Hoffer (1987) argue that the higher test scores of underprivileged students in Catholic schools compared with public schools indicate that Catholic schools better reflect the common-school ideal because they decrease the effects of family background on student achievement.

Hoffer's analysis, in conjunction with several other analyses of the HSB and NELS data, provides convincing evidence that students from homes with weak family structure and functioning and with background disadvantages do better in Catholic schools. This finding raises intriguing questions about why Catholic schools are successful in educating disadvantaged students and about what the implications of this accomplishment are for the future of Catholic education. The results may suggest to some that the scarce resources of Catholic educators should be targeted toward the underprivileged student population, perhaps particularly in inner-city schools, where the public schools have failed so badly. The findings also may suggest that Catholic schools are an appropriate laboratory in which to study ways to improve education in general, and the education of the disadvantaged in particular. The distinguishing characteristics of Catholic education, including a challenging curriculum, discipline, homework, and a community environment, may be particularly beneficial to any student who lacks the internal motivation or familial support to succeed in school.

To maintain and improve the quality of instruction in Catholic or public schools requires a well-trained body of professional educators. In her research comparing the characteristics of teachers in Catholic and public schools, Schaub (Chapter 4) finds that Catholic school teachers are less educated, less likely to be certified, and receive lower salaries than public school teachers. Further Catholic school teachers receive less professional training and have lower involvement in management decisions. On the other hand, Catholic school teachers are more satisfied with their working conditions and jobs than public school teachers. Further Catholic school principals have more autonomy than their public school counterparts.

These results suggest that the dedication of Catholic school teachers to the profession of teaching compensates for deficiencies in their training and in their remuneration, and accounts for their greater success in promoting student achievement. Indeed, critics have charged Catholic schools with taking advantage of the commitment of their teachers by maintaining a low salary scale. Professional standards that govern the licensing of public school teachers should be enforced by administrators of Catholic schools for their faculty as well. Improved professional training for Catholic school teachers may lead students in Catholic schools to attain even higher levels of academic achievement. A particular benefit might be increased success for underprivileged students in Catholic schools.

In general, the empirical studies reveal that Catholic schools, on average, have a small but consistent academic advantage over public schools. The advantage is evident in some curricular areas but not in others. The Catholic school advantage is greatest for students in the last 2 years of school. Of considerable significance is the finding that at-risk students benefit the most from Catholic education. Researchers conclude that Catholic schools realize their academic advantage by requiring students to take a challenging academic curriculum, holding them to high academic standards, requiring self-discipline, and fostering a spirit of school community.

Clearly, not all Catholic schools are better than public schools, and many public schools far outstrip good Catholic schools. Education in both school systems needs to be improved. By imitating the strengths and avoiding the weaknesses revealed in the research analysis, Catholic and public schools can learn from each other and raise the quality of education in all schools. In general, though, Catholic schools are holding their own compared with public schools and surpassing them in some ways. The academic accomplishments of Catholic school students demonstrate that Catholic schools are making a significant contribution to the education of American youth.

Religious Education in Catholic Schools

Given that Catholic schools are found to provide quality education for their students, they meet a necessary requirement for continued existence. However, the Catholic school system was founded not only to provide students with good schools, but also to offer them systematic religious instruction. Consequently, the second characteristic on which Catholic schools must be evaluated is their success in the area of religious education.

Bryk, Lee, and Holland (1993) present a comprehensive overview of the evolution of the Catholic school system in America. The authors divide the history of Catholic schools into three periods: colonial times to 1830; 1830–1960; and 1960 to present. They relate that in the colonial era, education was viewed both as a moral undertaking and as an informal, local endeavor. Both Catholics and Protestants established schools to transmit their religious beliefs and values to their children, as well as to prepare them for adult life. Nondenominational, or common, schools also were established, and little distinction was made between the two kinds of schools.

The formal public and Catholic school systems developed during the second half of the nineteenth century and continued to expand well into the 1960s. In response to Horace Mann's advocacy of a common school for all students, the public schools adopted a broadly humanistic philosophy and curriculum. Fearful that the public schools would promote Protestantism, Catholic leaders devoted extensive resources to forming their own schools, attempting to have a Catholic school in every parish. Catholic parents were commanded to send their children to Catholic schools. This attitude, coupled with the large influx of Catholic immigrants to the United States, fed the dramatic expansion of the Catholic school system, paralleling the expansion of the public schools.

By the time the second Vatican Council met in Rome in 1962, Catholic schools were the pride of the Church. They graduated well-educated, religiously conservative, and morally sensitive students who competed favorably in American society. Vatican II, however, effectively changed the face of the Catholic Church in America and, in so doing, had a dramatic impact on the nature of Catholic schools in this country. The Council rejected the separatism of American Catholics and their suspicion of the world and its activities. It encouraged Catholics to be engaged in secular culture, while at the same time retaining the ability to evaluate it based on Catholic belief and tradition. Lay persons were encouraged to assume leadership positions in the Church and to fulfill a social mission of pursuing peace and justice.

The new openness that characterized the Catholic Church after Vatican II had a dramatic effect on Catholic schools. Scores of priests and nuns left religious life to return to lay roles in the Church. The departure of these religious, especially the nuns who were primarily responsible for staffing Catholic schools, created a need for a large number of salaried teachers. This placed a staggering financial burden on the schools. Many schools closed, and those that stayed open began to charge tuition to remain financially viable.

In addition to the impact of Vatican II on Catholic schools, the social upheaval of the 1970s played an important role in their changing mission. In response to the civil rights movement, federal mandates required desegregating the public school system. This led a large number of White families to leave the city and flee to the all-White schools of the suburbs. Based on their renewed commitment to the poor, many Catholic schools remained in the city to teach disadvantaged and poor students. The demographic composition of Catholic schools changed dramatically, especially in the inner cities, where the student population became predominantly Black and Hispanic, and, in some areas, Asian (McLellan, Chapter 1; Riordan, Chapter 2; O'Keefe and Murphy, Chapter 6; Polite, Chapter 7; Nelson, Chapter 8). Many of these students were not Catholic, resulting in a different kind of student population than formerly characterized Catholic schools.

Post-Vatican II Catholic schools began to focus on social issues, urging students to engage in social activism and community service. While retaining their strong emphasis on academic excellence, Catholic schools emerged as proponents of justice and peace. Today, Catholic schools espouse pluralism in all its forms, and welcome students of any race, ethnicity, social class, and religion.

Contemporary Catholic schools aspire to the threefold ideal presented by the National Conference of Catholic Bishops in 1972. Their goal is to teach the message of hope contained in the gospel, to build community, and to serve humankind out of a sense of Christian community. The educational philosophy of contemporary Catholic schools is based on the directives of Vatican II, which replaced the previous understanding of the Catholic Church as a hierarchical, authoritarian institution with a view of the Church as the people of God. Catholic schools model the modern Church in affirming religious freedom and ecumenism, emphasizing the social mission of the Church, and focusing on the Bible as the Word of God.

Until the 1960s, religious instruction in Catholic schools was based primarily on the Baltimore Catechism. Students memorized the tenets of Catholicism presented in question-and-answer form in this catechism.

In 1977, Rome promulgated a document called *The Catholic School*. This document presents a new approach to teaching religion. Students are invited to examine the nature of humanity and society, the meaning of human existence, and morality, against the backdrop of the life of Christ. Religious training is based on respect for diverse cultures, races, and religions, and encourages engagement with others in a spirit of dialogue.

The mission of Catholic schools described by papal directives is an ideal, and Catholic schools vary in their success in attaining this ideal. Tensions exist in the Catholic Church between those who hold to pre-Vatican II thinking and those who are committed to rebuilding a Church based on the Vatican II vision. Many of these tensions are played out in Catholic schools as conservative clergy struggle to maintain control over the educational philosophy and theology that guide Catholic education. How this struggle is resolved will determine the kind of religious training Catholic schools will offer in the next few decades.

A number of chapters in this volume present important information about characteristics of contemporary Catholic schools that help determine the extent to which they are carrying out their post-Vatican II mission. Examining the appeal of Catholic schools to immigrants, Lawrence (Chapter 9) finds variation in the motivation of various immigrant groups to send their children to Catholic schools. Immigrants who are familiar with the Catholic tradition, such as Cubans and Filipinos, often choose Catholic schools to provide a specifically Catholic education for their children. Immigrants who do not have a Christian heritage often send their children to Catholic schools solely to escape the inadequacies and dangers of the public schools. As a result, Catholic schools in the inner cities serve students with a variety of religious backgrounds in accordance with the spirit of ecumenism.

At the same time, both McLellan (Chapter 1) and Riordan (Chapter 2) report that Catholic schools, on average, continue to serve a predominantly Catholic population. About 80% of enrolled students profess to be Catholic. Thus, while the percentage of Catholic students in Catholic schools has decreased over the past 20 years, Catholic children still remain a sizable majority in most Catholic schools. It is primarily inner-city and, to some extent, rural Catholic schools whose religious composition is more heterogeneous than that of Catholic schools a couple of decades ago. This is an important finding, since one argument in favor of closing Catholic schools is that they no longer serve Catholic students. The data do not support this argument.

A characteristic of Catholic schools that has changed over the past few decades is the social class of the students. For most of its history, the Catholic school system enrolled students who were primarily from the lower and lower middle class, many of them children of immigrants. However, as American Catholics became better integrated into American society and raised their standard of living, the social class of Catholic school children changed. A large proportion of today's middle- and upper-class Catholics were educated in Catholic schools and are the parents of today's Catholic school children. Riordan (Chapter 2) reports that in 1992, half of the students graduating from Catholic secondary schools came from families in the upper quartile of the income distribution. Thus, while many are aware that Catholic schools serve underprivileged students in the inner city, they are less aware that Catholic schools serve primarily children with privileged backgrounds.

The commitment of American Catholic schools to the education of both disadvantaged and advantaged students is in keeping with the spirit of Vatican II. The mission of Catholic schools to serve the poor in inner-city schools is an impressive expression of the orientation of the modern Church. Catholic schools are providing opportunities for learning and for social mobility to children who have the fewest resources and are least able to negotiate the public schools. Further, in keeping with the Council's emphasis on ecumenism, they are serving all students who enroll, regardless of the students' religion.

Contemporary Catholic schools that educate more affluent students also reflect the principles of Vatican II. These schools aim to promote learning in a community context. They strive to make students aware of their responsibilities to others. They encourage students to work for justice and equality, to fight discrimination, and to show respect for diversity in all its forms. Catholic schools aim to prepare leaders who will make a significant contribution to society through their involvement in and influence on secular society.

While not all Catholic schools are equally successful in meeting the challenges of Vatican II, most show some evidence of the new spirit of freedom and charity created by the Council. In general, Catholic schools demonstrate remarkable progress in following the Council's dictates. The Catholic school system may be viewed as a model of how an institution can respond to a call for reform and innovation. In short, Catholic schools may be judged to be quite successful in their ministry of religious education.

Social Development

The third dimension on which to evaluate Catholic schools is the social development of students. One of the aims of schooling is to teach students how to interact appropriately with their classmates and to prepare them for their future lives in society. Part of the informal instruction students receive daily in school involves their learning and practicing social skills. These skills include treating others respectfully, listening, turn taking, sharing, helping, playing fairly, organizing tasks and people, and developing leadership skills. Many students learn these skills easily and naturally, while others require more encouragement, discipline, boundaries, and feedback.

Although most schools are fairly successful in promoting students' social development, some students exhibit social and behavioral problems that challenge the best efforts of teachers and counselors. Among the serious problems associated with preadolescents and adolescents are drug and alcohol abuse, theft, violence, teenage pregnancy, truancy, and dropping out of school. Students who engage in these behaviors jeopardize their own health and welfare and have a negative influence on their peers. Educators, government officials, parents, and community members have developed programs to assist students with these difficulties and have been successful in many cases. These programs, such as DARE, a drug and alcohol education curriculum, provide information and advice on student social behavior.

The most severe behavioral problems of students are found in the public schools. Catholic schools usually screen their applicants and withhold admission from students with problems they feel unqualified to handle. Students who exhibit persistent antisocial behavior after admission usually are dismissed. One of the reasons Catholic schools have not admitted students with serious disabilities is that Catholic schools do not qualify for the federal, state, and local funds that the public schools receive to assist these students. As a result, Catholic schools generally are not faced with students who have profound psychological and social needs.

Both Catholic and public schools utilize many of the methods social scientists identify as successful in promoting student social development. Among these strategies are teaching conflict-resolution techniques, emphasizing honesty and respect for all persons and property, promoting social integration among racially and ethnically diverse students, and encouraging students to engage in social services activities and to develop a concern for the disadvantaged.

In evaluating the contribution of Catholic schools in the area of student social development, it is important to note that while Catholic schools do not serve youth who exhibit the most serious developmental and behavioral problems, they do influence the social behavior of a large number of American youth. In teaching students the importance of sociability, social responsibility, community, and service to the underprivileged, and by stressing ethics and moral behavior, Catholic schools make a significant contribution to the social development of their students.

Training for Citizenship

Finally, Catholic schools need to examine how well they are training students for citizenship and participation in a democratic society. Jacobs (1998) argues that Catholic schools have made an outstanding contribution in this regard in the past, pointing to the contribution of religious women and men engaged in Catholic education. He argues that religious educators have used Catholic schools as a forum where students could integrate their Catholic faith and practice with American democratic principles. Ultimately, this effort shaped a new American Catholic Church, one in which the American values of pluralism and equal opportunity were embraced along with Christian values of faith, mission, and service. Accordingly, Jacobs argues that Catholic schools have made a significant contribution to the nation's moral and intellectual fabric.

Catholic schools have played a major role in several political and social movements in the United States. At the beginning of the twentieth century, Catholic educators were among the first supporters of the worker's movement. Leo XIII's masterful encyclical, *Rerum Novarum* (On Capital and Labor), emphasizing social justice for labor, was taught in nearly every Catholic school. More recently, Catholic teachers and activists were among the leaders of the civil rights movement and the peace movement. The commitment of Catholic educators to justice and equality led to widespread involvement in efforts to promote racial justice and educational equality. The philosophy of Catholic education in the twentieth century has been based on respect for human life and a mission of participation in and service to community.

Catholic education has made a significant contribution to the ongoing debate about the relationship between individualism and communal responsibility. American society prioritizes individualism, self-determination, meritocracy, and individual freedoms. At the same time, it is concerned about the common good, and criticizes an accumulation of wealth and power in the hands of a few at the expense of the majority. Catholic education strikes a balance between individualism and community. Catholic educators support the transcendent value of the individual and stress the importance of individual rights and freedom. At the same time, they reveal their belief in the centrality of community by promoting social activism and a sense of responsibility to those in need (see, for example, Youniss & Yates, 1997). Students are taught that participation in the political process of a democracy is their responsibility in order to effect a more just social order. By teaching students to bring their ethical values and religious beliefs to their involvement in secular society, Catholic education makes a significant contribution to the preparation of students for citizenship in a democracy.

In summary, a comparative evaluation of the Catholic and public schools systems demonstrates that Catholic schools are making a significant contribution to the education of American youth. In each of three areas, academic achievement, social development, and democratic participation, Catholic schools show important accomplishments that are at least as impressive as those of the public school system. In the area of religious education, Catholic schools appear to effectively integrate religious faith and practice into the overall educational training of students and, in so doing, enhance that education in many ways. The data support the conclusion that continuing Catholic school education in America benefits both the individual students attending the schools and society in general.

FINANCIAL CONSTRAINTS ON CATHOLIC SCHOOLS

While the quality and mission of contemporary Catholic schools provide compelling evidence that Catholic schools play a major role in the education of American youth, one overriding concern about their future overshadows their successes. The Catholic school system is severely underfinanced (Harris, Chapter 3). The number of Catholic schools, teachers, and students in America has decreased dramatically over the past 3 decades. The primary reason for this decline is finances. With the large exodus of nuns from religious life after Vatican II, the voluntary support provided by numerous religious teachers disappeared. Salaried lay teachers took their place, creating a heavy financial burden for the schools and the parishes that supported them. When parishes began to charge tuition for attendance at Catholic schools, more students transferred to the free public schools. These fiscal pressures accounted for the dramatic reduction in the size of the Catholic school system.

The problem of financing Catholic schools has yet to be solved. Unless a viable source of funding is found, the number of Catholic schools will continue to decline. Thompson (1998) proposes more vigorous development efforts to raise private funding for Catholic schools. With the impressive number of well-established, professional Catholic school graduates in the country today, development efforts promise to be somewhat successful.

The recent debate about school choice has raised the question again of whether public moneys should support private schools. Small-scale experiments in which vouchers are provided to students attending Catholic schools are being conducted in a few states. Preliminary results indicate that children benefit from this arrangement. Another recent experiment allows public school teachers to instruct Catholic school children who are transported to public schools for certain classes or educational activities. This program too has been favorably evaluated. These experiments suggest a slight weakening of the reluctance of the federal and state governments to provide any support for private education.

Assuming that finances will always be a problem for Catholic education, even if some degree of public support is provided, plans for the future direction of Catholic education must take fiscal considerations into account. The worst case scenario would involve no public money for Catholic schools, meager success at fund-raising efforts, and the need to set tuition low to keep Catholic schools affordable to a wide population of students. In these circumstances, a number of Catholic schools would likely have to close. A more favorable situation would see funding for Catholic schools coming from various sources, both public and private. This would allow the Catholic school system to maintain its current size and to have some flexibility about its future direction. Catholic educators need to make plans for dealing with these and other financial contingencies. This planning exercise is salutary, not only to prepare strategies for operating Catholic schools under various financial constraints, but also to force Catholics to identify their preferences and order their priorities for Catholic education under different constraints.

The Catholic school system could move in a number of different directions in the future, depending on its understanding of the teaching mission of the Church and its financial resources. One new direction would respond to a renewed appreciation for the mission of the Church to serve the poor as well as a realization that Catholic schools have been singularly successful in educating the disadvantaged. Catholic educators might decide to focus primarily on the education of underprivileged students. The financial resources presently used for Catholic schools would be directed to Catholic schools in the inner city and, perhaps, to a limited number of rural areas. Catholic schools in the suburbs would be closed or would set tuition at a level that would subsidize inner-city schools. New inner-city schools could be established if resources permitted. Development efforts would be needed, since tuition would not be available from disadvantaged students. Financially viable parishes and dioceses might be taxed to support these schools.

An alternative strategy for Catholic educators would be to gear efforts to the education of the advantaged rather than the disadvantaged.

Given a sophisticated understanding of the social and political structure of our country and of the paramount role government and business play in shaping opportunities and constraints on human behavior and quality of life, Catholic educators could commit themselves to the education of leaders, preparing talented and promising young students to assume positions of leadership, power, and influence in society. Catholic schools might channel students into politics, business, and the professions to exert influence on public policy and to guard and protect the rights of less influential citizens, including children.

The option of staffing schools for both advantaged students and those in the inner cities or rural areas does not seem realistic under current financial constraints. Without a significant input of funds from new sources, Catholic schools will continue to close. These conditions make it imperative that Catholic educators consider moving their schools in a new direction, and choosing between service to the middle and upper class or to underprivileged students is one reasonable option.

Another strategy stems from an awareness of the mediocre education students receive in many public and some Catholic schools. Catholic educators might decide to focus their efforts on improving the academic excellence of existing schools in order to have a significant influence on the quality of education in this country. While research shows a weak Catholic school advantage at present, the difference between Catholic and public schools academically is small, at best. Catholic educators might decide to make Catholic schools models of learning and academic excellence, and through their accomplishments, influence the public schools to improve the quality of public education.

Another strategy represents a change in direction for Catholic schools from providing schooling for all Catholic students, or for disadvantaged students, to some other population that is being underserved in the public schools. One such population would be low-ability students. In the public schools, students who are considered slow learners are classified most often as special education students or are assigned to programs for children with learning disabilities. These classifications frequently do not match the students' learning needs. Many slow learners do poorly or fail in mainstreamed classrooms because they do not receive the instructional help they need. Many also flounder in special education or learning disability classes because they are placed with students having vastly different abilities and needs. As a result, a large number of students suffer academically and personally because they are unable to perform the work they are given or because they are not offered the kind of instruction that meets their learning needs. Catholic educators might decide that serving the needs of slow learners, who have few educational alternatives, is congruent with the Vatican II directives to serve the needy.

The financial constraints that are pressing on contemporary Catholic schools are the result of the rapid social change that has characterized social life at the end of the twentieth century. The alternative strategies for dealing with the financial crisis of Catholic schools represent responses to this social change. Debate about these strategies, based on Church mission and philosophy, will serve to revitalize Catholic schools and help them adapt to conditions in a new environment.

Regardless of the direction in which Catholic educators move the Catholic school system over the next few decades, and the decisions that are forced on them by financial considerations, their efforts will be more fruitful to the extent that they continue in dialogue with the public schools. The involvement of a community in educating its young, whether in public or private schools, affects the political, economic, and social fabric of the community. Parents and educators from both school systems have similar concerns and share many goals. By working together, supporters of public and Catholic schools can act as a strong political force to promote the needs of youth. Communities that have worked together in the past to improve education have been successful in attaining many of their goals.

Social science research has shown that Catholic schools compete favorably with public schools in the areas of academic achievement, social development, and training for citizenship in a democratic society. The quality of the academic, social, and civic training offered by Catholic schools furnishes a compelling argument for their continued existence. In addition, through its religious education, the Catholic school system provides a value-added dimension to education. Over and above their educational accomplishments, Catholic schools provide students with a perspective on life that promotes justice, responsibility, and social service. They challenge students to live generously in community, motivated by their religious faith. By providing this alternative to public schools, which at best offer a vague humanism to sustain individual and communal behavior, Catholic schools make a unique and significant contribution to American society.

Acknowledgments. I am grateful for support from the Institute for Educational Initiatives at the University of Notre Dame and express appreciation to Vladmir Khmelkov and Warren Kubitschek for helpful comments and editorial assistance.

REFERENCES

Bryk, A. S., Lee, V. E., & Holland, P. B. (1993). *Catholic schools and the common good*. Cambridge, MA: Harvard University Press.

Coleman, J. S., & Hoffer, T. (1987). *Public and private high schools: The impact of communities*. New York: Basic Books.

Coleman, J. S., Hoffer, T., & Kilgore, S. B. (1982). *High school achievement: Public, Catholic, and private schools compared*. New York: Basic Books.

Greeley, A. M. (1982). *Catholic high schools and minority students*. New Brunswick, NJ: Transaction Books.

Hallinan, M. T. (1994). School differences in tracking effects on achievement. *Social Forces, 72*, 799–820.

Jacobs, R. (1998). U.S. Catholic schools and the religious who served them: Contributions in the 18th and 19th centuries. *Catholic Education, 1*, 364–383.

Jencks, C. (1985). How much do high school students learn? *Sociology of Education, 58*, 128–135.

Schiller, K. S. (in press). In J. G. Cibulka (Ed.), *Educational choice: Lessons from public and private schools*. Westport, CT: Greenwood Press.

Thompson, L. (1998, April–May). Funding the essential Catholic school. *Momentum*, pp. 67–68.

Youniss, J., & Yates, M. (1997). *Community service and social responsibility in youth*. Chicago: University of Chicago Press.

About the Editors and the Contributors

James Youniss, Ph.D., is Professor of Psychology and Director of the Life Cycle Institute at the Catholic University of America. Recent books include *Community Service and Social Responsibility in Youth* (University of Chicago Press; Miranda Yates, co-author), and *Roots of Civic Identity: International Perspectives on Volunteer Service and Activism in Youth* (Cambridge University Press; Miranda Yates, co-editor). He is also co-editor with Jeffrey McLellan and John Convey, of the forthcoming book, *The Catholic Character of Catholic Schools* (University of Notre Dame Press).

John J. Convey is the Provost and the St. Elizabeth Ann Seton Professor of Education at the Catholic University of America. He received his Ph.D. in research and evaluation from Florida State University in 1974, a M.Sc. in mathematics from Ohio State University in 1968, and a B.A. in mathematics from La Salle College in 1962. During the 1986–87 academic year, he was a Senior Research Fellow in the Office of Research at the United States Department of Education. Dr. Convey is the author of *Catholic Schools Make a Difference: Twenty-Five Years of Research*, published by the National Catholic Educational Association in 1992. He served on the Education Committee for the United States Catholic Bishops from 1992 to 1994 and was the 1991 recipient of the C. Albert Koob Award, given by the National Catholic Educational Association for outstanding national service to Catholic schools.

Maureen T. Hallinan is William P. and Hazel B. White Professor of Sociology; Director, Institute for Educational Initiatives, University of Notre Dame; past president of the American Sociological Association; and president-elect (2000) of the Sociological Research Association. She holds a B.A. from Marymount College, an M.S. from the University of Notre Dame, and a Ph.D. from the University of Chicago. Her research is primarily in the sociology of education; she has studied the determinants and consequences of the organization of students for instruction, and the organizational effects on students' social relationships in schools. Her edited books include *The Social Organization of Schools: New Conceptualiza-*

tions of the Learning Process, Restructuring Schools: Promising Practices and Policies, and *Handbook of Sociology of Education.*

Joseph Claude Harris is a Catholic layman working as Controller for the Society of St. Vincent de Paul in Seattle. He received a B.D. from Mary-knoll Seminary, Maryknoll, New York, and an M.B.A. from City University in Bellevue, Washington. He is a member of the Institute of Management Accountants. He is the author of *The Cost of Catholic Parishes and Schools* (1996). He also has completed studies for the Life Cycle Institute at Catholic University on Sunday collections in the Church and school financing. His research articles have appeared in *America, Commonweal, Church, Chicago Studies,* and *The Review of Religious Research.* He currently is working on a study of the cost of parishes and elementary schools in the Archdiocese of Los Angeles.

Thomas B. Hoffer (Ph.D., University of Chicago, 1986) is a Senior Research Scientist at the National Opinion Research Center at the University of Chicago. He works primarily on the design, execution, and analysis of large-scale education surveys. His main areas of research interest are school organization and education policy. Recent publications include articles on high school graduation requirements in *Teachers College Record* (1997) and student outcomes in public and Catholic high schools in *Social Psychology of Education* (1998).

Stewart Lawrence has more than 15 years of professional research experience in Latin America and the United States. His areas of expertise include U.S. foreign and defense policy and U.S. and international migration. Mr. Lawrence obtained his master's degree in international affairs from Columbia University in 1989 and his M. Phil. in political science (also from Columbia) in 1991. Prior to joining the Life Cycle Institute in 1996, Mr. Lawrence served with the U.S. General Accounting Office, the Georgetown University Center for Inter-Cultural Education and Development, and the U.S. Catholic Conference. He is president of his own consulting firm, Puentes, Inc., which conducts community-based research and advocacy training for Latino social service groups nationwide.

Jeffrey A. McLellan (Ph.D., Catholic University of America, 1992) is a Research Associate at the Life Cycle Institute at Catholic University. Recent publications include articles on Catholic education in *Phi Delta Kappan* (1999) and *The Living Light* (1998) and editorship of a volume entitled *The Role of Peer Group Stability and Change in Adolescent Social*

Identity (1999) in the *New Directions for Child and Adolescent Development* series published by Jossey-Bass.

Jessica Murphy is currently an advanced doctoral student in Educational Research, Measurement, and Evaluation at Boston College. She is preparing a dissertation regarding the relationship between school climate and academic effectiveness in Catholic secondary schools. She works as an institutional researcher at Boston College.

M. Sheila Nelson is Assistant Professor of Sociology at the College of St. Benedict, St. Joseph, Minnesota, and St. John's University, Collegeville, Minnesota. She earned an M.S.W. from St. Louis University and her Ph.D. in sociology from Loyola University, Chicago. She has done research and published work on inner-city Catholic schools and small religious nonprofit organizations.

Joseph M. O'Keefe, S.J., is Associate Professor of Education at Boston College. During the 1999–2000 academic year he will hold the Jesuit Chair in Education at Georgetown University. He has authored a number of chapters and articles and has been the contributing editor of five books, most notably *The Contemporary Catholic School: Context, Identity and Diversity* (Falmer, 1996). His interests include urban education, the religious identity of schools, international comparative education, and the preparation of prospective teachers and administrators.

Vernon C. Polite is Associate Professor in the Department of Education at the Catholic University of America, Washington, DC. Dr. Polite earned his Ph.D. degree from Michigan State University in the area of K–12 educational administration. He specializes in research focused on organizational change, urban school leadership, and issues of race, class, and gender in education. Dr. Polite has served in a number of administrative positions in both Catholic and public schools. He is the editor of the book *African American Males in Schools and Society*.

Cornelius Riordan, Ph.D., is Professor of Sociology at Providence College. He received an M.A. in sociology from Clark University and his doctorate in sociology from Syracuse University, and he completed 2 years of postdoctoral study at Johns Hopkins University. His area of specialization is the social organization of schools and the educational outcomes related to various types of school organization. He is the author of a textbook in the sociology of education entitled *Equality and Achievement*. He has studied the effects over the past decade of single- and mixed-gender education at all levels of schooling and is the author of *Girls and Boys in School: Together or Separate?* and numerous professional papers on this subject. He was commissioned to write a paper for a report recently published by the American Association of University Women entitled *Separate by Sex.*

Maryellen Schaub currently is teaching at Pennsylvania State University. While at Catholic University of America, she developed the System for Catholic Research, Information, and Planning. She is a sociologist with research interests in comparative education.

Index